EDUCATION AND POWER

IDEOLOGY AND CURRICULUM

*CULTURAL AND ECONOMIC REPRODUCTION
IN EDUCATION*

MICHAEL W. APPLE

University of Wisconsin

EDUCATION
AND
POWER

ROUTLEDGE & KEGAN PAUL

BOSTON, LONDON, MELBOURNE AND HENLEY

First published in 1982
by Routledge & Kegan Paul Ltd
9 Park Street,
Boston, Mass. 02108, USA,
39 Store Street,
London WC1E 7DD,
296 Beaconsfield Parade,
Middle Park, Melbourne 3206
Australia and
Broadway House,
Newtown Road,
Henley-on-Thames,
Oxon RG9 1EN
Set in IBM 11pt Journal by
Columns, Reading, England
and printed in the United States of America

Library of Congress Cataloging in Publication Data

Apple, Michael W.

Education and Power
Bibliography: p.
Includes index.
1. Culture. 2. Social classes. 3. Education and
state. I. Title.
HM101.A646   306   81-19920

ISBN 0-7100-0977-1   AACR2

CONTENTS

ACKNOWLEDGMENTS

No matter how 'original,' all books are collective. This is certainly true of *Education and Power*, but in two distinct ways. The first is not often mentioned in acknowledgments. Yet in this case I think it needs to be said. This book could not have been written without the everyday struggles of working men and women on the left who have sought to build and maintain a movement that is emancipatory and democratic in both intent *and* practice. Nor could it have been written without the creative efforts of those authors who have participated in and theorized this movement over the past decades. Those who have sought to reestablish and maintain a non-reductive and non-mechanistic critical tradition of leftist scholarship have had a strong influence on me. Even though their influence was through an internal debate between what they wrote and my own reactions, puzzlements, agreements, and disagreements, and even though they can never know the current significance of their ideas, I thank them anyway. We are all in their debt.

Debts are not always so anonymous, of course. I am lucky enough to have friends and colleagues in Wisconsin and throughout the world who do not let friendship stand in the way of necessary criticism. A number of these deserve mention: Ron Aminzade, Jean Anyon, Stanley Aronowitz, Ann Becker, Basil Bernstein, Jean Brenkman, John Brenkman, Roger Dale, Henry Giroux, Andrew Gitlin, Herbert Kliebard, Henry Levin, Alan Lockwood, Madeleine Anton, Vandra Masemann, Linda McNeil, Fred Newmann, Gary Price, Fran Schrag, Richard Smith, Joel Taxel, Andrew Urevbu, Gary Wehlage, Lois Weis, Paul Willis, Erik Olin Wright, and Michael F. D. Young. Four others need to be singled out for special mention for their continued contribution to my thinking and rethinking: Michael Olneck, Steven Selden, Philip Wexler, and Geoff Whitty.

ACKNOWLEDGMENTS

In my past volumes, I gave a good deal of credit to the graduate students who work with me and who meet together for the now famous (or infamous) Friday seminar. This is even more the case here. The chapters in this study are the result of intense debates and discussions with my students. They too have taught me a considerable amount, as have the progressive elementary and secondary teachers with whom I have interacted over the last decade and the workers with whom I have worked to create materials for political education on the shop-floor and in offices.

David Godwin at Routledge & Kegan Paul continues to demonstrate how editorial excellence and support can be combined. Bonnie Garski and Barbara Seffrood are more than typists and secretaries, though they are very good at that. Their comments and suggested changes were always right on the mark. Their friendship, competence, and understanding is very much appreciated.

Rima D. Apple's uncanny ability to make me clarify what I want to say, her substantive and editorial suggestions, her consistent support, to say nothing of how much she continues to teach me about the histories of women, science, and medicine, all of this adds up to a debt no husband can fully repay.

Finally, I want to dedicate this book to Mimi Russak Apple who, even though she did not live to see it completed, would have understood its focus on struggles against exploitation. It is from the way both she and my father, Harry Apple, lived their lives that I first learned the importance of such struggle.

Portions of this volume have appeared in different form in *Curriculum Inquiry*, *Interchange*, the *Journal of Education*, the *Journal of Economic and Industrial Democracy*, and Robert Everhart, ed., the *Public School Monopoly*.

CHAPTER 1

REPRODUCTION, CONTESTATION AND CURRICULUM

I

THE SHADOW OF THE CRISIS

As I begin writing this the words of the noted sociologist Manuel Castells keep pressing upon me. 'The shadow of the crisis spreads over the world.' The images he brings to mind provide some of the driving force behind this volume. For behind the ups and downs of the 'business cycle' and behind the turmoil in education, both of which we hear so much about in the press, our daily lives and the lives of millions of people throughout the world are caught up in an economic crisis, one that will probably have lasting cultural, political, and economic effects.

It is affecting our very ideas about school, work and leisure, sex roles, 'legitimate' repression, political rights and participation, and so on. It is shaking the very economic and cultural groundings of our day to day lives for many of us. Castells's own images are worth quoting:

> Closed factories, empty offices, millions of unemployed, days of hunger, declining cities, crowded hospitals, ailing administrations, explosions of violence, ideologies of austerity, fatuous discourses, popular revolts, new political strategies, hopes, fears, promises, threats, manipulation, mobilization, repression, fearful stock markets, militant labor unions, disturbed computers, nervous police, stunned economists, subtle politicians, suffering people — so many images that we have been told were gone forever, gone with the wind of post industrial capitalism. And now they are back again, brought by the wind of capitalist crisis.[1]

The mass media bring us no escape from these images. If anything, their repetition and the fact that we cannot escape from seeing and experiencing them point to their reality. The crisis is not a fiction. It can be seen every day in the jobs, schools, families, government and health care and welfare agencies all around us.

In concert with this, our educational and political institutions have lost a large portion of their legitimacy as the state apparatus finds itself unable to respond adequately to the current economic and ideological situation. What has been called the fiscal crisis of the state has emerged as the state finds it impossible to maintain the jobs, programs, and services that have been won by people after years of struggle. At the same time, the cultural resources of our society are becoming more thoroughly commercialized as popular culture is invaded by the commodification process. They are processed and bought and sold. They too became one more aspect of accumulation.

The crisis, though clearly related to processes of capital accumulation, is not only economic. It is political and cultural/ideological as well. In fact, it is at the intersection of these *three* spheres of social life, how they interact, how each supports and contradicts the others, that we can see it in its most glaring form. The structural crisis we are currently witnessing — no, living — is not really 'explained' only by an economy, therefore (that would be too mechanistic), but by a social whole, by each of these spheres. As Castells puts it, this is the case because:

> the economy is not a 'mechanism' but a social process
> continuously shaped and recast by the changing relationships
> of humankind to the productive forces and by the class
> struggle defining humankind in a historically specific
> manner.[2]

What this implies is the following. It is not only in an abstraction like the economy that one can find the roots of the difficult times we face. Rather, the key words are struggle and shaping. They point to structural issues. Our problems are systemic, each building on the other. Each aspect of the social process in the state and politics, in cultural life, in our modes of producing, distributing, and consuming serves to affect the relationships within *and* among the others. As a mode of production attempts to reproduce the conditions of its own existence, 'it' creates antagonisms and

2

contradictions in other spheres. As groups of people struggle over issues of gender, race, and class in each of these spheres, the entire social process, including 'the economy,' is also affected. The struggles and the terrain on which they are carried out are recast. Therefore, the images of these struggles that Castells calls forth are not static, for people like ourselves live them in their daily lives (perhaps often 'unconciously'). And groups of these people constantly shape and are reshaped by these processes as the conflicts are engaged in.

While the crisis Castells describes is not wholly economic, the depth at which it is felt at an economic level needs to be pointed to if only to indicate how extensive it is.

Some of the figures are indeed shocking. While official unemployment rates of 7-8 per cent are bad enough, the real unemployment rate in the United States may be closer to 14 per cent. Though current figures are only now becoming available, the unemployment rate within the inner cities was as high as 60-70 per cent among black and hispanic youth as early as 1975.[3] Given the deterioration in the American economy (and those economies that are so interconnected with it), one has little reason to believe that this has been altered significantly downward.

Other findings concerning race and sex show another part of the picture. Even though women have struggled over the years to gain a more equal footing, recent data illuminate how difficult this will continue to be. As Featherman and Hauser have demonstrated, for instance, 'while the occupational and educational achievement of women have kept pace with men . . ., the ratio of female to male earnings has *declined* from 0.39 to 0.38 for husbands and wives.' In fact, there has been little change in the percentage of this earning gap that can be accounted for by plain old sex discrimination. Discrimination accounted for 85 per cent of the gap in 1962 and 84 per cent in 1973, not a very significant change over all.[4] While recent evidence suggests that this gap may be slowly changing in the professional sector[5] — and this is certainly a positive change — the fact is that only a relatively small percentage of women are actually employed in this sector.

What of other groups? The black and hispanic populations of the United States have much higher rates of under and unemployment than others, rates that will significantly increase in the near future. A large proportion of these workers are employed in what might be called the 'irregular economy,' one in which their work

3

(and pay) is often seasonal, subject to repeated layoffs, poorer pay and benefits, and little autonomy. Like women, they seem to suffer a dual oppression. For not only is the social formation unequal by class — a point brought home, for instance, by the significant class differential in income returns from education — but added to this are the powerful forces of race and gender reproduction as well. Each of these forces affects the other.[6]

Certainly gains have been made by specific portions of these groups. However, the raw statistics of these gains cover something rather consequential. The economy itself has shifted less markedly, either in its benefits or power based on race, sex, or class composition, than we might have supposed. The bulk of the advance has occurred through employment in the state.

One fact documents this rather clearly. Government — at the local, state, and national levels — employs over 50 per cent of all of the professional blacks and women in the United States.[7] It has only been through protest and struggle within the state that this has been effected.[8] These jobs were not 'given,' but are the result of groups of people pressuring year after year. Without such state hiring, the gains among these groups would have been drastically lower. As we shall see later on, in fact, the role the state plays in our economy and culture needs to be given a good deal of attention if we are to understand how an unequal society reproduces itself and how crises are dealt with. This will be of special importance in my discussions of the contradictory role of the school in such reproduction.

Conditions also seem to be worsening because of what has been called the dynamics of uneven development. That is, there is an increasing dichotomization between the haves and the have nots. We can see partial evidence of this in the fact that the wages workers in low-wage industries have been getting dropped over a twenty-year period from 75 per cent of the average pay in high wage industries to 60 per cent. A dual economy is created with an ever widening gap which, according to a number of political economists, will be next to impossible to reverse.[9]

But what of conditions on the job itself? I shall cite but a few pertinent statistics, though many more could fill up the pages of a number of books. In health and safety, the United States consistently lags behind other industrialized nations, with many occupations having a death and injury rate three to four times what one finds in England and Europe.[10] Profit is more important than

4

people, it seems. Yet many people do not even realize this. Both blue- and white-collar work is often maddeningly boring and repetitive. Workers have little formal control over their labor and this centralization of control is growing in offices, stores, universities and schools, factories, and elsewhere.[11] Pensions are being lost and hard-won benefits weakened. While service jobs increase (to be largely filled by lower-paid women), other jobs are disappearing as runaway corporations move their plants to areas with a less organized, cheaper, and more docile work-force. And even these additional service jobs are suffering more and more from added workloads, a lack of responsibility for the organization of their jobs, increasing insecurity, and a paucity of serious social services to support them. Furthermore, it is estimated that conditions may worsen since the economy is currently producing only about half of the total new jobs that will be required in the future.[12]

For many women it is often worse. Since so many of them work in 'pink-collar' jobs and in the competitive low-wage sector (that is, stores, restaurants, small offices, and labor-intensive industries such as clothing and accessory manufacturing), they are frequently condemned to relative material impoverishment.[13] The same is true of minority workers, a large portion of whom work in the competitive sector. Working conditions here are much worse and, again, unemployment and underemployment, inadequate health and pension benefits, and weak or non-existent labor unions seem to be the rule.[14]

When this is coupled with the deteriorating purchasing power of most workers' pay, the class and sex differential in that pay, the loss of control on the job, the decline of cities and cultural supports and human ties, and the astronomical costs in mental and physical health these conditions entail, it makes one pause even further. For the images that Castells calls forth describe the conditions that an increasing portion of the population within and outside the boundaries of the United States will face. What these conditions signify, the structural reasons for them, are not made evident due to the hegemonic control of the media and the information industries.[15] We castigate a few industrialists and corporations, a small number of figures in government, a vague abstraction called technology, instead of seeing the productive and political apparatus of society as interconnected. In part, though, we cannot blame ourselves for not recognizing the situation. The unconnected version is what we are presented with by the cultural apparatus in its dominant forms. It takes constant attention to detail by even the most politically sensitive of the working men and women in our society to begin to put it all together, to see these images as realities that are generated out of the emerging contradictions and pressures of our social formation and its mode of production. We live through a crisis in legitimation and accumulation — where the productive and reproductive apparatus of a society (including schools) are riven with tensions, where the very essence of the continued reproduction of the conditions necessary for the maintenance of hegemonic control is threatened — yet it is so hard to see the *patterned* impact all this has on the practices in our daily lives. This is especially difficult in education where an ameliorative ideology and the immense problems educators already face leave little time for thinking seriously about the relationship between educational practices and discourse and the reproduction of inequality.

As we shall see, though, the men and women who work in our offices, stores, shops, factories, and schools have not been totally quiescent in the face of all this, a fact that will be made rather clear in my later discussions of cultural forms of resistance. But, the facts that the objective conditions they face are not easy and the perspectives made available to understand them are not very powerful must be recognized at the outset.

This gives a view of the side on which many workers and employees sit. But what about the other side, the side that has much greater control of our culture, politics, and economy? The picture here is one of rapid centralization and concentration of economic and cultural resources and power. A few examples are sufficient to indicate the extent of, say, corporate control. The top one hundred corporations increased their control of industrial assets from 40 per cent in 1950 to nearly 50 per cent in 1969, a figure that is even higher today. Of the more than two million businesses in the United States today, the two hundred largest corporations take home over two-thirds of the total profit in the entire country. After-tax corporate profits in 1970 were three times what they had been just ten years earlier. In insurance, the top ten concerns control over 60 per cent of all assets. This very same phenomenon is found in banking and the communication industries, as well as in the growing national and international power concentrated in financial and industrial corporate conglomerates. The investment patterns of these industrial and financial concerns reveal what one would expect, the maximization of capital accumulation and profit — with human welfare, public goals, high employment, and so on distant runners up when they are considered at all. From all of this, it should be quite clear that the interests of capital control our economic life and our personal well-being to no small extent.[16]

These data present a less than attractive view of the structural conditions in which many of our citizens find themselves and of the unequal power in our society. Yet, one could still claim that these are aberrations. On the whole we are becoming a more equal society; just look around you. Unfortunately, this may be more wish than fact. As the authors of *Economic Democracy* note:

> As numerous academic and government studies have demonstrated, the distribution of wealth and income in the United States has changed little in the direction of greater equality since the turn of the century and hardly at all since World War II.[17]

Even with this maldistribution and the widening centralization and concentration, we know that stagnation and inflation beset the economy. Capital accumulation and legitimation are threatened. The debt level of these very same corporations has risen markedly, in part because of the financing of technological innovations due to increased international competition.[18] New markets 'need' to be developed; workers need to be brought under greater control and discipline; productivity needs to be increased; new technologies need to be developed at an ever-growing rate; and the techniques and expertise required for engaging in all of this need to be generated. The role of the worker is critical here since it has been found that the rate of exploitation of one's workers is an exceptional predictor of the profit levels of an industry.[19] That is, one of the most important means by which firms may deal with the economic 'problems' they confront is to refocus on their work-force and increase the level of exploited labor they can gain from it.

The state and the school will not be immune from these pressures. Social austerity 'needs' to be regained. Governmental policies need to correspond to the requirements of capital. Educational practices need to be brought more closely into line with work and the costs of the research and development prerequisites of industry have to be socialized by having them taken over by the state and the university. These conditions in the workplace and the political sphere also create their own problems, however. Intensified competition makes the replacement of technologies necessary well before they are fully paid for by profits. Workers react against a good deal of this. Progressive groups, educators, and parents may challenge the closer linkages between the state, factories, boardrooms, and schools. Blacks, hispanics, and many other workers reject the position that they must pay for the economic contradictions plaguing society. And inflation and social tension are raised again. Hence, in the midst of this, the seeds of continued conflict and crisis grow.

This gives the barest glimpse of the actual circumstances many of our citizens experience. If Castells and so many others are correct, we cannot expect it to get better soon in any significant way. What we can do, however, is to face the structural crisis honestly and see how it works its way out in one of our major institutions of reproduction, the school. We must do this even if it means criticizing some of the basic ways our educational institutions currently operate. To do this, though, we need to understand much more thoroughly the connection between education and the ideological, political, and economic spheres of society and how the school partakes in each of them.

At the same time, we should take existing criticisms of schools and suggestions for their reform and place them as well within the crisis in these three spheres. However, it is not just these connections and criticisms that should concern us. We need also to be aware of possibilities for action. For just as this crisis generates contradictions and tensions that are emerging at all levels of our social formation, so too will these emerge in schools. Finding them will be undoubtedly difficult, but important as well. It may be the case that these contradictions and tensions will actually open up possibilities for us to act in education, in much the same way that, for instance, the crisis in our offices and factories is generating pressures for greater worker control and autonomy.[20]

These issues noted above are the tasks I shall attempt throughout this book. How are schools linked to outside agencies in complex and contradictory ways? What responses do people inside and outside the school make to these contradictions and pressures? Do most recent analyses of the linkages and responses —

even some of the more interesting Marxist investigations — uncover enough of this? How are the processes of cultural and economic reproduction and contestation linked in schools? Are current proposed reforms adequate to deal with this complexitiy? What can progressive educators and others do about this situation? Perhaps the best way to engage in this is to begin by documenting in the rest of this chapter how the concerns about schools and economic and cultural reproduction have grown in sophistication. Here I shall trace out my own and others' progressive realization of what schools do in this regard and how they respond to structural contradictions and reproductive crises. In so doing, I shall outline and prefigure a number of the arguments that will appear in the following chapters.

II

EDUCATIONAL CRITICISM

In the previous section of this chapter I documented some of the elements of the structural crisis that we are beginning to see. I pointed out how this has begun to impact on the labor process, on parts of our culture, and on the legitimacy of our institutions. As economic and cultural institutions, schools will 'reflect' these changes in the labor process, culture, and legitimacy. Partly because of this, they have been and will be subject to the same kinds of serious criticisms that are currently being marshalled against other institutions in the political, cultural, and economic spheres.

It is not inconsequential that a central thrust of radical criticism of our institutions during the last decade or so has been on the school. It has become increasingly obvious over this same time period that our educational institutions may serve less as the engines of democracy and equality than many of us would like. In many ways, this criticism has been healthy since it has increased our sensitivity to the important role schools — and the overt and covert knowledge within them — play in reproducing a stratified social order that remains strikingly unequal by class, gender, and race. As individuals as diverse as Bourdieu, Althusser, and Baudelot and Establet in France, Bernstein, Young, Whitty, and Willis in England, Kallos and Lundgren in Sweden, Gramsci in Italy, and Bowles and Gintis, myself, and others in the United States have repeatedly argued, the educational and cultural system is an exceptionally important element in the maintenance of existing relations of domination and exploitation in these societies.

While there may be serious disagreements among these people about how this goes on, still none would deny the importance of examining the relationship between schooling and the maintenance of these unequal relations. And while some of us may also disagree with parts of the logic of each other's analysis, we simply cannot look at the schools, and the knowledge within them, in quite the same way as we did before this corpus of work appeared.

While this criticism has been healthy, it has perhaps had two side effects that are, paradoxically, the opposite of each other. On the one hand, it has caused us to give too much importance to the school. We may see the school as *the* issue, instead of as part of a larger framework of social relations that are structurally exploitative. That the issue is much larger can be seen in the recent study by Jencks *et al.*, *Who Gets Ahead?* It documents the fact that not only are economic returns from schooling twice as great for individuals who are economically advantaged to begin with, but for, say, black students, even finishing high school will probably not bring any significant benefits. Thus, even if we could alter the school to equalize achievement, the evidence suggests that it might not make a significant difference in the larger framework in which schools exist.[21]

The second side effect is nearly the mirror image of the possible overemphasis on the power of the school. This is the rather pessimistic stance that says that since schools *are* so integrated into this larger framework and since they seem basically to mirror what a 'society needs,' especially in a time of crisis, then they can be ignored. Nothing of value can be gained by acting in them because they are fundamentally determined institutions. I believe that both of these side effects can have negative consequences. As I present my arguments here, we shall need to be cautious of these effects. Behind my own sense of this lay these two cautions, therefore: the realization that understanding and acting on schools is not enough, but also knowing that and ignoring them is simply wrong. It is the result of an incorrect analysis and is misguided politically. As I shall argue, in fact, the educational system — because of its very location within a larger nexus of social relations — can provide a significant terrain over which serious action can evolve.

In this section of the introductory chapter I shall be forced to speak rather generally at times, skating over what are serious issues and controversies within structurally oriented economic and cultural scholarship on schools. How does one summarize one's work over a decade, as well as other people's efforts, when that work has grown in sophistication considerably over those years? How can one trace the rapid development of critical ideas about what schools do, without at the same time showing how these ideas about what happens within schools have been fundamentally influenced by one's political practice and by the intense debate going on now within the leftist community on the relationship between culture and mode of production? Obviously, all of this can't be done. Therefore, I have chosen to handle this problem in three ways. First, I shall lay out what Marxist oriented educational scholarship is about by making some general points about how one should interpret the central issue, that of reproduction. I then want to trace the development of my own thinking on these matters by illuminating the concerns I had during the years when I wrote *Ideology and Curriculum*. In so doing, I want to show how my analysis has progressed in more recent work, a progress that, again, has been strongly influenced by the exceptional work being currently done within Marxist literature, and by my own involvement in political activity. The third aspect, possible action, is just as critical and will be developed throughout the coming chapters.

Since I cannot give a sense of all of the debates that are continuing to influence the work of people like me, I shall outline in my Notes some of the major controversies that remain unsettled. This will leave a good deal unsaid, for in order to show how, say, my own political work — with poor, black, white, and hispanic groups to secure their and their children's economic and cultural rights, with politically progressive workers on the development of materials for political education, on economic justice, etc. — has been so important in my latest analyses, I would have to transform this book into an autobiography. For now I shall leave that style to others. I do want to stress, however, that none of what is written here can be thoroughly understood without reference to the concrete practice of the men and women with whom I act.

CURRICULUM AND REPRODUCTION

For the major part of this century, education in general and the curriculum field in particular has devoted a good deal of its energy to the search for one specific thing. It has searched long and hard for a general set of principles that would guide educational planning and evaluation. In large part, this has reduced itself to attempts at creating the *most efficient method* of doing curriculum work. One need only trace the internal history of the dominant traditions in the field — from Thorndike, Bobbitt and Charters in the early years of the twentieth century to Tyler and to the even more vulgar behaviorists and systems managers today — to begin to realize how strong the emphasis on curriculum as efficient method has become.[22]

The focus on method has not been without its consequences. At the same time that process/product rationality grew, the fact that education is through and through a political enterprise withered. The questions we asked tended to divorce ourselves from the way the economic and cultural apparatus of a society operated. A 'neutral' method meant our own neutrality, or so it seemed. The fact that the methods we employed had their roots in industry's attempts to control labor and increase productivity, in the popular eugenics movement, and in particular class and status group interests, was made invisible by the stunning lack of historical insight in the field.[23] At the same time, we seemed to assume that the development of this supposedly neutral method would eliminate the need to deal with the issue of whose knowledge should be or already was preserved and transmitted in schools. While a number of alternative traditions continued to try to keep this kind of political question alive, by and large the faith in the inherent neutrality of our institutions, the knowledge that was taught, and our methods and actions, was ideally suited to help legitimate the structural bases of inequality.

The key to this last sentence is the concept of legitimation. (Like Wittgenstein, I am claiming that the meaning of our language and practices is in their use.) And the use in this case has tended to be twofold. As I sought to demonstrate in *Ideology and Curriculum*, the traditions that dominate the field assist in the reproduction of inequality while at the same time serving to legitimate both the institutions that recreate it and our own actions within them. This is *not* to claim that individual children are not often being helped by our practices and discourse; nor is it to claim that all of our day to day actions are misguided. It is to claim that macroeconomically our work may serve functions that bear little resemblance to even our best intentions.

How are we to understand this? A fundamental problem facing us is the way in which systems of domination and exploitation persist and reproduce themselves without being consciously recognized by the people involved.[24] This is of particular import in education, where our commonly accepted practices so clearly seek to help students and to ameliorate many of the 'social and educational problems' facing them. On the face of it, such a focus on these 'problems' should seem helpful. Yet, it ignores something that has been made rather clear in recent sociological literature.

The essentials of this literature are stated rather pointedly by DiMaggio when he argues that commonsense classification of individuals, social groups, or 'social problems' tends to confirm and reinforce these structurally generated relations of domination. For 'purposeful, reasoning, well intentioned actors' often contribute — simply by pursuing their own subjective ends — to the maintenance of these structural relations.[25] These purposeful, reasoning, and well-intentioned actors, hence, may be latently serving ideological functions at the same moment that they are seeking to alleviate some of the problems facing individual students and others. This is as much due to the linkages between economic and cultural institutions — what many Marxists have called (not unproblematically) the relationship between base and superstructure[26] — as it is to the personal characteristics of these people. Thus, one can examine schools and our action on them in two ways: first, as a form of amelioration and problem-solving by which we assist individual students to get ahead; and, second, on a much larger scale, to see the patterns of the *kinds* of individuals who get ahead and the latent outcomes of the institution. These larger social patterns and outcomes may tell us much about how the school functions in reproduction, a function that may tend to be all too hidden if our individual acts of helping remain our primary focus.

So far I have been using words like function and reproduction. These concepts point to the role of educational institutions in preserving what exists. But, they also imply a good deal more that deserves our attention if we are not to be utterly mechanistic.

What do we mean when we look at how schools 'function' to

reproduce an unequal society? Unlike sociological functionalism, where order is assumed and deviance from that order is problematic, Marxist and neo-Marxist analyses signal something else by that term (or at least they should). Rather than a functional coherence where all things work relatively smoothly to maintain a basically unchanging social order, these analyses point to 'the *contested* reproduction of a society's fundamental relations, which enables society to reproduce itself again, but only in the form of a dominant and subordinate (i.e. antagonistic, not functional) social order.'[27]

For schools are not 'merely' institutions of reproduction, institutions where the overt and covert knowledge that is taught inexorably molds students into passive beings who are able and eager to fit into an unequal society. This account fails in two critical ways. First it views students as passive internalizers of pre-given social messages. Whatever the institution teaches in either the formal curriculum or the hidden curriculum is taken in, unmodified by class cultures and class (or race or gender) rejection of dominant social messages. Anyone who has taught in working-class schools, in schools located in our inner-city ghettos, and elsewhere knows that this is simply not the case. Student reinterpretation, at best only partial acceptance, and often outright rejection of the planned and unplanned meanings of schools, are more likely. Clearly, schools need to be seen in a more complex manner than simple reproduction.

The reproduction account is too simple in another way. It undertheorizes and hence neglects the fact that capitalist social relations are inherently *contradictory* in some very important ways. That is, as I claimed earlier, just as in the economic arena where the capital accumulation process and the 'need' to expand markets and profits generates contradictions within a society (where, for example, rising profits and inflation create a crisis in legitimacy in both the state and the economy),[28] so too will similar contradictions emerge in other dominant institutions. The school will not be immune to these.

For instance, as a state apparatus schools perform important roles in assisting in the creation of the conditions necessary for capital accumulation (they sort, select, and certify a hierarchically organized student body) and for legitimation (they maintain an inaccurate meritocratic ideology and, therefore, legitimate the ideological forms necessary for the recreation of inequality).[29]

However, these two 'functions' of schools are often in conflict with each other. The needs of capital accumulation may contradict the needs for legitimation, a situation that is currently rather intense. In the school we can see this in the relative overproduction of credentialed individuals at a time when the economy no longer 'requires' as many high salaried personnel. This very overproduction calls into question the legitimacy of the ways schools function.[30] On a more concrete level, we can see the contradictions of the institution in the fact that the school has different ideological obligations that may be in tension. Critical capacities are needed to keep our society dynamic; hence schools should teach students to be critical. Yet critical capacities can challenge capital as well.[31] This is not an abstract idea. These ideological conflicts permeate our educational institutions and are worked out every day in them.

The emphasis on working out contradictions in the last few paragraphs is not just important for thinking about how schools may be caught in conflicts of accumulation and legitimation not necessarily of their own making. It also provides a fundamental principle for thinking about how ideology itself works, a working that has been a constitutive part of my own and others' inquiries about reproduction.

Just as the school is caught in contradictions that may be very difficult for it to resolve, so too are ideologies filled with contradictions. They are not coherent sets of beliefs. It is probably wrong to think of them as only beliefs at all. They are instead sets of lived meanings, practices, and social relations that are often internally inconsistent. They have elements within themselves that see through to the heart of the unequal benefits of a society and at one and the same time tend to reproduce the ideological relations and meanings that maintain the hegemony of dominant classes.[32] Because of this, ideologies are contested; they are continually struggled over. Since ideologies have both 'good and bad sense' within them, people need to be won over to one side or the other, if you will. Particular institutions become the sites where this struggle takes place and where these dominant ideologies are produced. The school is crucial as one of these sites.

Here it is not just the institution that is important. Actors (real people) must elaborate dominant ideologies. As Gramsci — one of the most influential figures in the analysis of the relationship between culture and economy — notes, this has been one of

15

the prime tasks of 'intellectuals,' spreading and making legitimate dominant ideological meanings and practice, attempting to win people over and create unity on the contested terrain of ideology.[33] Whether we accept it or not, educators are in the structural position of being such 'intellectuals' and, therefore, are not isolated from these ideological tasks (though many of them may struggle against it, of course). Again Gramsci's insights are helpful. The control of the cultural apparatus of a society, of both the knowledge preserving and producing institutions and the actors who work in them, is essential in the struggle over ideological hegemony.

All of these general comments about how recent scholarship has looked at ideology and reproduction raise some exceptionally complex issues, of course. Reproduction, the state, legitimation, accumulation, contradiction, ideological hegemony, base/superstructure, all of these are strange concepts to a field involved in building efficient and neutral methods. Yet, if we are to take seriously the political nature of education and curriculum and the unequal benefits and results of schooling,[34] they are essential. By and large, then, if we conceive of the internal qualities of schools and the knowledge found within them to be intricately connected to relations of domination, what is it that the use of these concepts entails in an analysis of schools and curriculum?

In his discussion of the various ways Marxists have looked at schooling (and these ways are not all alike; they *do* differ radically),[35] Stuart Hall captures the essence of part of the approach taken by those of us who have been influenced by this scholarship, and in particular by the original work of Gramsci. A quote from one of his longer passages summarizes some of the background of this position rather clearly.

> [This position] attributes the fundamental determination in securing the 'complex unity' of society to the relationships of the economic structure, but regards the so-called 'superstructures' as having vital, critical 'work' to do in sustaining, at the social, cultural, political, and ideological levels, the *conditions* which enable capitalist production to proceed. Furthermore, it regards the superstructures as having the role, above all, of drawing society into 'conformity' with the long-term requirements and conditions of a capitalist economic system (for example, in the work of

16

Gramsci). This suggests that, though the superstructures are more determined than determining, the topography of base/superstructures is not so important as the relatively autonomous 'work' which the superstructures perform for the economic structure. This is regarded as difficult, contested 'work,' that operates through opposition and antagonism — in short, by means of class struggle which is present at all the various levels of society — where simple correspondences are hard to come by. Far from assuming a simple recapitulation between the various structures of society, this approach sees the 'work' which the superstructures [like schools] perform as necessary precisely because, on its own, the economic system cannot ensure all the conditions necessary for its own expanded reproduction. The economic system cannot ensure that society will be raised to that general level of civilization and culture which its advanced system of production needs. Creating an order of society around the fundamental economic relationships is just as necessary as production itself; the relations of production alone cannot 'produce' such a social order. Here, then, the relationship is not one of correspondence but of coupling — the *coupling* of two distinct, but interrelated and interdependent spheres. Gramsci is one of the outstanding theorists of this position. The nature of the 'coupling' envisaged is described in Gramsci's phrase, the 'structure-superstructure complex.' Again, simplifying, we may call this the paradigm of *hegemony*.[36]

While some of these points should be and are currently being widely debated, notice what is being argued here. 'Superstructural' institutions such as schools have a significant degree of relative autonomy. The economic structure cannot ensure any simple correspondence between itself and these institutions. However, such institutions, with the school among them, perform vital functions in the recreation of the conditions necessary for ideological hegemony to be maintained. These conditions are not imposed, though. They are and need to be continuously rebuilt on the field of institutions like the school. The conditions of existence of a particular social formation are rebuilt through antagonistic relations (and sometimes even through oppositional forms, as we shall see later on in this book and as I discuss my own genesis

17

through these concepts and positions in this chapter). Above all, hegemony doesn't simply come about; it must be worked for in particular sites like the family, the workplace, the political sphere, and the school.[37] And it is just this process of understanding how hegemony comes about, how it *is* partly produced, through the day to day curricular, pedagogical, and evaluative interactions in schools, that has been my primary concern.

IDEOLOGY AND CURRICULUM
AS A FIRST APPROXIMATION

What emerges from this general discussion of the way we might interpret schools? No simple one-way, conflict free, base/super-structure model will do. Contestation is central to reproduction. Even concepts like reproduction may be inadequate. It is easier for me to say this now, and to begin to understand fully the signifi-cance of what this perspective articulated by Hall implies today, than it was even three years ago when I was completing the work on *Ideology and Curriculum*.

To be honest, all of these points about reproduction, contra-diction, and contestation did not dawn on me all at once; nor was I able to appreciate either how they could be employed or what they might mean. Given my own interest, and that of people like Bowles and Gintis, Bourdieu, Bernstein, and others, in *reproduc-tion* — an interest that was critically important I believe at that particular historical moment, but an interest that at the beginning tended to exclude other elements of what might be happening in schools — these points have had to be struggled with, worked through, and have ultimately been slowly incorporated. At times, this involved (and still does) serious self-criticism of my own and others' previous work, building on and correcting mistakes, and fleshing out what now seems too simple and mechanistic.

Given this painstaking movement away from a focus on simple reproduction by a number of people like myself, in what follows I would like to employ the development of my own work as a paradigm case both for understanding how the exceptional growth of literature on how such things as, say, reproduction, contradiction, and contestation are accomplished has influenced scholarship that seeks to situate the school within a larger nexus of social relations and for seeing the logic of the arguments I shall

18

make in the later chapters of this book.

In my previous work I focused on the role school curricula played in the creation and recreation of the ideological hegemony of the dominant classes and class segments of our society. In essence, the fundamental problematic that guided my work was the relationship between power and culture. While I was not totally clear on it, I intuitively grasped the fact that culture has a dual form. It is lived experience, developed out of and embodied in the day to day lives and interactions of specific groups. Yet, it also has another characteristic. Here I am referring to the ability of certain groups in society to transform culture into a commodity, to accumulate it, to make of it what Bourdieu has called 'cultural capital.' In many ways, it seemed to me that cultural capital and economic capital could be thought about in similar ways.[38] Yet both of these senses of culture — commodified and lived — were partly underdeveloped in my original investigations, perhaps because of the debates and issues into which I wanted to intervene.

Much of my analysis of schooling in *Ideology and Curriculum* concentrated on two issues: (1) a debate with liberal theories of curriculum and education in general, by attempting to show what is actually taught in schools and what its ideological effects might be; and (2) a debate within leftist scholarship on education about what schools do.

The first of these issues grew out of my general agreement with individuals like Bowles and Gintis, Althusser, and others that schools are important agencies for social reproduction. Our attempts at reforming these agencies tended to be misguided, in large part because we misrecognized the socio-economic functioning of the institution. Along with these other individuals, I set out to document how this functioning actually went on. The kinds of questions I asked were unlike those that tended to dominate our efficiency-minded field. Rather than asking how we could get a student to acquire more curricular knowledge, I asked a more political set of questions. 'Why and how are particular aspects of a collective culture represented in schools as objective factual knowledge? How, concretely, may official knowledge represent the ideological configurations of the dominant interests in a society? How do schools legitimate these limited and partial standards of knowing as unquestioned truths?'[39]

These questions provided the fundamental set of interests

guiding my work. As I mentioned earlier, I was taken with the fact that, in our long history from Bobbitt and Thorndike to Tyler and, say, Popham and Mager of transforming curriculum into only a concern with efficient methods, we had almost totally depoliticized education. Our search for a neutral methodology and the continuing transformation of the field into a 'neutral instrumentation' in the service of structurally non-neutral interests served to hide from us the political and economic context of our work. The kind of political/economic scrutiny I was engaged in was very similar in many ways to that being done by Katz, Karier, and Feinberg in the history and philosophy of education, by Bowles and Gintis and Carnoy and Levin in the economics of education, and by Young, Bernstein, and Bourdieu in the sociology of education. While there were similarities, however, there were and are serious disagreements among many of us on the left who examine and act on educational institutions. These disagreements provided the context for the second issue I noted above.

All too much of this kind of neo-Marxist scholarship treated the school as something of a black box and I was just as dissatisfied with this as I was with the dominant tradition in education. It did not get inside the school to find out how reproduction went on. In many ways, oddly, it was an analogue of the Tyler Rationale in curriculum, in that the focus tended to be scientistic and to place its emphasis on input and output, consensus, and efficient production. The interpretations placed upon the school were clearly different from those of Tyler and the efficiency minded curriculum 'experts,' yet schools were still seen as taking an input (students) and efficiently processing them (through a hidden curriculum) and turning them into agents for an unequal and highly stratified labor force (output). Thus, the school's major role was in the teaching of an ideological consciousness that helped reproduce the division of labor in society. This was fine as far as it went, but it still had two problems. *How* was this accomplished? Was that *all* schools did?

I spent a good deal of time in *Ideology and Curriculum* attempting to answer these questions. I interrogated schooling using a variety of techniques — historical, economic, cultural, and ethnographic. In the process, it became clear that at least three basic elements in schooling had to be examined. These included: the day to day interactions and regularities of the hidden curriculum that tacitly taught important norms and values; the formal corpus of school knowledge — that is, the overt curriculum itself — that is planned and found in the various materials and texts and filtered through teachers; and, finally, the fundamental perspectives that educators (read here Gramsci's points about the role of intellectuals) use to plan, organize, and evaluate what happens in schools.[40] Each of these elements was scrutinized to show how the day to day meanings and practices that are so standard in classrooms — while clearly there to help individual children — tended to be less the instruments of help and more part of a complex process of the economic and cultural reproduction of class relations in our society.

One word in this last sentence highlights the question of 'Is that all schools do?', the word cultural. Like Bernstein, Bourdieu, and, especially, Gramsci, it was evident to me that schools were cultural as well as economic institutions and examining the reproduction of the social division of labor would not exhaust how schools contributed to the creation of ideological hegemony. Thus, once again the form and content of the curriculum became of great significance if we were to see how cultural domination works and how 'unity was created.' What the investigators who dealt almost totally with the problem of economic reproduction were neglecting was the culture preserved, transmitted, and rejected within the institution. The way the curriculum was organized, the principles upon which it was built and evaluated, and, finally, the very knowledge itself, all of these were critically important if we were to understand how power was reproduced. Here I meant not just economic power but cultural power as well, though the two are considerably interwoven.[41]

Yet the focus on curriculum and culture still left out one very important aspect of schools, and it is here that I also tried to go beyond the theorists of economic reproduction such as Bowles and Gintis. They attempted to see the school as a place where economically rooted norms, dispositions, and values were taught, something I had also documented in both the ethnography of what is taught in kindergartens and in the analysis of social studies and science curricula reported in *Ideology and Curriculum*. This position tended to see schools and their overt and hidden curriculum as part of a mechanism of *distribution* only. This was all well and good. After all, schools do distribute ideological knowledge and values. However, it neglected an essential factor in what our educational apparatus also does. I wanted to argue that the

educational system constitutes a set of institutions that are fundamental to the *production* of knowledge as well. As the reader will
see in Chapter 2, this was and is a key element in my argument
about how we should interpret education. Schools are organized
not only to teach the 'knowledge that, how, and to' required by
our society, but are organized as well in such a way that they
ultimately assist in the production of the technical/administrative
knowledge required among other things to expand markets, control production, labor, and people, engage in the basic and applied
research needed by industry, and create widespread 'artificial'
needs among the population.[42] This technical/administrative
knowledge was able to be accumulated. It acted like a form of
capital, and, like economic capital, this cultural capital tended to
be controlled by and serve the interests of the most powerful
classes in society.[43] Economic and cultural capital were inextric-
ably linked. The kinds of knowledge considered most legitimate in
school and which acted as a complex filter to stratify groups of
students were connected to the specific needs of our kind of social
formation. Schools produced knowledge of a particular kind, then,
at the same time as they recreated categories of *deviance* that
stratified students. Deviance creation and the production of
cultural capital were indissolubly connected.

Thus, I began to see the need to interpret schooling as both a
system of production and reproduction. Our analysis of what gets
into schools and why, of what counts as legitimate knowledge and
values, would be incomplete unless we saw the complex and
contradictory roles schools play. As some of the 'new' sociologists
of education argued, schools process both people and knowledge.
But the 'processing' of knowledge includes more than its differential distribution to different kinds of people, but also its production and ultimate accumulation by those in power.

While all of this may seem horribly abstract, its roots were
and are in something much more concrete. As someone who had
taught for years at both the elementary and secondary level and
who had worked continuously with teachers and administrators as
a professor, I was searching for ways of understanding my and
their actions. Teachers, for example, blamed themselves as individuals (or their pupils) for the failures of students, just as I did. It
more and more, however, seemed to me *not* to be a question of
the amount of effort teachers and curriculum workers put in.
Indeed, few groups of people work harder and in more uncertain,

difficult, and complex circumstances than teachers and administrators. Rather, it became clearer that the institution itself and the connections it had to other powerful social agencies generated the dominant rules and practices of educators' lives. Blaming teachers, castigating individuals, was less than helpful. Figuring out how and especially why the institution did what it did in ways that went beyond these individual actions, that constrained these actions in ideological and material ways, seemed much more ethical. In this way we could make much better decisions on warranted curricular and pedagogical action. While an understanding of control was but a small step in challenging that control, it was a step I felt was essential if we were ever to see the control for what it was and to begin to realize the differential benefits — both economic and cultural — that resulted from it.

At the same time, as I became even more aware myself of these differential benefits and the structures in which education found itself, it altered my own practice politically. The analysis, while still deficient in ways I was beginning to grasp, was compelling in other ways. It required an even deeper involvement in socialist politics and action at a variety of levels, thus, ultimately acting back on my original analysis. My original work did not seem to 'theorize' adequately the kinds of things either myself or the groups of workers, parents, and progressively oriented teachers with whom I was working were doing. This became all the more pressing.

CONFLICT AND CONTRADICTION IN
LABOR AND CULTURE

After reading the prior section of this chapter, concerning simple reproduction theories and their problems, it is probably clear to you that part of the problem was the very fact that the dominant metaphor behind most of the analysis that went into *Ideology and Curriculum* was the idea of reproduction. I had broadened it to include cultural as well as economic considerations and I had argued for a notion of the school as a productive, as well as reproductive, apparatus. However, the orientation here still remained at too functional a level. It saw schools, and especially the hidden curriculum, as successfully corresponding to the ideological needs of capital; we just needed to see how it was really accomplished.

What was now more obviously missing in my formulations at this time was an analysis that focused on contradictions, conflicts, mediations and especially resistances, as well as reproduction. For while I had argued against mechanistic base/superstructure models where economic form totally determines cultural form and content, and while I wanted to show that the cultural sphere had some degree of relative autonomy, I had a theoretically underdeveloped notion of determination. It was a notion that led me to drift back to a logic of functional correspondence between what schools taught and the 'needs' of an unequal society and one that could not fully account for what else might be going on.

In struggling with this problem, my colleague Erik Olin Wright's work on the nature of determinations became quite helpful. He identified a number of basic modes of determination, some of which indicated a situation where an institution or a practice simply reproduced a given ideology or social order. But he also showed a good deal more could be going on. There could be meanings and practices that contradicted the overt and covert interests of a dominant class. There were important 'institutions' — such as the state — that mediated the interests of capital. And, most importantly, there could be concrete actions and struggles, though sometimes not conscious ones, by real groups of human actors that existed and which might be both mediating and transforming existing structures and meanings in significant ways.[44]

I began to realize that functionalist accounts of the hidden curriculum — accounts that sought to demonstrate both that students, like workers, were effectively socialized and that the power of technical/administrative forms used by capital was unchallenged — were part of the very process of ideological reproduction I wanted to struggle against. This meant that I had to examine two areas — resistances at both the school and the workplace. If Wright (as well as my own personal experience) was correct, then I should be able to find contradictory processes at work in these institutions, not only a correspondence between what industry wants and what goes on. And these contradictory processes should be exacerbated as the structural crisis unfolds.

This growing awareness of the way contestation and resistances operated, and my own political work with people involved in factories, schools, and offices, led me to examine the rapidly growing research on the day to day control of labor. Something quickly became rather apparent. When one examines the labor process, the actual life of men and women in our offices and factories, it becomes clear that what is found is a more complex picture than one has been led to expect from the literature on the hidden curriculum where simple correspondences between the school and the economy emerge in some straightforward fashion. This complexity is quite important since the truth of correspondence theories is dependent upon the accuracy of their view of the labor process. Rather than finding workers at all times being guided by the cash nexus, by authority, by expert planning, and by the norms of punctuality and productivity, however, the actual organization and control of the labor process illuminates the extent to which workers at all levels often resist and engage in action that is rather contradictory. A quote from Chapter 3 will give a sense of my later argument.

> Rather than the labor process being totally controlled by management, rather than hard and fast structures of authority and norms of punctuality and compliance, one sees a complex work culture. This very work culture provides important grounds for worker resistance, collective action, informal control of pacing and skill, and reasserting one's humanity . . . . Men and women workers seem engaged in overt and informal activity that is missed when we talk only in reproductive terms.

Clearly, then, workers resist in subtle and important ways, I believe. They often contradict and partly transform modes of control into opportunities for resistance and maintaining their own informal norms which guide the labor process. Whatever reproduction goes on is accomplished not only through the acceptance of hegemonic ideologies, but through opposition and resistances. We should remember here, though, that these resistances occur on the terrain established by capital, not necessarily by the people who work in our offices, stores, and industries.

We need also to remember a point I noted earlier, one that I shall argue in greater detail in Chapters 3 and 4. These informal cultural resistances, this process of contestation, may act in contradictory ways that may ultimately tend to be reproductive. By resisting and establishing an informal work culture that both recreates some sense of worker control over the labor process and rejects a good deal of the norms to which workers are supposedly socialized, workers may also be latently reinforcing the social relations of corporate production. Yes, they can partly control the skill level and pacing of their work, but they do not really impinge on the minimal requirements of production; nor do they effectively challenge the 'rights' of management. Resistances on one level may partially reproduce the lack of control on another.

All of these analyses of life in our workplaces were of no small import to me. My work on 'the other side of the hidden curriculum,' on what the labor process actually looked like, had given me a considerable amount of insight into the way oppositional cultural forms developed in day to day life. My interest in ideology and the relative autonomy of culture remained strong, for if resistance and contestation were real, then they could be employed for serious structural change as well. They could be used to 'win' people to the other side, if you will. Base/superstructure models were clearly too limiting here both theoretically and politically and I was going beyond them in some important ways now. My attempts to go further — to deal with culture as well as economy more seriously, to articulate the principles of knowledge production as well as reproduction — were also stimulated by something else, however. A significant amount of progress was being made on the very topic of cultural production and reproduction, especially by Marxist ethnographers.

Recent ethnographic investigations, in particular those carried out by people such as Paul Willis at The Centre for Contemporary Cultural Studies at the University of Birmingham, provided critical elements that enabled me to apply some of what I had learned about the labor process to the school. Willis and others demonstrated that rather than being places where culture and ideologies are imposed on students, schools are the *sites* where these things are produced. And like the workplace, they are produced in ways that are filled with contradiction and by a process that is itself based on contestation and struggle.[45] Once again resistance and the importance of lived culture came to the fore. The general points I laid out in my earlier discussion about reproduction were now no longer mere abstractions. The heritage of mechanistic perspectives was now being pushed aside some more.

These ethnographic investigations helped make it abundantly plain that there was no mechanistic process where the external pressures from an economy or the state inexorably mold schools and the students within them to the processes involved in

26

legitimation and in the accumulation of economic and cultural capital. Students themselves have power based on their own cultural forms. They act in contradictory ways, ways that both support this reproductive process and partially 'penetrate' it.[46] As my discussion of some of the major literature on class and cultural resistances in Chapter 4 will show, groups of working-class students often expressly reject the world of the school. This resistance will be filled with contradictions and will generate, in part, attempts by the state to intervene in times of intense social and ideological upheaval.

Besides Willis's work, other studies in the United States showed similar things. For example, Robert Everhart's ethnography of junior high school students illuminates how these predominantly working-class youths spend a large amount of their time 'goofing off' and recreating cultural forms that give them some degree of power in the school setting.[47] While these students do not totally reject the formal curriculum, they give the school only the barest minimum work required and try to minimize even those requirements. These students, like the lads in Willis's work, resisted. They gave only what was necessary not to endanger the possible mobility some of them might have. Yet, they already 'knew' that this was only a possibility, one that was not guaranteed at all. Most of them would, in fact, remain within the economic trajectories established by their parents. The elements of self-selection, of cultural forms of resistance, that both reproduced and contradicted the 'needs' of the economic apparatus, all of this demonstrated the relative autonomy of culture. It also provided a critical element in any serious evaluation of what schools do. For without getting inside the school, without seeing how and *why* students rejected the overt and hidden curriculum, and without linking this back to non-mechanistic conceptions of reproduction and contradiction, we would be unable to comprehend the complexity of the work that schools perform as sites of ideological production.[48]

The notion of a specifically Marxist ethnography was very significant here. For unlike vulgar representations that look for the imprint of economic ideology on everything, a more sophisticated approach would see ideology differently. It was not a form of false consciousness 'imposed' by an economy. Rather, it was part of a lived culture that was a result of the material conditions of one's day to day practices. It was a set of meanings and practices that indeed did have elements of good sense as well as reproductive elements within it. And because it had these elements of good sense, just as in the case of the workers whom I had examined, that made it objectively possible to engage in activity centered on political education that would challenge the ideological under-pinnings of the relations of patriarchy, dominance and exploita-tion in the wider society. The objective possibility of political education is something to which I shall return in later chapters.

As all of this was going on, as I began to make much better sense of how a more refined conceptual framework could help me understand the political and cultural practices I was seeing (and engaging in), I began to realize that I now could also begin to answer more coherently even some of the more traditional ques-tions that plagued education. If I wanted to understand why our reform efforts often failed, why even our most creatively designed curricula seemed not to be able to reach many of the most 'dis-advantaged' students, the research tools and conceptual frame-work that emerged from Marxist oriented ethnographies provided major insights. We were much closer to understanding this fully because of these studies of resistance, contestation, and lived culture.

EDUCATION AND THE STATE

The original stimulation I had received from Wright on contra-dictory processes and institutions that mediate economic pressures and which have their own needs, needs that may not be totally reproductive of the interests of capital, pointed me to an area that provided an ideal counterpart to my focus on the creation of ideological hegemony and the relative autonomy of culture. This was the political sphere, the state, and its own interaction with ideology and economy. The state became an essential ingredient in my analysis as I began to realize that the power, amount, and scope of state regulation of and intervention into the economy and the entire social process tends to increase in part as a function of the 'gradual unfolding of the process of capital accumulation,' of the need for consensus and popular support of this process, and the accompanying continuous 'declassing' of people by reorganizing political and legal discourse around individuals as economic agents,[49] among others. Hence, there was a dynamic interplay between the political and economic spheres which was found in education. While the former was not reducible to the latter — and, like culture, it had a significant degree of relative autonomy — the role the school plays *as a state apparatus* is strongly related to the core problems of accumulation and legitimation faced by the state and a mode of production in general.[50]

It seemed odd to me that we had so thoroughly ignored the state in education, except for some predominantly liberal research on the 'politics of education.'[51] After all, the mere recognition that approximately one-sixth of the labor force in the United States is employed by the state,[52] and that teaching itself is a form of work which will respond to changes in the over-all conditions of state intervention in the labor process, should make us sit up and take notice of it in all of our discussions surrounding education in the first place. This is especially the case if we are interested, as I was, in the building and rebuilding of hegemonic ideologies through state apparatuses like the school.

It became considerably more clear to me that the notion of hegemony is not free floating. It is in fact tied to the state in the first place. That is, hegemony isn't an already accomplished social fact, but a process in which dominant groups and classes 'manage to win the active consensus over whom they rule.'[53] As a part of the state, education, then, must be seen as an important element in attempting to create such an active consensus. Linkages to my earlier concerns became readily apparent. First, the literature on the state enabled me to go further in my arguments against the dominant theories of education, theories that acted as if education was an essentially neutral enterprise.

Just as importantly, however, the investigations on the state let me deepen my arguments against some of the other figures on the left who seemed to be still relatively economistic. Unlike them, I believed that the fact that education is an aspect of the state and is an active agent in the process of hegemonic control should not cause us to assume that all aspects of curriculum and teaching are reducible to the interests of a dominant class.[54] Like most aspects of liberal theories, this assumption too was simply incorrect. The state itself is a site of conflict among classes and class segments, and among gender and racial groups as well. Because it *is* the site of such conflict, it must either force everyone to think alike (a rather difficult task that is beyond its power and would destroy its legitimacy) or generate consent among a large

29

portion of these contending groups. Thus, to maintain its own legitimacy the state needs gradually but continuously to integrate many of the interests of allied and even opposing groups under its banner.[55]

This involves a continual process of compromise, conflict, and active struggle to maintain hegemony. The results, therefore, are not a simple reflection of the interests of an economy or dominant classes. Even reforms proposed to alter both the way schools are organized and controlled and what is actually taught in them will be part of this process. They too will be part of an ideological discourse that reflects the conflicts within the state and attempts by the state apparatus both to maintain its own legitimacy and that of the surrounding process of accumulation.

This had important implications for my analysis of schools and the day to day curricular and pedagogical activity that goes on within them. It meant that I had a better way of understanding why these curricular and teaching practices are never the result of 'mere' imposition; nor are they generated out of a conspiracy to, say, reproduce the conditions of inequality in a society. The fact that exactly the opposite is the case, that they will be guided by an urge to help and make things better, can be understood if we recognize that only in this way can various social interests *be* integrated within the state. By integrating varied ideological elements from differing and often contending groups around its own unifying principles, consensus can be gained[56] and the sense that practices based on these hegemonic principles actually help these contending groups can be maintained.

How is it that the state is able to appear as a set of 'neutral institutions' acting in the general interest?[57] The most effective hegemonic strategy seems to be 'to integrate popular democratic and economic corporate claims into a programme that favours state intervention in the interests of accumulation.'[58] That this is exactly the strategy being employed currently will become very clear in my discussions of the state's contradictory role in accumulation and maintaining hegemonic social relationships in Chapters 2, 4, and 5. There we shall see how the school is a site where the state, economy, and culture are interrelated and how many of the current reforms being proposed and curriculum innovations now in place 'reflect' these interrelations.

IDEOLOGY AND CURRICULUM FORM

So far I have talked about the state, the labor process, and the hidden and overt curriculum in two sites. I have described my own realization of how ideologies work in contradictory ways in both the workplace and the school. At the same time, I have argued that the usual ways the left has examined these sites has tended to be somewhat limited. Even given the movement of my own thinking over the last years, we should be careful, however, not to overstate the case against reproduction metaphors. For I do not want to imply that the logic and ideology of capital do not enter into the school and its curriculum in some very powerful ways. In fact, as will become clear in Chapter 5, such a logic is having a profound impact on day to day school practice. In order to understand this, we need to return to the idea of culture not as a lived experience, but as commodified form. This provides another opening into how schools act as sites of ideological production and reproduction.

Throughout my inquiries over the past decade, I have maintained that if we are to understand fully how ideologies work in schools we need to look at the concreta of day to day school life. Currently of immense import here is the way the logic and modes of control of capital are entering the school through the *form* the curriculum takes, not only in its content. And this relationship between form and content will be critical in my analysis of reproduction and contradiction here.

If we are to understand why some of these notable things are happening in schools and to our lives inside and outside of them, we need to comprehend the historical progression of our social formation. Without being reductive, we do need to understand changes and crises in our economy and in the ideological form and content that are in part both generated by it and act upon it. Curricular knowledge once again became rather significant for me in this regard.

It is important to interrogate two aspects of curriculum. The first concerns the content itself. What is there? Just as crucially, what is missing? In Macherey's words, thus, one interrogates the silences of a text to discover ideological interests at work.[59] Following Raymond Williams, I have called this analysis of the actual stuff of the curriculum the 'selective tradition.'[60]

The second aspect to be examined is the form. How is the

content, the formal culture, put together? What is going on at the level of the organization of the knowledge itself? Let me provide an example here, one that will be considerably deepened later on. For a variety of economic, political, and ideological reasons, a large amount of curricula in the United States is organized around individualization. That is, no matter what the specific content of the mathematics, social studies, science, reading, and so forth, it is put together in such a way that students often work at individual skill levels, on prespecified individual 'worksheets,' on individual tasks. Take one of the most popular sets of reading curricula, for instance, that manufactured by Science Research Associates (a subsidiary of IBM), the SRA Reading Kit. Here, students are given tests to establish appropriate skill levels; they are individually placed at a specific color-coded level; and they then proceed through the standardized sequence of material, working on individual stories and 'skill builders.'

Notice the form itself. Most important pedagogic, curricular, and evaluative activity are designed in such a way that students only interact with the teacher on a one to one level, not with each other (except during 'breaks'). The teacher 'manages' the system. This both increases efficiency and helps discipline. One could ask, what could be wrong with that? This is the wrong question if one is interested in ideological reproduction and how the school responds to crisis. A better question is, what is the ideological coding in the material? How does it organize our experiences in ways similar to the passive individual consumption of prespecified goods and services that have been subject to the logic of commodification so necessary for continued capital accumulation in our society?

Perhaps an example taken from another element of the cultural apparatus of a society, and one that aided me quite a bit in my own initial understanding of these questions, may be helpful here. It is taken from Todd Gitlin's provocative examination of how the formal device of prime-time television entertainment encourages viewers to experience themselves as anti-political, privately accumulating individuals. He points to the following characteristics as important in the reassertion of hegemony. The 'standard curve of narrative action' where standard characters deal with a new version of a standard situation, the thickening of the plot where 'stock characters' show their standard stuff, the resolution of the plot over twenty-two or fifty minutes, all of these regularities of the repeated formula are 'performances that rehearse social fixity.' They 'express and cement the obduracy of a social world impervious to substantial change.'[61]

These formula are not isolated, however. They need to be seen in relation to temporal structures and commercialization. For, by organizing the 'free time' of individuals into end-to-end interchangeable units, television 'extends, and harmonizes with, the industrialization of time. Media time and school time, with their equivalent units and curves of action, mirror the time of clocked labor . . .' In this way, free time is industrialized, duration is homogenized, and, given the formula employed, even personal excitement is routinized by the standard plot structure used. The form of this aspect of the cultural apparatus is the important component here.[62]

Even the form of the social experience of the actual viewing process contributes to the recreation of ideological experience. One sits isolated as a viewer, often only engaging in social interaction during commercials.[63] Commercials determine the times at which things happen in the plot. The very fact that commercials are so dominant speaks to the consequences on the contours of our consciousness over all. They play a large part in getting us 'accustomed to thinking of ourselves and behaving as a *market* rather than a *public*, as consumers rather than citizens.'[64] Notice that this extended example of the ideological impact of one element, television, of the larger cultural apparatus did not look at the content — what happened, whose perspectives were presented, and the ideological role of the selective tradition at work in this. While these issues are of critical importance, we miss what is just as important if we neglect the form that the content takes — its organization of our meanings and actions, its temporal sequences and interpersonal implications, its integration with the processes of capital accumulation and legitimating ideologies. Exactly these kinds of questions need to be asked about curriculum form and social interaction in schools as well. For it is on the grounds of the dominant curricular forms that control, resistance, and conflict are worked out. And, it is on this very same field that the structural crisis becomes visible and questions about the hidden curriculum, state intervention, and the control of the labor process are integrated at the level of school practice.

In order to see the implications of these arguments fully we need to remember a point that was implied in my brief discussion of the state. Schools are places of teachers' *work*. This is something we tend quite regularly to forget. Yet alterations in curricular form like those I have been discussing also have a profound impact on such work. They embody a fundamentally changed relationship between a person's labor, skills, consciousness, products, and other people. At the same time, by stressing these changes as I shall in Chapter 5 — and they will be just as contradictory as the changes we see today in any aspect of the labor process in general — we shall have a key to laying out possible actions progressive groups may take within schools and among teachers. This dual realization — that new curricular forms engender both new modes of control and possibilities for political action — opens up a door to our understanding of what happens in schools and provides us with a key building block in our analysis. How? Certain principles based in large part on the technical/administrative knowledge originally produced by the educational apparatus have guided the organization and control of places where people work in corporate economies. These principles have entered not only into the shop-floor in factories but have found their way more and more in all aspects of the productive apparatus of society. Blue- and white-collar labor, manual and mental labor, selling and assembling, yes, and even teaching, have slowly but surely been incorporated into the logics of these forms of organization and control. In ways that are not inconsequential, teaching is a labor process, one that, to be sure, has its own specific characteristics that are not reducible to working on a shop-floor, an insurance company office, or as a salesperson, but one that is a labor process none the less. And it is on the terrain of the school as a workplace that the technical/administrative knowledge that was once produced by the school enters back into the school to control and rationalize the work of both teachers and students.

In fact, as I shall argue, because of the current structural crisis in the economic, political, and cultural spheres of social life, the primary elements used to organize and control the labor process in our society — among them the separation of mental from manual labor, the divorce of conception from execution, the logic of deskilling and controlling a work-force — all are being reconstituted in complex and paradoxical ways in schools at the present time. And like other workplaces and cultural settings, these elements are subject to acceptance and rejection at one and the same time. By returning to the day to day life of schools to examine this in Chapter 5, we can complete the circle of our inquiries into how schools both reproduce and contradict the 'needs' of our unequal society.

III

THE CIRCULATION OF TECHNICAL/ ADMINISTRATIVE KNOWLEDGE

This chapter has, of course, only introduced what are clearly complicated issues of the state, class, culture, reproduction, resistance, contradiction, knowledge, and schooling. However, my prior claims about curricular form and its relationship to the labor process of teaching returns us to the conceptual point at which I began the middle section of this chapter, the school as a productive, as well as reproductive, apparatus.

One strand weaves its way through these arguments — the importance of technical/administrative knowledge and its accompanying ideology. The school helps produce it as a form of 'capital;' it is found and contested in the workplace as a form of control; it enters the state and the school. Each of these sites transforms it until it reenters the school and is reproduced and produced again. Thus, a continuous yet contradictory process can be envisioned.

I want to make this point more clearly since it can act as a summary of many of the arguments I have made and will make here. Technical/administrative knowledge can be thought of as having a circulation as it is embodied in the economy, the state, and the school.

In many ways, this can be thought of as something of a circular process. Technical/administrative knowledge is produced over the long term in and through the organization of education. As we shall see in Chapter 2, its accumulation for use by those in power (through patent laws, hiring practices, credentialing processes, and so forth) is a strong tendency in our social formation. These forms of knowledge, or 'cultural capital' — and the ideology of rationalization which both supports and is in part engendered by it — is employed in the economy and *increasingly in the state* as the state itself becomes caught in the larger crisis of capital accumulation and legitimation. In both the workplace and the school, however, workers and students mediate, transform, and even reject parts of it. In the process, it is altered somewhat but its circulation still spreads as the crisis continues. Hence, through a set of complex interconnections, the logic of capital embodied in technical/administrative knowledge returns to its source — the educational apparatus — as a form of control.

This is complicated, but so are the ties between the three spheres I have noted. If it were simple, the economic conditions that I described earlier which are now being faced by so many people might themselves be dealt with simply. Of course, they are not. For our problems are as much due to a lack of understanding of the connections among economy, culture, and politics, as they are due to both a lack of will and because of the objective conditions that make it so hard to build and maintain a large movement of working men and women to change them.

Now that I have laid out the growth of the conceptual, and political, framework I have employed here and prefigured in general my basic arguments, let me be a bit more specific about the content of each of the coming chapters.

Chapter 2 begins with culture as commodity by pointing out a number of the limitations of current economistic theories of what schools do, including some of the more respected Marxist approaches. In it, I deal with the dialectical interplay between the school as a productive and reproductive apparatus. By focusing on culture as a commodity, the ties between the school's function in assisting in the production of the technical/administrative knowledge needed for capital accumulation and the control of labor on the one hand, and the school's role in stratifying a student population and 'creating' deviance on the other, are documented.

Chapters 3 and 4 turn to culture as lived experience and the contradictory role such a lived culture performs. Here, we shall see it as a fundamental grounding for the possible development of resistance and alternatives to the ideological practices of capital and the state at the same time that it partly reproduces the conditions of existence of these very same ideological practices.

More specifically, Chapter 3 will again challenge the dominant economistic theories of reproduction, especially those concerned with the hidden curriculum. It will examine the labor process at the workplace itself by following up on Erik Olin Wright's points about the possibility of non-reproductive activity going on in particular sites. The focus will be on the day to day lives of *workers* in shops, factories, offices, and elsewhere. Rejection and contradiction, as well as reproduction, will be its guiding themes.

Chapter 4 will go further into my account of the processes of rejection, mediation, and transformation. There I shall analyze the way class- and gender-related cultural forms are lived out in many *students'* everyday patterns of interaction. It will continue my documentation of the exceptional importance of going beyond simplistic base/superstructure theories by showing the relative autonomy of culture. The connections and contradictions between the economic and the cultural/ideological will be apparent. At the same time, I shall link these connections and contradictions back to the crisis they cause in the state by scrutinizing the reforms currently being proposed to enable the school to respond more adequately to the structural crisis — such as tax credits and voucher plans. Finally, as in the previous chapters, suggestions for action will be made.

Chapter 5 returns us to the commodification process where technical/administrative knowledge reenters the school. Here cultural form and content is exhibited in its reified existence as the state and capital attempt to control both the content of what is taught, the form of its transmission, and the labor process of teaching. The chapter will analyze the curricular form now increasingly being found in schools and will relate it back to the arguments made previously about the labor process. In essence, Chapter 5 will enable us to see one of the major ways the state can integrate popular democratic and corporate claims together so that both legitimation and accumulation can be fostered.

Chapter 6 will summarize the arguments made and will examine the prospects for the success of progressive action in both the school and the surrounding institutions. Such progressive action is even more necessary today, for the shadow of the crisis is widening.

CHAPTER 2

TECHNICAL KNOWLEDGE, DEVIANCE AND THE STATE: THE COMMODIFICATION OF CULTURE

In a little book of stories written for children who are just beginning to learn how to read, there is an interchange that goes something like the following. Boris the Bear and Morris the Moose meet in the forest. Boris, obviously the smarter of the two and someone who is in the know, asks his friend if he likes riddles. Morris stands there. He puzzles over this question. Suddenly, in a flash of insight he responds with something like, 'Well, I don't know. How do they taste?' Boris, exasperated, a look of contempt now flashing from his eyes, yells at his companion, 'Listen, a riddle is not something to eat!' Morris now understands, of course. And he says, 'Of course. I know. It is something to drink.'

Now I find myself in something of the position of Morris. Borises by the score keep telling me the one way to interpret a particular phenomenon, though in this case it happens to be the school and not a riddle. The bulk of these Borises, including many curriculum reformers and educational researchers, tell me schools are the engines of a meritocratic democracy. A smaller portion, and one that I must admit I feel quite close to in many ways, interpret schools more structurally. They tell me schools are simply mechanisms for the reproduction of the division of labor. Yet I know the first group of Borises is clearly wrong[1] and unfortunately the second group seems to be too enamored with a black box vision of schooling. For my own experience inside the black box and my research on the ideological and economic place of the day to day pedagogic and curricular activity within it, lead me to wonder, as Morris did, if this is all a riddle can do and be. Can we understand what schools are and do without reducing schools, like that riddle, to one function, yet at the same time without giving up the structural interests that guide the reproduction theorists? Can we build a more subtle 'external' theory of schools — a theory that is a bit more complex than that embodied in the unidimensional theory of the recreation of a hierarchical work-force, and which still helps us explain both some of the internal qualities we know schools have and the connections between these qualities and an unequal economy?

It is clear that we are part of the way towards that goal. This is partially because the impressive development of ethnographic and ethnomethodological studies has led to a concomitant growth in our understanding of the internal ways (and the constraints on these ways) that teachers and students 'negotiate' their respective realities in classrooms.[2] It has also led to clearer descriptions of ways in which teachers impute such things as deviance to students within the school.[3] However, while these kinds of investigations help us unpack the meanings educators and children either have imposed on them or act on in their day to day lives, they are at times less adequate than they might be in offering possible *reasons* for particular kinds of meanings to evolve and particular conceptions of deviance to dominate. Describing any X is obviously not necessarily the same as explaining why X exists in the first place.

This process of explanation can be accomplished in two ways. One can explain the conditions of existence of X within an institution, focusing 'internally' on what supports or contradicts action in the immediate environment in which this X is found. Or, as I would like to do in this chapter, one can focus on the relationship between this X and the 'external' modes of production and ideological and economic forces in which X is embedded. My focus, hence, *will* be structural. It will seek to uncover the connections between the creation and imputation of such things as certain kinds of deviance in schools and the unequal economic and cultural conditions that might give a number of the reasons for the existence of these kinds of conditions in these institutions. This is *not* to deny the importance of internalistic appraisals of schooling; nor is it to assume that structuralist analysis of school life, like Boris's notion of a riddle, can explain everything.[4] In fact, micro-social descriptions of our commonsense practices are essential for those who want to take a macroeconomic perspective, if only to make us remember what is brought out in the work of Gramsci and Williams. As they continually remind us, ideological hegemony, as a part of the actual workings of control, is not something one sees only on the level of macro-social behavior and economic relations; nor is it something that resides merely at the top of our heads, so to speak. Instead, hegemony is constituted by our very day to day practices. It is our whole assemblage of commonsense meanings and actions that make up the social world as we know it,[5] a world in which the internal curricular, teaching, and evaluative characteristics of educational institutions partake.

Even with all this in mind, however, I do want to claim that until we understand the ties that exist between these internal curricular and pedagogic practices of schools and the 'external' structures of domination of a society, we shall have a necessarily incomplete explanation of X. Hence, while we are beginning to have fairly thorough descriptions of the internal workings of schools and the imputation of deviance, these need to be complemented by a structural theory of schooling and the place of deviance within it. Such a theory would have to link together the kinds of knowledge considered important in schools (high status or legitimate knowledge), the kinds of students who are labeled as deviant, the ideological, political, and economic 'needs' of the society in which schools are embedded, and finally, the role of the state in all of this, in a way that responds to the complexity of this better than the simple economic reproduction theories now extant.

WHAT SCHOOLS DO AND DO NOT DO

At the outset, it should be clear that there is a danger in even employing a concept such as deviance. Its traditional usage tends to bring out conceptions of people who are different *and* inferior. In this accepted view, schools are basically meritocratic institutions. They lead to large-scale mobility among groups and individuals in a population. Any lack of mobility, any failure in achievement, is defined as a lack within the individual or group who has failed. One might say here that deviance is 'earned' by the deviant, since the overt and hidden curriculum, the social relations of the classroom, and the categories by which educators organize, evaluate, and give meaning to the activities found in schools are perceived as being basically neutral. This claim of neutrality is, of course, less accurate than this proposition would have us believe. As I noted in Chapter 1, the formal corpus of school knowledge and the hidden curriculum often embody ideological commitments.[6] The categories educators employ to think about, plan, and

40

evaluate school life are consistently biased towards extant and unequal social regularities.[7]

And, finally, schools are not as meritocratic as many educational researchers would have us think. Though many individuals still accept the notion that schooling serves to maximize the possibility of personal mobility, leading in some direct fashion to the ability to live a better life later on, recent analyses suggest otherwise. For if we did in fact live in a meritocratic order, 'we would expect to find the relationship between test scores and measures of adult success rising over time, and the relationship between family background and adult success falling.'[8] Neither of these is the case. Instead, current evidence seems to indicate that there has been little consistent loosening of the ties between origins and attainments through schools.[9]

Rather than looking at the internal and external characteristics of schools in this way, a way that seems to be both an empirical and ideological misperception, I want to argue that one fundamental latent social role of the school is 'deviance amplification.' That is, the school *naturally generates* certain kinds of deviance. This process of natural generation is intimately related to the complex place schools have in the economic and cultural reproduction of class relations — on the one hand to the school's function as an ideological state apparatus[10] and through this in producing agents (with the 'appropriate' dispositions and values) to fill the needs of the social division of labor in society, and on the other hand to the place of educational institutions in producing the particular kinds of knowledge forms required by an unequal society. It is the interplay (an interplay too often covered by black box theories) between these two factors, and especially the latter, that will concern me here. In essence, we shall want to interpret this as a problem of beginning to unpack the ties that bind the school's economic and cultural roles together.

How are we to understand this? First, let us examine some general propositions, ones that seem to have some empirical warrant, about what schools seem to accomplish as institutions embedded within our society. Schools seem to do a number of things. They are reproductive organs in that they *do* help select and certify a work-force. Here the reproduction theorists are not wrong. But schools do more. They help maintain privilege in cultural ways by taking the form and content of the culture and knowledge of powerful groups and defining it as legitimate

41

knowledge to be preserved and passed on. In this way, they act as agents of what Raymond Williams has called the 'selective tradition.' Schools, hence, are also agents in the creation and recreation of an effective dominant culture. They teach norms, values, dispositions, and culture that contribute to the ideological hegemony of dominant groups.[11]

Yet this is not all, for schools help legitimate new knowledge and new classes and strata of social personnel; and it is often in the battle over a place in the school curriculum between the cultures of older and newly emergent classes and groups that one can see class and gender conflicts and economic contradictions working themselves out in the activities of people as they go about their routine lives.[12]

Notice that this listing of the major social functions of educational institutions by necessity includes cultural as well as economic concerns. Schools allocate people and legitimate knowledge. They legitimate people and allocate knowledge. Now one can talk about this combination (and they are *not* separate functions, but interpenetrate each other) positively or negatively. It is basically good, bad, or contradictory. But one must talk about control of *both* culture and economy together if one is to understand what schools do. Thus, as we shall see, the control of knowledge and economic power will go together, but not in the ways we are used to thinking about them.

SCHOOL KNOWLEDGE: DISTRIBUTION OR PRODUCTION?

That there is a relationship between knowledge and an economy is not a new idea, of course. It is often recognized, though in a different light, by both Marxists and non-Marxists alike. For example, two recent approaches — one supposedly neutral, the other on the left — are among the responses to this relationship and have dominated our thinking about what schools do. Basically, though each is no more than an ideal type that covers real differences within them, these can be called human capital and allocation theories. In general, human capital theory claims that schools are critical agencies for industrial growth and for mobility. Schools will maximize the distribution of technical and administrative knowledge among the population. As students learn this knowledge, they can 'invest' their acquired skills and expertise and will climb the ladder to better occupations. This will provide higher rates of individual mobility and will also guarantee the supply of well-trained people that is required by an expanding economy. Widespread technical training, mobility, and economic growth are linked. Conscious 'manpower' planning and the stimulation of scientific, technical, and career oriented curricula in schools become essential here.[13]

Almost as a direct response to the assumptions held by many members of the human capital school, allocation theorists assert the opposite. Schools are not there to stimulate widespread class mobility. Rather, they basically act as sorting devices. They allocate individuals to their 'proper places' within the hierarchical division of labor and distribute the dispositions, norms, and values (through the hidden curriculum) that are required by workers for their effective participation on their particular rung of the occupational ladder. The teaching of differential hidden messages (by class position), the relatively small importance of technical competence, and a lack of class mobility are linked here.[14] For human capital theorists, 'owning' some knowledge leads to greater personal power in the economic arena. For allocation theorists, internalizing hidden knowledge — those dispositions, norms and values — leads to power remaining in the hands of others.

Now the allocation theories of the political economists of education have taught us a good deal, of course. Though they have systematically underconceptualized the important role played by the formal corpus of school knowledge in the reproduction for which they want to account,[15] they have provided an important political base from which one can interpret the covert messages schools seem to teach so powerfully.

Elsewhere, for instance, I have reported ethnographic research that has shown how the hidden curriculum in schools effectively teaches 'essential' norms and ideological distinctions to students, norms and distinctions 'required' by a labor market.[16] This research tended to confirm part of the arguments put forth by the political economists that a major economic role of the school was just this hidden teaching. Thus, for Bowles and Gintis, this covert teaching brought about by the social relations of the classroom was differentially distributed. In essence, rather than one public school system in advanced capitalism, there are two. Each of these systems teaches different norms, values, and dispositions depending on

43

one's social class and economic trajectory.[17] The school, here, acts as a filter between the home and the labor market. It defines one as normal or deviant and these definitions of deviance roughly correspond to the needs of the economy outside the school. This is partly accurate, though it is rather mechanistic.

In fact, as I noted earlier, while my political sympathies lie with the structural concerns generated by the positions of the allocation theorists rather than the human capital theorists, both groups ignore, and therefore miss, an important role of the school. Both groups of individuals assume at least in terms of the knowledge found within the institution, that schools are *distribution* institutions. The first assumes that a major function of the educational apparatus is to maximize the distribution of technical knowledge so that individuals can also maximize their chances of attainment in a competitive market. The flaws in this (a vision of a competitive and open market, etc.) are clear.[18] The other is certainly a structural position, yet it too assumes that the only serious way to interpret the school is as a mechanism which distributes norms and dispositions that reinforce and reproduce economically based class positions. This is correct in many ways and certainly serves to debunk a good deal of the meritocratic beliefs that are still widespread, beliefs that take as given the 'fact' that the distribution of this technical knowledge guarantees advancement in a society that is at root unequal. However, both positions, and especially any position that wants to understand fully the school's place in the reproduction of inequality, must be complemented by a concomitant focus on the school as a productive, not only distributive, institution.

While this certainly does not exhaust everything accomplished by an educational system, we shall need to look at schools as aspects of the productive apparatus of a society in two ways: first, as institutions that help produce agents for positions outside of the school in the economic sector of society; and second, as institutions that produce the cultural forms directly and indirectly needed by this same economic sector. I shall argue that there is an interplay, one that is quite complex, between the school's role in the production of agents for the social division of labor (a role that the political economists of education have recognized) and the school's place as a mode of production of cultural capital. In essence, I shall argue that in order to understand this interplay, we shall have to begin to 'decipher the logic' of the corporate accumulation process, since the production, accumulation, and control of particular kinds of knowledge is an integral aspect of this process.[19]

As Erik Olin Wright has argued, capital accumulation lies at the heart of the reproduction of corporate societies.[20] Speaking metaphorically, while the school is not the pumping station of this economy, it resides in the same body and contributes to the accumulation process as it exists today. Let us look at this body just a bit closer.

SCHOOL KNOWLEDGE AND CAPITAL ACCUMULATION

I want us to think about knowledge as a form of capital. Just as economic institutions are organized so that particular classes increase their share of economic capital, cultural institutions like schools seem to do the same thing. Schools play a fundamental role in assisting in the accumulation of cultural capital.

Now I am using the idea of cultural capital in a particular way, one that is different from that of Bourdieu and others. For Bourdieu, for instance, the style, language, cultural dispositions, and so on of dominant groups — i.e. their cultural capital — can be cashed in in schools so that their dominance is preserved.[21] Thus, they get ahead because of the 'possession' of this cultural capital. There is some strength to such a conception of cultural capital. However, it fails to catch the school's role in the *production* of a kind of capital. Bourdieu's work is still something of an allocation theory. For him, cultural capital is used as a device to allocate students, by class, to their 'proper' position in society. Students without it are, by definition, deviant. What such an approach does not catch is that schools also act as one of the primary modes of production of the cultural commodities needed by a corporate society. This will require some further explication.

In my recent investigation, in *Ideology and Curriculum*, of the ideological role of school knowledge I argued the following:

> Our kind of economic system is organized in such a way that it can create only a certain amount of jobs and still maintain high profit levels for corporations. In essence, the economic apparatus is at its *most efficient* when there is a (measured)

unemployment rate of approximately 3 or 4-6 per cent (though we know that this is a notoriously inaccurate measure to which must also be added the issues of much higher rates for blacks [and other groups] , high levels of under-employment [and the underpaid and unpaid labor of women]). To provide useful work for these individuals would require cutting into acceptable rates of return, and would probably require at least a partial reorganization of so called 'market mechanisms' which apportion jobs and resources. Because of this, it would not be a misplaced metaphor to describe our economic system as *naturally generating* specifiable levels of under and unemployment. We can think of this model as one which is primarily concerned with the maximization of the production of profit and only secondarily concerned with the distribution of resources and employment.

Now a similar model seems to hold true when we think about knowledge in its relationship to such an economy. An advanced corporate economy requires the production of high levels of technical knowledge to keep the economic apparatus running effectively and to become more sophisticated in the maximization of opportunities for economic expansion. Within certain limits, what is actually required is *not* the wide-spread distribution of this high status knowledge to the populace in general. What is needed is to maximize its production. As long as the knowledge is continuously and efficiently produced, the school itself, at least in this major aspect of its function, is efficient. Thus, certain low levels of achievement on the part of 'minority' group students, children of the poor, and so on can be tolerated. It is less consequential to the economy than is the generation of the knowledge itself. Once again, production of a particular 'commodity' (here high status knowledge) is of more concern than the distribution of that particular commodity. To the extent that it does not interfere with the production of technical knowledge, then concerns about distributing it more equitably can be tolerated as well.

Thus, just as in the 'economic market place' where it is more efficient to have a relatively constant level [or corporate or state controlled variation in the level] of unemployment, to actually generate it really, so do cultural institutions 'naturally' generate [deviance] and levels of poor achievement. The distribution or scarcity of certain forms of cultural capital is of less moment in the calculus of values [generated by this social formation] than the maximization of the production of the particular knowledge itself.[22]

Thus, schools do not 'merely' act as mechanisms for the distribution of a hidden curriculum and the distribution of people to their 'proper' places outside of them. They are important elements in the mode of commodity production in a society.

What could be wrong with this? Of course schools produce knowledge. Isn't this commonsensical? It is in what seems so commonsensical, however, that we can begin to uncover some of the ties between school knowledge, the reproduction of the division of labor, and the accumulation process. To do this, we need to understand how technical/administrative knowledge is actually employed. We need to situate it back into the structural relations that helped generate it, because technical knowledge is *not* necessarily a neutral commodity within the context of a corporate economy. This is especially important today since it is becoming increasingly clear that there is nearly a total corporate monopolization of technical knowledge and technological intelligence.[23]

Andre Gorz's position becomes of particular import here. He maintains that 'it must always be remembered that the "means of production" are not only plant and machines; they are also the technology and the science incorporated in machines and installations, which dominate the workers as a "productive force distinct from labour." '[24]

Broadly speaking, technical knowledge is essential in a number of ways in any advanced industrial economy. The *way* it is employed in ours, though, is the critical factor. Given the enormous growth in the volume of production there has been a concomitant need for a rapid increase in the amount of technical and administrative information. This is coupled with the continued increase in the need for 'market research' and human relations research which each firm requires to increase the rate of accumulation and workplace control. All of this necessitates the machine production of information (and the production of more efficient machines as well). These products — the commodity of knowledge — may be non-material in the traditional sense of that term, but there can be no doubt that they are economically essential products.[25] When one adds to this the immense role played by defense-related industries in corporate accumulation — something I pointed out in my notes to Chapter 1 — the importance of this kind of cultural capital increases.

While it is not a hard and fast rule, and has tended to vary in different periods, historically in economies like our own technical knowledge has been produced and organized in such a way that it has tended to benefit corporate concerns. For example, in his interesting, but sometimes problematic, analysis of the role of technical innovations in the growth of a capitalist economy, Stephen Marglin notes that the bias of technological change has nearly always been consistent with industrial organization and reorganization. That is, the technical efficiency brought about by the accumulation *and control* of technical/administrative knowledge was sponsored and introduced by corporate managers so that they could increase their share of economic profits, not merely for efficiency of organization. The social function of the hierarchical division of labor based on technical criteria, hence, was not only technical efficiency, but accumulation. At the same time, it increased the power of management to control and supervise workers by the very fact that a technically based hierarchy of labor broke down crafts and skills into atomistic units so that they could be reorganized on the factory floor.[26] Part of the historical working out of this process is graphically illustrated in Harry Braverman's treatment of the progressive atomization and loss of control within blue- and white-collar jobs.[27]

The importance of the use, control, and accumulation of technical cultural capital is made even more clear if one examines the history of our more technically and scientifically based industries. For instance, in the extractive, petroleum, steel, rubber, and above all the automobile industry the systematic introduction of 'science' as a means of production presupposed, and in turn reinforced, industrial monopoly.

Hence, in his recent analysis of the history of the relationship among science, technology, educational institutions, and industry, Noble argues that:

> This monopoly meant control not simply of markets and
> productive plant and equipment but of science itself as well.
> Initially the monopoly over science took the form of patent

control — that is the control over the *products* of scientific technology. It then became control over the *process* of scientific production itself, by means of organized and regulated industrial research. Finally it came to include command over the social prerequisites of this process: the development of the institutions necessary for the production of both scientific knowledge and knowledgeable people, and the integration of these institutions within the corporate system of science-based industry. 'The scientific-technical revolution,' as Harry Braverman has explained, 'cannot be understood in terms of specific innovations . . .' Rather, it 'must be understood in its totality as a mode of production in which science and exhaustive engineering have been integrated as part of ordinary functioning. The key innovation is not to be found in chemistry, electronics, automatic machinery . . . or any of the products of these science-technologies, but rather in the transformation of science itself into capital.'[28]

Thus, as industry tied itself more and more to the division and control of labor and to technical innovations, if it was to expand its markets and consumption it needed to guarantee a relatively constant accumulation of two kinds of capital, economic and cultural. These needs required much larger influence in the places where both agents and knowledge were produced — the school and especially the university. This process of influence has heightened today, often in the form of state intervention, a form of intervention I shall describe in greater detail shortly.

Noble's previous statement about the importance of patent control illuminates a critical point for it is here that one can see an area where the accumulation of technical knowledge plays a significant economic role. Controlling the production of technical knowledge was important for systematic patent production and the monopolization of a market. While the primary aim of a good deal of industrial research was to find technical solutions to immediate production problems, the organization and control of knowledge production was essential if one was to 'anticipate inventive trends and take out patents to keep open the road of technical progress and business expansion.'[29] The control of major aspects of science and technical knowledge was accomplished by way of patent monopolies and the organization and reorganization of university life (and especially its curricula). Thus, as Noble again so clearly shows, industry and ideologies it has spawned played and continue to play an exceptionally important role in determining (that is, in setting structural limits on) the kinds of curricula and pedagogical practices deemed appropriate or legitimate for a significant portion of university and technical institute life. Given the economic crisis we currently face, one should expect an even greater influence of the interests of capital in the near future as well.

In one respect, using the universities to generate and preserve technical knowledge based on basic and applied research was quite efficient. The cost and the risk of both the production of trained personnel to work in industry and the production of the fundamental research upon which so much of science-based industrial research depends is to a large extent placed upon the public.[30] In part, this explains why the overt curricula of schools — the legitimate knowledge within the black box — seems to be organized towards the university. That is, the fact that a large portion of schooling is pointed toward college and technical schools (and as Karabel has shown which of these schools one attends is often dependent upon one's personal trajectory within one's economic class)[31] provides further evidence of the interpenetration of the school's dual role in the production of both agents and cultural commodities.

I have argued so far that we need to see schools as productive as well as distributive institutions in order to get a fuller picture of what they seem to do. At the same time, by looking at the ties between economic and cultural production, we can fill in even more of that picture. I want to go just a bit further here in exploring these ties.

The focus on the production of technical knowledge allows us to see how schools help maintain a distinction that lies at the heart of the social division of labor — that between mental and manual labor.[32] Those students who are identified as being able to produce — through their later surplus labor — important quantities of technical/administrative knowledge are increasingly 'placed' on the mental side of this dichotomy. This is done internally by the 'natural' workings out of the curricular and guidance program of the school. Those who reject or are rejected by this particular calculus of values are 'placed,' again through the internal guidance and curricular programs of the school, in a trajectory that allows

50

surplus labor to be extracted from them later on in the form of service and/or manual labor.[33] The fact that the culture, language, and values of dominant groups are employed in the initial teaching in these schools helps produce the fact that the children of the poor and ethnic minorities will be found on the manual side of this dichotomy. This process is obviously not as smooth as it sounds. Students do not necessarily sit still in the face of these conditions, a point I will return to in my discussion of the internal qualities of schools and of the lived culture of students in Chapter 4.

Notice again how this seems to work in both aspects of the productive role of the school by also assisting in the production of agents to fit the needs of the social division of labor. On the one hand, those individuals who are not 'seen' as contributing to the maximization of the production of technical/administrative knowledge are regarded as deviant and hence can be effectively sorted out into various levels, again with the appropriately differentiated norms and values. On the other hand, 'experts' are produced who serve an important ideological function. In Wright's words, 'experts of various sorts at all stages of the production process help to legitimize the subordination of labor to capital, by making it appear natural that workers are incapable of organizing production themselves.' In essence, because of the extensive division between mental and manual labor, to a large extent workers are ultimately excluded from the knowledge necessary for both understanding and directing important aspects of the production process.[34] The corporate accumulation and control of technical knowledge is tied in intimately with this division, a division that, as we have seen, is critical to the accumulation and control of economic capital as well.

This relationship between the accumulation of economic and cultural capital means that it is *not* essential that everyone have sophisticated technical knowledge in one's head so to speak. As long as the knowledge is available, the school is relatively efficient in this aspect of its productive function. As the conditions of the maximization of the production of technical/administrative knowledge are satisfied, and as students respond to or reject much of the messages of school life basically by class (and race and gender), the school can employ this knowledge as a complex filter to sort out students according to their prospective places in a hierarchical market. Origins become again tied to attainments (though again

51

not through any mechanistic process since there is *individual* mobility as well).

All of this needs to be continually situated back into the accumulation process. Reserves of capital need to be generated for times of crisis in an economy. To accomplish this, two other kinds of reserves seem also to be needed: (1) a reserve of workers, workers who can be inserted into positions when these become available; and (2) cultural capital, the knowledge forms that can be used to create new techniques for production, for patent monopolies, for the stimulation of needs and markets, and for the division and control of labor. Thus, one might hypothesize that technical knowledge functions through schools as a reserve knowledge force in the same way that an economy needs a reserve force of workers. Both of these reserves will play important roles in an economic crisis.

This is quite involved, I realize. However, the basic point in this section of my analysis has been something of a structural claim. While the content of technical knowledge is not necessarily ideological on the face of it, the uses to which it is put in corporate economies and the way it functions in and through schools are 'determined' by the actual structural patterns that currently exist. That is, the domination of corporate control, use, and ultimate accumulation of technical knowledge sets limits on the forms it will take in this society, and ultimately on the kinds of knowledge and people selected as legitimate within the schools of capitalist societies.[35]

I noted in my introductory comments, however, that in order to understand these complex interconnections we would need to see the relations not only between knowledge, deviance, and economic and cultural reproduction. We would also have to begin to grapple with the power of the state. It is to this that we shall now turn.

THE ROLE OF THE STATE

In his comparative investigation of state power and state apparatuses, Goran Therborn has recently argued that the state apparatus, in its very organization and functioning, can often be seen as expressing relations of class dominance.[36] This is not an inconsequential point in my argument since the role of the state (with the school as a critical arm of it) becomes increasingly important in understanding what schools do.

Since it has become more and more difficult for individual corporations to guarantee a flow of technical knowledge and both technically specialized and semi-skilled personnel, the educational apparatus of the state, through its curricular, funding and testing priorities and policies, takes on a prominent responsibility. The state, which since the 1930s in the United States has been guided by allocative policies to redistribute some of the resources that have been produced by the economy, enters more and more into productive policies. This is clearly true in the economy where the state regulates, controls, subsidizes special interests, sponsors research, and supplies monetary support for the production of 'essential' goods, often those directly relating to the defense industry. It acts nationally and internationally as a force in 'guaranteeing' supplies which contribute to the productivity of the economy.[37]

Unlike previous periods before, say, World War II when the state would intervene into the economy for limited objectives, state intervention has grown so rapidly today that it is an essential part of advanced capitalist countries. Though different countries will differ in how they intervene — e.g., nationalization of certain industries in France and Italy; massive public spending in the United States — there can be no longer any doubt about the extent of such intervention.[38] This intervention usually consists of a number of principal forms. First, the state subsidizes capital directly by fiscal measures such as loans and credits, and indirectly by furnishing energy, transportation, etc. A second form, and one that is quite important for my arguments here, involves the state's role in assuming more of the social costs of private capital. That is, it socializes the costs of such things as scientific research and the education and training of labor power. In this way, even though these expenses are fundamental primarily for increasing the profitability and productivity of industry, the costs are 'spread out' to all of us. Thus, even though the benefits are disproportionately accumulated by capital, the expenses are assumed by the bulk of the working population through the state. Industry can increase its share of technical/administrative knowledge without individual capitalists having to increase their own expenses in technological research.[39]

There are other functions of state intervention, of course.

The state's contribution to the expansion of outlets for the sale of goods, its maintenance of a huge military establishment here and abroad, and its absorption of 'surplus' workers by increasing the proportion of salaried civil servants, all of these provide important services to the economy.[40] Finally, the state plays an increasing role in what has been called the 'reproduction of social relations' and the organization of the social division of labor. Thus, numerous laws and regulations in education, health, mass media, the family, property relations, and so on tend to reproduce the forms of social and contractual relations needed by capital,[41] though they may also be stimulated by the specific needs of the state *itself*, of course.

Each of these forms of state intervention has been largely generated out of the continuing and now worsening crisis in capital accumulation. In order to deal with it the state has developed and will continue to develop strategies to attempt to deal with crises in 'the whole process of production, reproduction, circulation, and regulation of capital, commodities, resources, and labor.'[42]

In summary, then, it is clear that the state has moved to the very center of our economy by sustaining capital accumulation, providing services, creating new markets and protecting old ones, and absorbing a large portion of the 'surplus' population into public employment. In so doing, a systematic trend can be observed: *the socialization of costs and the privatization of profits*.[43] We have a classic pattern operating here. Many investments in 'human capital' and resource development are absolutely necessary for industry, but, as I noted earlier, are quite expensive. The state will take on the large initial cost of basic research and development. It then 'transfers' the fruits of it back to the 'private sector' once it becomes profitable.[44] The state's role in capital accumulation is very evident here in its subsidization of the production of technical/administrative knowledge.

The emphasis on such knowledge has important implications for the legitimation needs of the state, as well as the needs for accumulation in the economic sphere. With the growing power of the new petty bourgeoisie in the economic and cultural apparatus, the focus on technical/administrative knowledge enables the school to do two things. It increases its own legitimacy in the eyes of this crucial class segment and, just as importantly, it enables this same class segment to *use the educational apparatus to reproduce itself.*[45] Middle-level managers, semi-autonomous employees, technicians, engineers, accountants, government employees, and so on can both see the school positively (which in a time of intense doubting of our basic institutions is not inconsequential) and use it for the reproduction of their own credentials, positions, and privilege for their ultimate employment in the state and industry.[46]

The specific needs of the state apparatus, hence, must be considered here. The school does not only respond to the 'needs of capital,' but must also preserve its own legitimacy to its other clientele. In this case (though not necessarily in all others), there is a specific conjuncture of interests between the requirements of industry in the production of cultural capital and the interests of a large portion of the new petty bourgeoisie in their own mobility. Particular kinds of state intervention, therefore, arise in part from this conjuncture.

The effects of both of these concerns for accumulation and legitimation, and the ideologies fostered by them, can be observed in education in general as well as in its specific 'productive' role. Like the economy, examples of this pattern of intervention are becoming more visible. They include the emphasis on competency-based education, systems management, career education, futurism (often a code word for 'manpower' planning), continued major funding for mathematics and science curriculum development (when compared to the arts), national testing programs, community colleges and technical institutes, and so on. All of these and more signal the sometimes subtle and sometimes quite overt role of state intervention into schooling to attempt to maximize efficient production of both the agents and the knowledge required by an unequal economy.[47]

These points about the economic sphere and education can be made clearer if we look more closely at the American (internal) economy. Where there is a misallocation of commodities and resources brought about by the workings of the 'market,' the state has stepped in to reallocate resources to the have-nots at a minimal level. Thus, when high unemployment is naturally generated in times of crisis, depression, and recession, the state increases funds for unemployment compensation. When health care under corporate control is not responsive to a large proportion of the poor and disenfranchised, the state begins to enter that arena. When pension funds are lost due to inflation and the crisis of the economy, the state acts to guarantee some level of support. Notice that all of these kinds of actions, though seemingly helpful, signify two things. First, and again most noticeable, is the increasing pace of state intervention. Second, each of these interventions is designed both *not* to challenge the basic workings of the economic apparatus and to maintain the legitimacy of the political institutions in the eyes of the populace. The very fact that the conditions that cause the necessity for active intervention are naturally generated out of the productive apparatus of the society is covered by the seemingly less expensive intervention (compared to the economic value of and state commitment to corporate capital accumulation) by the state.

It is crucial to realize that this pattern of intervention is not a neutral act in terms of the distribution of benefits when it is examined closely. As Vicente Navarro has demonstrated in his research on the effects of state intervention in two of these social arenas — health care and inflation — the pattern of benefits generated by these programs has consistently benefited the top 20 per cent of the population, often at the expense of the bottom 80 per cent.[48]

This same pattern — the state intervenes to support production, legitimation, and accumulation and to alleviate the worst effects of 'misallocation' — with the benefits disproportionately going to those who control the accumulation of economic and cultural capital — is found in education. It (the state) will also act to remediate the negative outcomes that are generated out, if only to maintain its own legitimacy. By defining large groups of children as deviant (slow learners, remedial problems, discipline problems, etc.), and giving funding and legislative support for special teachers and for 'diagnosis' and 'treatment,' the state will fund extensive remedial projects. While these projects will seem neutral, helpful, and may seem aimed at increasing mobility, they will actually defuse the debate over the role of schooling in the reproduction of the knowledge and people 'required' by the society. It will do this in part by defining the ultimate causes of such deviance as within the child or his or her culture and not due to, say, poverty, the conflicts and disparities generated by the historically evolving cultural and economic hierarchies of the society, etc. This will be hidden from us as well by our assumption that schools are primarily organized as distribution agencies, instead of, at least in part, important agencies in the accumulation process.

Thus, just as in current economic relationships where one of the major results of the labor of a large portion of the work-force is to increase the accumulation and control of economic capital by a relatively small portion of the population, and then to ameliorate the worst effects of this through state-funded social programs, the same could be said in the cultural sector of a society. The cultural apparatus of a society, especially the school, is organized in such a way that it assists in the production of a commodity − through the surplus labor of its personnel − which is ultimately controlled and accumulated by a small portion of the population. Those groups of people who 'cannot' contribute to the maximization of its production are labeled and stratified. They then become the recipients of relatively small amounts of state money to remediate some of the major effects, under the assumption that this is merely a problem of misallocation. That is, that the school is organized to *distribute* this technical knowledge. However, such an estimation of what schools do seems to function as an ideological misrecognition. For I have maintained that just as the economy is organized *not* for distribution but for accumulation, so too are schools in a complex and often contradictory way roughly organized not for the widespread distribution of cultural commodities but for their production and accumulation by a corporate class and the new petty bourgeoisie.

My arguments here are not meant to imply that all of this is a conscious conspiracy. First, even when it is the result of conscious curricular and more general educational policies, consciousness of purpose is not the same as conspiracy.[49] Second, it is quite difficult for it to be otherwise given existing institutional arrangements. It is the result of 'structural causation,' not the conscious manipulative planning by a few industrialists.

Nor am I arguing for a form of technological determinism, where the forces of technical knowledge drive out all that is good and true in our lives. Rather, I am arguing that one of the major mechanisms through which an unequal social order reproduces itself involves the selection, organization, production, accumulation, and control of specific kinds of cultural capital. In an advanced corporate society, a significant element involves one particular kind of cultural commodity, that of technical/administrative knowledge. This knowledge is not something of an imperative, pushing everything out of its path. Rather, it merely defines what is possible, not what is necessary. The imperatives are

57

not determined by what can be done, but by the ideological and social decisions concerning what must be done.[50] This 'must' can only be understood by situating the institutions, like schools, which are partly organized to produce this kind of cultural commodity, back into the context of the social arrangements which determine the uses to which the commodities are put.

This is actually a rather contradictory process, one in which the school is sometimes caught with little hope of resolution. On the one hand, the school must assist in accumulation by producing both agents for a hierarchical labor market and the cultural capital of technical/administrative knowledge. On the other hand, our educational institutions must legitimate ideologies of equality and class mobility, and make themselves be seen positively by as many classes and class segments as possible. In a time of fiscal crisis, this structural contradiction is exacerbated. The need for *economic* and ideological efficiency and stable production tends to be in conflict with the other *political* needs. What we see is the school attempting to resolve what may be the inherently contradictory roles it must play.

WHAT CORRESPONDENCE PRINCIPLES DO NOT EXPLAIN

This discussion of certain of the relationships that tie schools to the larger social fabric has been quite skeletal, I realize, especially since I have limited myself to the articulation of something akin to the principles of correspondence linking together some aspects of school curricula, the state, and economic form. Yet, in our attempts not to become like Boris, and to eliminate some of the confusion of Morris, we need to remember that no explanation of what schools do can be adequate if it limits itself to such correspondence theories. In fact, as I shall demonstrate in my next two chapters, and as I have shown here, correspondence principles that link the activity of schools *directly* with the needs of a corporate economy cannot fully account for either the nature of education's place in the political sphere, its relative autonomy, internal history, or the diversity of the institution; nor can they fully understand the actual practices and meanings of teachers, students and workers as they go about their respective lives in classrooms and in the workplace.[51] Because of the contradictory situation in which they find themselves, schools may 'attempt' to stratify students and may employ categories of deviance so that different students can be given specific forms of help. Our educational institutions may, hence, ultimately give differential treatment to students on the basis of class, gender and race due to these categories, and help reproduce the social division of labor as Bowles and Gintis have maintained. However, this is not a mechanistic process where 'external pressures' from an economy or the state inexorably mold schools and the students within them to the processes involved in the accumulation of economic and cultural capital.

As we shall see later on, something of a process of self-selection as well as institutional selection goes on. A hierarchical supply of differentiated workers is naturally generated as well because some of the students define the *school* as deviant, as not fitting their own cultural and economic responses. In this way, the school can still engage in both the production of agents and the maximization of technical knowledge. Thus, both the creation of agents and the production of cultural commodities can be dealt with in the same historical moment. At the same time, the school can still also act as an important legitimator of the existing social order. For everyday life within the black box of the educational system 'upholds those meritocratic values that justify differential rewards, and the separation of the "successful" from the "failures" provides daily object lessons in inequality.'[52] Thus, the curricular and pedagogic practices that are used to organize the routines in most schools — the differentiated curriculum, the grouping practices, the hidden curriculum — do play a large part in enabling students to internalize failure based on this sorting process as an *individual* problem. ('It is my fault. If only I had tried harder.') For large groups of students, the deviant label the school affixes to them as they act upon their own lived culture becomes them. In the words of Goffman, their moral career is such that they live out the label.[53]

FINDING SPACES IN WHICH TO ACT

By focusing on educational institutions not only as part of a system of distribution, but as a specific system of production, I have tried to begin to uncover some of the actual mechanisms that operate in schools so that we can also begin to understand more fully the interpenetration between the cultural and economic reproduction of our society. One might want to claim that the kinds of theories that dominate how we understand the riddle of schooling — ones that focus on distribution — have provided a relatively effective, though subtle, form of social control.[54] They organize our thoughts about and research on schools as if they were designed as distribution mechanisms. In one way schools are. They do seem to 'attempt' to distribute, or at least provide the conditions for the generation of, a hidden curriculum, one that is often differentiated by class, race, and sex and one that helps make legitimate the structural arrangements of which schools are a part.

Yet, in another way, in the field of education in general the focus on distribution has caused a large proportion of educational research to examine a rather limited range of phenomena. Curriculum and more general educational researchers, hence, tend to look at the techniques teachers employ in their teaching, at better curriculum designs and so on, assuming that changes in these will make schools more efficient in distributing the supposedly neutral information that these institutions must teach. What, however, if this is *not* the educational apparatus's only job?

In arguing both against these dominant theories and research traditions and for a perspective that examines schools as aspects of a set of productive arrangements, I have claimed as well that the state will assume an increasingly critical role not only in the actual organization of production on an economic level, but will do the same at a 'cultural' level as well. It will actively intervene to guarantee the production of particular kinds of cultural commodities (here technical knowledge) by sponsoring sanctions, programs, institutions, and people related to the maximization of this process of commodity production. I have hypothesized that this will be related to changes and crises in the accumulation and legitimation process within (and among) corporate economies and to changes in the class structure.

However, talking about knowledge as a form of capital, about culture as commodity, and tying these things back into the problem of accumulation, needs always to be seen as a set of metaphors. As we know, commodities embody *sets of relations* among concrete actors and classes.[55] Such metaphors can tacitly assume a relatively non-contradictory appraisal of schooling, conflict, class, and culture. Obviously, therefore, I have described only one moment in a more complex set of contradictory arrangements and struggles. It is a description that must be complemented by historically oriented analyses of mediation and contradiction, in Willis's words, of penetrations and limitations.[56]

Thus, as I have been at pains to note, I realize that what I have presented here is only an outline, one that is inadequate in a number of ways. The metaphors I have employed to begin to unpack some of the structural reasons which might explain why X exists (in this case as particular kinds of schools and deviance) may lead us to think in overly deterministic terms. They may also tie us a bit too closely to black box theories of schooling. However, while I have spent the last few years arguing strongly against such economically mechanistic and simple correspondence approaches to explaining what schools do,[57] this does not mean that we can ignore the relations schools have to the economic mode of production in which they exist. Linking the internal pedagogical, curricular, labeling, and guidance practices of schools to the accumulation and control of economic and cultural capital outside of them, while necessarily less grounded in the day to day interaction of classrooms than some of us would like (or that in fact I am used to), is at least an initial step in a more generative appraisal of the role of schools in our less than meritocratic order.

Finally, we should not be made overly pessimistic by analyses such as this. Indeed, there *are* contradictions that arise directly out of the process I have described that can and need to be exploited. The increasing role that the state plays, for instance, in the cultural and economic production process means that these interventions are in the *political* arena and can potentially become political conflicts, not merely technical ones.[58] Hence, they can provide the opportunity for opening up more debate, more collective action, more political education, and so on. This, when coupled with the clear trend toward what Wright has called the 'proletarianization' of state workers that I shall analyze in more detail in Chapter 5, makes political linkages among committed actors that much more structurally possible. That the rapid growth of state intervention can provide opportunities for political work, since it opens up the state itself for criticism, is made clear by Castells in his discussion of some of the contradictions being generated currently in our society. Castells describes the process in this way:

The long term contradiction that comes from the need of capital to develop the productive forces is a . . . fundamental one. It concerns the social conditions of scientific research and technological innovation. Scientific research and technological innovation require massive investments that are only profitable in the long term. They also require a great deal of autonomy in decisionmaking in relation to the requirements of particular units of capital. In other words, the process of technological innovation can only be effective under conditions of production that evade capitalist logic. A continuing high rate of innovation can only exist in a society where human creativity is favored by the type of social organization and the characteristics of the work process. It requires a highly developed system of education, not just professional training and ideological manipulation. It demands an increasing non-capitalist sector of social services able to provide information to the workers as well as improving their initiative. It implies, primarily, that there must be a good deal of initiative in the process of production, which basically contradicts the model of authority in the organization of a capitalist firm. Many of these social functions are necessary for the development of the productive forces, but they are incompatible with capitalist logic. Therefore, they are assumed by the state . . . [Thus], *in order to expand and avoid the barriers existing in the process of accumulation, capital grows by generating, in an increasing proportion, a sector of activities, rules, and apparatuses that denies its own logic.* Capital pursues its accumulation by increasing reliance on the state.[59]

He goes on documenting the contradiction between legitimation and accumulation that can give rise to difficulties.

Capital must develop productive forces in order to continue its accumulation. But the social conditions necessary for the development of productive forces are increasingly contradictory to capitalist social relationships. Since capital shapes society, the state is used more and more as a basic mechanism to absorb, smooth, and regulate the contradictions that emerge in the process of accumulation. However, the state is not a purely regulatory capitalist

62

apparatus. It expresses the contradictions of society and must also fulfill the functions of legitimating the dominant interests and integrating the dominated class into the system. The growing state intervention to support the capitalist logic in all spheres of economic and social life *undermines the basis for its legitimacy* as the representative of the general interest.[60]

It is in just these ways that the political sphere becomes a site of struggle, a struggle that may ultimately threaten the legitimacy of the economic sphere itself.

What programs should be worked for within the state, however? If the state is placed in a vulnerable position because of these contradictory pressures, what kinds of concrete educational action might be focused upon? As Carnoy and Shearer argue, one necessary focus will be on schools of engineering, schools where a large part of the technical knowledge is ultimately generated. Centers of 'democratic engineering' need to be established. This can be done by creating new schools or through political work in established institutions that train engineers for industry. Political debate over the ends and means of these institutions can be started. The emphasis in each of these kinds of facilities would be on democratic attitudes and values. At the same time, 'these schools of democratic engineering could also begin pilot programs in technological education for workers so that as firms with more democratic work places were established, workers could be educated in line with their expanded responsibilities.'[61]

Similar kinds of action are necessary in administration and management. There are institutes for democratic management currently in operation that are coupling the need for economic and technical proficiency with cooperative and democratic planning and values.[62] The more equal distribution of these technical and administrative skills to men and women workers in our offices, stores, and industries is quite an important task. It points to the need for the development of models of worker education — through existing unions, study groups, feminist groups, the creative use of media such as cable television, job rotation arrangements, workers' colleges at universities and/or self-organized locations, and so on — to reduce the ideological power of the expert and begin the democratization of technical/administrative knowledge.

This will become even more critical as corporations attempt to deal with the crisis in accumulation by closing down industries and/or moving their plants to other locations. In order to maintain their jobs and provide an economic base for their communities, social services, and schools, workers and employees in these industries will need high levels of management, financial, and technical skills to refinance, reopen, and run these enterprises themselves. Their education should begin now, before the crisis deepens any further. This will provide greater opportunities for these people to demonstrate that there *are* workable alternatives to the existing modes of corporate control of the workplace and will provide, as well, for the possibility of the development of alternative educational practices among workers that will break down the authoritarian practices which may now be dominant.

Within the school itself — at levels well below that of the university — new models of democratic administration need to be experimented with. As the management techniques that are employed by the state come increasingly from industry, the same conflicts between production and efficiency on the one hand and flexibility and initiative will undoubtedly emerge. This may provide for groups of teachers, parents, and students to begin to establish less authoritarian and bureaucratic management forms in the schools, ones that will prefigure the democratic alternatives now slowly growing at many workplaces and ones that will be less romantic and more thoughtfully political than those attempted in the late 1960s and early 1970s in education.

Finally, the fact that the state itself may lose some of its legitimacy allows for a more honest appraisal of institutions within the state, such as the school. Rather than blaming teachers for the 'failure' of education, by working closely with parents and groups of working men and women, politically minded educators can begin to demonstrate some of the structural relationships between the ways schools may function now and the reproduction of inequality and help in the formation of linkages between progressive teachers and these groups. The possibility and importance of such 'coalitions' is something to which I shall return later on.

There are many Morrises for whom the riddle of what schools do needs to be unpacked. While, unlike Boris, we may not yet have a fully worked out appraisal of what the riddle means, one thing is clear. What the riddle means will not be explained unless we situate the internal qualities of the institution, and its relationships with 'external' agencies, back into a more complex analysis of our social order. Such an analysis may be hard to do, especially since, at least in the USA, we shall have to re-teach ourselves traditions on the left which until recently had become horrible atrophied, traditions that focus on contradictions and possibilities as well as on reproduction. Yet our more 'intellectual' pains need at all times to be compared with pain of a different sort. We need only remember John Masefield's lines:

> To get the whole world out of bed,
> and washed, and dressed, and warmed, and fed,
> to work, and back to bed again,
> Believe me, Saul, costs worlds of pain.[63]

A collective commitment to help eliminate this kind of pain is what we need to be about.

CHAPTER 3

THE OTHER SIDE OF THE HIDDEN CURRICULUM: CULTURE AS LIVED-I

INTRODUCTION

In Chapter 2, by treating culture as part of the larger process of commodification and accumulation, I examined the ways in which the educational system produces particular kinds of knowledge that are ultimately accumulated and used in the economic sphere, and how its political role sometimes complements and contradicts this. I cautioned us not to assume, though, that there is necessarily always a successful correspondence between what industry needs in terms of cultural capital or the norms and dispositions — the ideology — of its workers and what happens in schools. Because students are stratified based on the categories of deviance generated in part by the productive function of the educational system, this does not mean that we need to accept the idea that the 'bottom layers' of these students necessarily get a hidden curriculum that prepares them simply to fit into and accept their place on the lower rungs of the 'economic ladder.'

In fact, we should be very careful about assuming that the ideologies and processes of control that accompany the growth of technical/administrative knowledge are always successfully employed. I shall demonstrate in this and the next chapter that, because culture is also lived, because of what might be called the intersection of the economic and cultural spheres, these ideologies and processes may not lead to a straightforward imposition of control in either the workplace or the school. Just as the school's role as a productive and reproductive apparatus needs to be interpreted as being generated out of contradictory pressures upon it, so too do we need to see that the actual employment and ultimate effects of technical/administrative knowledge in the workplace itself are also a result of similar contradictions. Once again, the notion that a simple process of reproduction is going on will have to be cast aside.

BEYOND SIMPLE REPRODUCTION

The laws of physics determine the shape any object will take in an ordinary mirror. The image may be distorted by imperfections in the glass, but, by and large, what you see is what you have got. The internal composition of the mirror reproduces the external object standing over it. This set of laws may be good for thinking about optics, but it is questionable whether it is adequate for thinking about schools. We, especially many of us on the left side of the political spectrum, tend to act as if it is adequate, however. We see schools as a mirror of society, especially in the school's hidden curriculum. A 'society' needs docile workers; schools, through their social relations and covert teaching, roughly guarantee the production of such docility. Obedient workers in the labor market are mirrored in the 'marketplace of ideas' in the school. As I shall try and show in this chapter, though, such mirror image analogies are a bit too simple *both* in the school and in the supposedly mirrored external object, the workplace.

The assumptions behind most recent analyses of the hidden curriculum can generally be grouped around a theory of correspondence. Broadly, correspondence theories imply that there are specific characteristics, behavioral traits, skills, and dispositions that an economy requires of its workers. These economic needs are so powerful as to 'determine' what goes on in other sectors of a society, particularly the school. Thus, if we look at our educational institutions we should expect to find that the tacit things that are taught to students roughly mirror the personality and dispositional traits that these students will 'require' later on when they join the labor market.

One of the most recent explications of this kind of analysis is, of course, found in Bowles and Gintis's *Schooling in Capitalist America*. Here the hidden curriculum is differentiated by economic class and by one's expected economic trajectory. The arguments presented by Bowles and Gintis have led a number of investigators to argue that this differential hidden curriculum can be seen in the fact that working-class students are taught punctuality, neatness, respect for authority, and other elements of habit formation. The students of more advanced classes are taught intellectual open-mindedness, problem-solving, flexibility, and so on, skills and dispositions that will enable them to function as managers and professionals, not as unskilled or semi-skilled laborers. Though the socio-economic causes of this differentiated hidden curriculum are seen as quite complex, still the fundamental role of the school is seen as the rough reproduction of the division of labor outside of it. The school is a determined institution.

Now social phenomenologists, philosophers of science, critical social theorists, and others have maintained that how we act on the world, be it the educational, economic, or political world, is in part determined by the way we perceive it. While this point can be so general as to be relatively inconsequential, it is important that the ties between perception and action are not ignored. This is especially true in any serious analysis of schooling that wishes to go beyond correspondence theories. Correspondence theories tend to 'cause' us to see the school only in reproductive terms. Its logic sees the institution as acting only to reproduce a social order. Both the form and content of the formal corpus of school knowledge and the hidden curriculum help create the conditions for the cultural and economic reproduction of class relations in our society.

There certainly is evidence to support this kind of assertion, some of which I have contributed myself.[1] However, by seeing the school in only reproductive terms, in essence as a passive function of an external unequal social order, it is hard to generate any serious educational action whatsoever. For if schools are *wholly* determined and can do no more than mirror economic relations outside of them, then nothing can be done within the educational sphere. This is pessimistic, of course, and is an argument to which I shall return later on in this discussion. Yet there is something besides its pessimistic perspective that we must point to. It is, in some very important ways, also inadequate as a theory of the relationship both among all social institutions and between the school and other powerful socio-economic forces. For the concept of reproduction does not exhaust the nexus of relationships that ties institutions and people to each other. It may be an important element; however, there will be constitutive aspects of day to day life that can best be described not as mirror images of what larger economic and social forces require, but as genuinely contradictory. Thus, by focusing on schools only as reproductive institutions, we

68

may miss the dynamic interplay between education and an economy and be in danger of reducing the complexity of this relationship to a bare parody of what actually exists at the level of practice.

In order to go beyond this, we need to think more clearly about the range of ways institutions and people may be 'determined.' What 'modes of determination' actually exist, modes which go beyond 'mere' reproduction? While these are actually heuristic devices that might enable us to see how the institutions of a society are dialectically interrelated, we can distinguish at least six modes of determination which represent the structural constraints and contradictions present in a given society. These include: (1) structural limitations; (2) selection; (3) reproduction/nonreproduction; (4) limits of functional compatibility; (5) transformation, and (6) mediation.

These can be specified further: to what extent any institutional structure like the school or the workplace can vary (an example of structural limitation); the mechanisms such as funding patterns, economic and political support, and state interventions that exclude certain possible decisions (an example of selection); what aspects of a set of institutions or relations are functional to the basic recreation of, say, a mode of production or an ideological practice (an example of reproduction/nonreproduction); what aspects of institutional structures and cultural practices are *not* merely reproductive but are genuinely contradictory (an example of the limits of functional compatibility; what processes work their way through and help shape the interaction among these elements, such as class struggle (an example of mediation); and, finally, what concrete actions and struggles are now altering these institutions and processes in important ways (an example of transformation).[2] Given this set of relationships, relationships that enable us to go well beyond mirror image analogies, in this chapter I shall take two of these − mediation and transformation − and use them to begin to unpack some of the possible complexity associated with the hidden curriculum and culture as lived not commodified.

In Chapter 1, I argued that the traditional literature on the hidden curriculum has been guided by an overly restricted view of socialization. The conceptual weaknesses of this approach (Is a one-way perspective on socialization an adequate metaphor for illuminating what happens in schools?) make its continued dominance questionable. Yet as we shall see in much more depth in the next chapter, just as important is an empirical issue. Is it accurate? Do students always internalize these norms and dispositions unquestioningly? One way of uncovering this is to work backwards, starting from the places where people actually work.

THE HIDDEN CURRICULUM AND THE NORMS OF THE WORKPLACE

The status of theories of the hidden curriculum does not only depend on the accuracy of their perception of what actually occurs in classrooms. There is another end to the rope which binds schools to outside agencies. Here I am talking about the workplace itself. For one could describe the reality of what is taught to students with exceptional clarity and still be wrong about the actual effects this hidden teaching has, if the norms and values that organize and guide the day to day subjective lives of workers are *not the same* as those found in schools.

In the rest of this chapter, hence, I want to give a portion of the other side of this picture. I want to claim that the hidden curriculum literature, because of its overly deterministic model of socialization and its exclusive focus on reproduction to the exclusion of other things that may be happening, has a tendency to portray workers as something like automatons who are *wholly* controlled by the modes of production, technical and administrative procedures, and ideological forms of our society. In more theoretical terms, agents exist (as abstract social roles), but they have no agency. In a real sense, then, structures exist, actors don't.[3]

I also want to claim something else. I want to argue that such overly deterministic and economistic accounts of the hidden curriculum are themselves elements of the subtle reproduction, at an ideological level, of perspectives required for the legitimation of inequality. What I mean to say is simply this. The analyses recently produced by a number of leftist scholars and educators are themselves reproductions of the ideological vision of corporate domination. By seeing schools as total reflections of an unequal 'labor market,' a market where workers simply do what they are told and passively acquiesce to the norms and authority relations of the workplace, these analyses accept as empirically accurate the

70

ideology of management.

In order to unpack these issues, we shall have to examine the labor process itself. A good deal of the recent writings on the relationship between the hidden curriculum and the labor process has been strongly influenced by work such as Harry Braverman's exceptionally important historical investigation of the growth of corporate procedures for ensuring management control of the production process.[4]

Braverman makes a powerful case for the relentless penetration of corporate logic into the organization and control of day to day life in the workplace. In his portrayal, workers are continually deskilled (and, of course, some are 'reskilled'). The skills they once had – skills of planning, of understanding and acting on an entire phase of production – are ultimately taken from them by management and housed elsewhere in a planning department controlled by management.[5] In order for corporate accumulation to proceed, planning must be separated from execution, mental labor separated from manual labor, and this separation needs to be institutionalized in a systematic and formal manner. The archetypical example of this is, of course, Taylorism and its many variants. In plain words, management plans, workers merely execute. Thus, a major organizing principle of the workplace must be 'taking the managers' brains from under the workman's cap.'[6]

This kind of analysis is a major contribution, not the least in its 'demystification' of a number of assumptions held by many educators, policy analysts, and others. In particular, it serves to raise serious questions about our assumption that there is a widespread historical tendency toward increasing the skill level in industrial occupations throughout our economy. It is just as correct, Braverman maintains, to see the opposite of this. One can see the corporate expropriation of skill and knowledge, the rationalization of the workplace, and the increasing centralization of control of work so that all important decisions are made away from the point of production.[7]

Braverman also sees something else, though, to complete this story. As the process of deskilling – or what can be called the degradation of work – proceeds, workers also continuously lose power. While it is never totally successful, as corporate logic and power enter even more aspects of their lives and institutions, workers become appendages to the production process. They are ultimately confronted by the fruits of the knowledge originally

71

generated in part out of the educational apparatus and by the uses of Taylorism and scientific management, by human relations management techniques, or finally by the threat of authority. In the face of all this, workers can do little. Caught in management's web, they are relatively passive, obedient, and hard working. The cash nexus replaces craft and worker control.

While Braverman does not expressly point to this, the differentiated hidden curriculum in school has served to prepare them well, for if this is what the inexorable logic of corporate control is like, then we should expect that workers will need particular norms and dispositions to function within a hierarchical labor market. They will need habits that contribute to the smooth and rational flow of production. They will need to acquiesce to 'expert' authority. They will not need collective commitment, a sense of craft, creativity, or control.

However, just as there are serious weaknesses in looking at schools in only reproductive terms (and thereby missing what I shall document in Chapter 4 – the possible ways day to day life and the internal history of schools mediate and often provide the possibility for some students to act against powerful social messages), so too can this view, so powerfully put by Braverman, cause us to neglect similar things that may occur in the workplace. Let us look at this much more closely.

What do we find at the level of execution, on the shop-floor itself? Do the inexorable logic and techniques of capital call forth the lessons learned (or at least taught) in the hidden curriculum in school? Here, an examination of the separation of conception or planning from execution may be helpful. Recent research on the history of the relations between management and labor, especially of Taylorism, paints a somewhat different picture than that of Braverman. It is becoming increasingly clear that what is missing in this account is the actual response of workers to these expected norms and organizational strategies and their ability to resist them. This general point is clearly documented by Burawoy.

> It is one thing for management to appropriate knowledge, it is another thing to monopolize it. Braverman himself says '. . . since the workers are not destroyed as human beings but are simply utilized in inhuman ways, their critical intelligent, conceptual faculties, no matter how deadened or diminished, always remain in some degree a threat to capital.' Rather

than a separation of conception and execution, we find a separation of workers' conception and management's conception, of workers' knowledge and management's knowledge. The attempt to enforce Taylorism leads workers to recreate the unity of conception and execution but in opposition to management rulings. Workers show much ingenuity in defeating and out-witting the agents of scientific management before, during and after the 'appropriation of knowledge.' In any shop there are 'official' or 'management approved' ways of performing tasks and there is the workers' lore devised and revised in response to any management offensive.[8]

In essence, study after study has confirmed the fact that a large proportion of working adults have been able to continue their own collective setting of informal production norms and their ability to 'defy' the supervisor and the 'expert.'[9] In fact, one of the major results of the attempts to separate conception from execution totally and to emphasize worker compliance and obedience to management in the pursuit of management's expanding production goals was exactly the opposite of what managers intended. Rather than always creating a 'compliant work-force,' it quite often *promoted* resistance, conflict, and struggle. It heightened collective action by workers at the point of production and in so doing also often undermined both management control and the norms that were 'required' in the workplace.[10]

These forms of resistance have an exceptionally long history, as we know. That there was a constant and bitter struggle in which workers were deeply concerned with 'management prerogatives' is documented by the fact that the early waves of industrial strikes were often most fiercely fought around union rules and recognition, and around sympathetic strikes with other workers who had similar grievances. The bitterest losses were these strikes. Strikes over wages were eminently successful,[11] thereby giving us some insight into why unions became somewhat more economistic.

Yet even wage demands often hid (and still do) a smoldering anger at managerial methods. For example, in the famous strikes by munitions workers when Taylorism was introduced, the issue seemed to be over pay scales of tool makers that ranged from thirty-eight to ninety cents an hour depending on one's job assignment. However, these machinists were demanding a standard

73

wage rate for all of them. This was actually an indirect challenge to a whole array of management practices, including management's 'right' to divide labor and establish new and often arbitrary job classifications that were to be taken out of the workers' hands.[12]

Even relatively unskilled workers struggled over both wages and control. Indeed, again it is hard to separate the two out even analytically. When management engaged in 'speed ups' or used what seemed to be arbitrary authority to increase the pace of the work — thereby getting more production out of the same labor in the same time — laborers' resistances often took the form of 'continuous, covert, self-organization by small informal groups at work.'[13] These served both to buttress their own informal systems of control and to prevent further economic exploitation.

During economic crises, similar things came to the fore. In times of economic difficulty when it looked as if layoffs were in the offing, many workers traditionally slowed down. Both organized and unorganized workers found ways of protecting older workers who might not be able to keep up with the expanded pace of the work, and engaged in other action to maintain both jobs and control.[14] These are historical examples; yet we must be very careful of assuming that they are merely of historical interest. Rather, the control of production by workers was not a static thing that existed and then ceased to exist at any one point in time. Instead, it was, and is, a continuous struggle which has taken *a variety of forms*.[15]

Partial support for my claims here — that workers at a variety of levels have and do often subtly resist, that they are not as truly and fully socialized to be obedient operatives as correspondence theories would have it — can be found in the literature on bureaucratic control. This is summarized in a recent investigation of the growth of bureaucratic mechanisms in the workplace by Daniel Clawson. He argues, after a thorough review of research on the topic, that the rapid growth of bureaucratic controls is evidence of the struggle by blue- and white-collar workers. For if all workers could be counted upon to be obedient and respect authority, if they continued to work as hard as they could, if they didn't 'take materials that didn't belong to them,' and if they always followed what management wanted them to do, then the enormous cost of bureaucratic and hierarchical supervision and control would not have to be paid.[16]

While there is clearly a danger in overstating this case, it is largely confirmed by other investigators. For example, a number of writers argue that not only is the growing bureaucratization of the workplace a response to workers' attempts to maintain some element of control, but bureaucratic control has itself often engendered even more conflict.

Richard Edwards makes this point rather well.

> Thus bureaucratic control has created among American workers vast discontent, dissatisfaction, resentment, frustration, and boredom with their work. We do not need to recount here the many studies measuring alienation: the famous HEW-commissioned report, *Work in America*, among other summaries, has already done that. It argued, for example, that the best index of job satisfaction or dissatisfaction is a worker's response to the question: 'What type of work would you try to get into if you could start all over again?' A majority of both blue and white-collar workers – and an increasing proportion of them over time – indicated that they would choose some different type of work. This overall result is consistent with a very large literature on the topic. Rising dissatisfaction and alienation among workers, made exigent by their greater job security and expectations of continuing employment with one enterprise, directly create problems for employers (most prominently reduced productivity).[17]

This very conflict has forced employers to introduce plans for job enrichment, job enlargement, worker self-management, worker-employer co-management, and so on. Yet we should not forget that these very plans may ultimately threaten the control of employers over the workplace. Thus, as Edwards contends, 'the trouble is that a little is never enough. Just as some job security leads to demands for guaranteed lifetime wages, so some control over workplace decisions raises the demand for industrial democracy.'[18]

As David Montgomery reminds us, the history of the growth of management control of the workplace is not a simple story of imposition. A complete account must always emphasize 'the initiatives of the workers themselves, rather than the ways in which they were manipulated by those in authority over them.'[19] As he goes on to note, worker resistance and their own articulate programs for control have often been the *causes*, not only the effects of the rapid evolution and diffusion of management practices. Even such practices as 'modern' personnel management were developed as 'cooptive and repressive responses' to initiatives coming from workers.[20]

How are we to understand all of this? Correspondence theories would have it that schools are exceptionally successful in teaching specific norms that are lived out at the workplace. Yet, at best, if these recent investigators of the actual working out of the labor process are correct, this supposed correspondence can only partially describe what *is* lived out at the workplace. We shall need to go into this in somewhat more detail.

If we are to understand the actual lives of workers at a variety of levels of the 'occupational ladder,' an important key is what has been called *work culture*. Work culture is not easily visible to the outsider and, like studies of the hidden curriculum, requires living within it to come close to comprehending its subtleties and organization. However, even with its subtle character, informal practices, and clear variations, it can generally be defined as 'a relatively autonomous sphere of action on the job, a realm of informal, customary values and rules which *mediates* the formal authority structure of the workplace and distances workers from its impact.'[21] In essence, work culture, as a 'relatively autonomous sphere of action,' is not necessarily only a reproductive form. It constitutes a realm of action that in part provides both strength and the possibility of transformative activity.

This very work culture provides a ground for the development of alternative norms, norms that are quite a bit richer than those pictured by theories of bare correspondence. These norms provide a locus for worker resistance, at least partial control of skills, pacing, and knowledge, collectivity rather than complete fragmentation of tasks, and some degree of autonomy from management.

On close examination, there are a number of norms that pervade the workplace in many industries, norms that give more than a mere semblance of autonomy and which 'are manifested every day in the forms of interaction that reproduce the work culture.' Among the strongest of these is cooperation as exemplified in work sharing arrangements. An instance of this is the practice of workers saving finished pieces in the wood and metal working industries. These pieces are lent to other workers 'who have had a hard day (because of machine breakdown, because they do not feel good, etc.).'[22]

Significant counter examples to passive acquiescence, deskilling, and loss of control are found elsewhere as well. Industrial workers in, say, steel mills in particular have maintained a significant degree of worker autonomy by developing and redeveloping a shop-floor culture that allows them a very real role in production. Even within highly mechanized industries, worker 'militancy' to protect what is not mislabeled as 'solidarity' is clear. Steve Packard's account of day to day life in the steel mills documents this rather well. Here is one example.

> One day a white craneman was assigned to a good crane that should have gone to a black. Black cranemen decided to sabotage production until this bullshit was straightened out. They had mild support from most white cranemen, who also thought the foreman was wrong.
>
> Nothing can operate without the cranes bringing and taking steel, so blacks quietly stopped the whole mill. They kept the cranes in lowest gear and worked in super slow motion. Foremen soon began hatching out of their offices, looking around, rubbing their eyes in disbelief. It was like the whole building popped LSD or the air had turned into some kind of thick jelly: everything but the foremen moved at one tenth of normal speed.[23]

Here is a prime example of how the control of workers by management is less than total, to say the least. The unspoken cultural life within the mill, the power of workers' cooperation, provides substantial reins on the norms of profit, authority, and productivity sought by the employers.[24]

This resistance, as we know, has often been turned into avenues that are overly economistic. We strike and bargain over wages and benefits, not as often over control and power.[25] In certain industries, of course — coal-mines provide one example here — the tradition of overt resistance is still very visible. Yet, overt and formally organized resistance (or even the relative lack of it at times) is not as significant to my argument as the fact of informal resistance to control at the point of production.[26]

For rather than being left, as Noble puts it, with a corporate juggernaut on one side and impotence and total despair on the other, we find evidence to the contrary again at the level of informal practices. Thus, in the metal-working industry, new technologies have been developed over the years with the express purpose of increasing production and deskilling occupations. They, thereby, would increase the rate of capital accumulation in two ways — more goods sold and less salary paid to workers who were mere 'button pushers.' Among the most significant of these technologies was the development in recent decades of numerical control. In brief, numerical control entails the specifications of a part that is to be produced on the machine being broken down into a mathematical representation of that part. These representations are then themselves translated into a mathematical description of the desired path of the cutting machine that will make the part. This leads, finally, to a system of control in which hundreds or thousands of discrete instructions are translated into a numerical code which is automatically read by the machinery. Numerical control, hence, is a means of totally separating conception from execution, of 'circumventing [the worker's] role as a source of the intelligence in production (*in theory*)' and of management getting greater control over, and compliance from, its employees.[27]

The stress on 'in theory' is important here. The introduction of numerical control has not been uneventful. Let me be specific here. Overt and covert resistance was and is quite common. Strikes and work stoppages have not been unusual. At the Lynn, Massachusetts General Electric plant, the introduction of numerical controls caused a strike that shut down the factory for a month. Workers saw the issue clearly. As one machine operator put it:

> The introduction of automation means that our skills are being down-graded and instead of having the prospect of moving up to a more interesting job we now have the prospect of either unemployment or a dead-end job. But there are alternatives that unions can explore. We have to establish the position that the fruits of technical change can be divided up — some to the workers, not all to management as is the case today. We must demand that the machinist rise with the complexity of the machine. Thus, rather than dividing his job up, the machinist should be trained to program and repair his equipment — a task well within the grasp of most people in industry.

Demands such as this strike at the heart of most management prerogative clauses which are in many collective bargaining contracts. Thus, to deal with automation effectively, one has to strike at another prime ingredient of business unionism: the idea of 'let the management run the business.' The introduction of [numerical control] equipment makes it imperative that we fight such ideas.[28]

This is clearly overt and organized resistance and struggle. But what about the informal norms of the work culture on the shop-floor? What happens there? Do workers there embody the norms of obedience to authority, punctuality, etc. when there is not a strike? While in theory under numerical control all that a machine operator must do is to press buttons to stop or start the machine and continue to load and unload it, this rarely happens. Here too the actual process of work at the point of production does not necessarily correspond to the norms 'required.' On the shop-floor, one often finds workers engaged in what is called 'pacing' or 'the 70 per cent syndrome' — the collective restriction of output on the floor by workers cooperating to set the speed at which the machine is fed at 70-80 per cent of capacity. One can again often find workers running the machine harder to get enough products to help each other out. And, finally, there are the more subtle forms of resistance in terms of negative and uncooperative attitudes and the lack of 'willing acceptance of authority.' As some managers note: 'When you put a guy on an N.C. machine, he gets temperamental. . . . And then, through a process of osmosis, the machine gets temperamental.'[29]

WOMEN AT WORK

So far I have painted a picture of workers who were predominantly male and industrial in my attempt to uncover whether the hidden curriculum literature is correct in seeing a correspondence between what is supposed to be taught to working-class children in schools and what is 'required' in their later participation in a stratified labor market. Yet what about women? If male workers then and now often showed serious signs of collective commitment, struggle, and attempts to maintain control of their skills and knowledge (though often informally) — and hence act against and do not necessarily reproduce the expected norms of the labor market — can we say the same for other groups of workers?

Even given the relative recency of a large body of research on women's day to day work, a number of striking points emerge from the literature. Women were often quite effective in resisting the production requirements and norms handed down by management in factories. In the shoe and garment industries, 'the effective unionization of women operatives was likely to have a remarkably radicalizing impact on the organization.' Sharing, mutual respect, resistance to management control, all of these counterbalancing norms came to the fore even more noticeably when, say, women shoe workers were organized along with men. Here, at least, women workers were quite aggressive in their relationship with their employers.[30]

This was not the case 'only' with women in factories. Much the same is found in areas of employment which for a variety of economic and ideological reasons have consciously sought to hire women, such as clerical and sales work.[31] Perhaps the most interesting aspect of this can be seen in the latter areas, that of working in retail stores.

Examples of subtle resistance among saleswomen abound. For instance, when management directives designed to tighten up obedience out on the sales floor interfered with the established informal rules which maintained the work culture, they were often quite effectively sabotaged or altered. If these directives included extra duties, they were often merely refused or fought back informally. Saleswomen would engage in sloppy or 'eccentric' work when setting up new displays. As a group, they might take back the time management had extracted from them for these extra duties by unilaterally extending the lunch-hour. Or, they could visibly insult the authority of management by, say, purposely ignoring the requirements of the store's dress code.[32]

The countervailing norms of the work culture frequently went further. Since so much of a saleswoman's work was public, since it was carried out on the sales floor, many employees developed rather clever ways of turning back management harassment and abuse of authority. Saleswomen could easily embarrass a buyer or a floor manager in front of his or her superiors or an important customer. Further, solidarity against management directives and control was repeatedly enforced by informal sanctions. A saleswoman who transgressed the work culture could find her stock mysteriously messed up. Shins could be banged into by drawers. And like floor managers, the transgressor could be embarrassed before customers and higher management.[33] All of this does not leave one with a sense of total worker internalization of and acquiescence in the face of the imperatives of the norms and values of management ideology.

The resistance and collective commitment went further in many stores. The work culture on the sales floor also developed important ways of controlling the pacing and meaning of work, ways that mirror those found in my earlier discussion of day to day life on the shop-floor. Just as in the factory, where workers found ways effectively to transform, mute, or work against the demands of management, so too did clerks develop a work culture that could effectively set limits on output and dampen competitiveness among departments in sales. These tactics are nicely illustrated in the following discussion.

> Each department had a concept of the total sales that constituted a good day's work. Saleswomen used various tactics to keep their 'books' (sales tallies) within acceptable limits: running unusually low books would imperil a worker's status with management just as extraordinarily high books would put her in the bad graces of her peers. Individual clerks would avoid customers late in the day when their books were running high, or call other clerks to help them. Saleswomen managed to approximate the informal quota with impressive regularity, ironing out the fluctuations in customers' buying habits in ways the management never dreamed of. They adjusted the number of transactions they completed to compensate for the size of the purchases; if they made a few large sales early in the day, they might then retire to do stockwork. During the slow summer season or during inclement weather, they were more aggressive with the smaller volume of customers; at peak seasons, they ignored customers who might put them over their quota.[34]

Managers were not the only recipients of these kinds of informal practices. Customers came in for their share, too, a share that naturally arises since, unlike the factory, the sales floor involves not just the production of goods but the 'production of customers.' Through subtle ways – picking and choosing among waiting customers, pretending not to notice customers while doing stock work or having a conversation with one's peers, disappearing into the storeroom, rudeness, and so on – saleswomen communicated a hidden message to both management and the customer. We take customers on our terms not yours. While you might have a superior class position, we have the upper hand here – we control the merchandise.[35]

There are, of course, other examples one could point to. One would expect similar informal 'cultural' practices to be found in secretarial work, for instance. However, the major point to be kept in mind brings into serious question the myth – and it may be just that – of the passive woman worker. As we have seen, men and women do have some agency. It may be informal and relatively disorganized, and hence may be at a cultural not a political level. But it exists in ways that are not simply reproductive. To speak metaphorically, the reproductive mirror has some serious cracks in it.

AGAINST ROMANTICISM

In this chapter, I have sought to bring together a set of counter-examples to illuminate the partial quality of the research being done on the hidden curriculum in schools. I have argued that correspondence theories – even if they develop the ethnographic and statistical sophistication required to unpack what schools actually teach – are *dependent upon* the accuracy of their view of the labor process. The exclusive use of the metaphor of reproduction, however, leads them to accept the ideology of management (i.e., workers at all times are guided by the cash nexus, by authority, by expert planning, by the norms of punctuality and productivity) as a real description of what goes on outside the school. When the metaphor of reproduction is complemented by investigations describing other modes of determination such as mediation and transformation, among others, and when one examines the actual organization and control of the labor process, one finds a somewhat different picture of important aspects of the day to day life than one might expect.

Rather than the labor process being totally controlled by the ideological, technical and administrative rubrics of management, rather than hard and fast structures of authority and norms of punctuality and compliance, one sees a complex work culture. This very work culture provides important grounds for worker resistance, collective action, informal control of pacing and skill, and reasserting one's humanity. In the counterexamples I have given here, men and women workers seem engaged in overt and informal activity that is somehow missed when we talk only in reproductive terms. These terms make us see the school and the workplace as black boxes.[36]

These are not unimportant points, for the organization and control of work in corporate economies *cannot* be understood without reference to the overt and covert attempts of workers to resist the rationalizing control of employers.[37] A theory of the hidden curriculum that loses sight of this risks losing its conceptual vitality, to say nothing of its empirical accuracy.

Castells points out the significance of workers' resistance in structural terms.

> The main structural barrier in capitalist production and circulation is the workers' resistance to exploitation. Since an increase in the rate of surplus value is the basic element required for the accumulation of capital, the struggle over the relative amount of paid and unpaid labor is the first determinant of the rate of exploitation and, therefore, of the rate of profit and the speed and shape of the accumulation process. This is not an undetermined factor. Historically, labor's resistance tends to increase and capital is increasingly unable to appropriate the same amount of labor in absolute terms.[38]

When all this is said, however, we still must be very careful of appropriating an overly romantic outlook here. I have focused on the other side of the norms and dispositions that guide the workplace, norms and dispositions signifying struggle, resistance, conflict, and aspects of collective action that counterbalance the obedience, compliance, bureaucratic authority structure, and relations to the experts that management seeks to impose. Yet, while we need to see how the actual lived conditions at the workplace both mediate ideological and economic 'requirements' and have transformative potential, we need to remember at all times that power *is* often unequal in factories, offices, shops, and stores. Struggle and conflict may indeed exist; but, that does not mean that it will be successful. The success is determined by the structural limitations and selection processes that occur in our day to day lives.

There are powerful features within and outside the productive process that militate against a sense of collectivity and that exacerbate a sense of isolation and passivity. The 'serial organization of production,' where assembly lines spread workers out over the vast interior landscape of factories (and now many offices), provides one obvious example.[39] This is coupled with status and rank distinctions within the workplace so that even in areas not overtly like the factory – in the hospital, for instance – 'there are often injunctions against fraternizing with workers of marginally different ranks and penalties against workers who seek to exercise initiative in the interests of good patient care.'[40] Obviously, these are not exhaustive examples. (My earlier discussion of Taylorism and even newer time and motion measurement and control systems such as numerical control documents this.) However, they do point to how what might be called atomization or the creation of the abstract individual can and does go on.[41]

Any honest appraisal must not ignore Braverman's analysis quoted earlier. Management *has* historically attempted to incorporate resistance and to extend its dominion over the workplace; while, as we have seen, it has met with varying degrees of success, it is also clear that many management techniques that were developed in response to worker knowledge and informal control and resistance have been relatively fruitful in two ways.

First, while the early principles of scientific management were less than successful – and in fact often generated even more resistance on the part of workers – in actually controlling what went on in factories and offices, we need to remember that they had a second aim. And in this aim capital has been quite successful. The technical and administrative procedures were also introduced as part of a much larger ideological strategy to discredit the prevailing work practices in the public eye. Thus, labels such as 'soldiering' were affixed by Taylor and others to all worker-controlled craft rules and informal work-sharing arrangements. In this way, the public (and ultimately labor itself) could see that it was important to 'relieve labor of responsibility not its own,' since in fact it was 'immoral to hold up to this miscellaneous labor, as a class, the hope that it can ever manage industry.'[42] The fact that only recently has labor begun again to raise serious questions about sharing that 'labor of responsibility,' points to the relative success of management's strategy here.[43]

Second, in large part through the process I described in Chapter 2, management did accumulate a reservoir of techniques and knowledge that could be employed when the time seemed right to continue both its rationalization of production and reassertion of control of labor.[44]

Among these techniques are some I have already mentioned: the rationalization of production (cost accounting systems, centralization of authority, formalization of bureaucratic and supervisory structures and procedures), the redivision of labor (transforming skilled into less skilled and standardized jobs, differential training and knowledge for management and workers, a strong division between mental and manual labor), and the design of technology (numerical control devices to eliminate worker knowledge and control, assembly line production where the pace of the line regulates the pace of the work). Other techniques include: hiring practices (a battery of tests given to prospective employees, selection of employees by economic background for low paying work, exclusion or inclusion by race or sex), corporate welfare policies (human relations training added on to Taylorism, 'high' raises in times of expanding economy, bonuses, health and pension plans often granted 'in trade for' more management control and no-strike provisions), union policies (unions used to discipline militant workers and to standardize grievance procedures thereby eliminating wildcat strikes), and workplace location (the runaway shop where corporations move their factories and offices to locations where abundant and more compliant labor is available, threats of plant closings).[45]

There clearly may be many more. And even here these do not account for the ideological and economic pressures outside of the workplace which may 'cause' men and women to accept both their work and their social life as pregiven and natural.[46] Nor do they account for action by the state itself, as it regulates and assists in the process of capital accumulation, which will at times provide serious barriers to collective action.

Still more could be said about the informal work culture as well. Many of these informal 'attempts' at transformation, and the ways the work culture may mediate management ideology and pressures, may be turned back against the workers themselves. This is a critical point.

85

For example, in some machine shops, workers 'steal back' time and control by using their machines to create useless but often intricate objects called 'homers.' Or they find ways of playing complicated games among themselves with the machines. Often the playing of games and the making of homers is apparent to management, but it does not intervene since it keeps workers both busy and relatively happy on the job and does not usually threaten production to an inordinate degree. In essence, the workers' resistance to boredom and administrative/technical control *and* their own lived cultural forms produce what Michael Burawoy has called a type of Utopian escape.[47] Leisure is defined as filling time with making useless objects; it becomes the absence of serious meaningful work. Struggle on the shop floor becomes transformed by the process of individual commodity production into playing games. While play may be culturally creative here — and this is not to be ignored — the ultimate contradictory effect may be to continue the depoliticization of the relationship between one's labor, one's products, and the process and control of production.

A question we must ask, hence, is if, as I have maintained, these countervailing and relatively autonomous norms and practices exist, where, when, and how *specifically* may they ultimately be contradictory, perhaps even lending partial support to ideological and economic rubrics of control at an even deeper level?[48] It is a question that will not be easy to answer; but, we cannot understand either the hidden curriculum or the labor process without asking it.

At the very least, the search for such an understanding requires us to take much more seriously the idea that the cultural sphere is not totally reducible to the economic. Paul Willis makes this point rather markedly when he argues against the prevailing tendency on the left to make culture — even that found among workers in the workplace itself — only an epiphenomenal 'response' to or reflection of dominant economic or 'productive' relations. As he puts it:

> There is no question, for me, of counterposing the 'cultural' with the 'productive' or the 'real' as if the former had no actual constitutive role in the basic social relations which govern the form of our society. I am arguing against the *trivialization* of the notion of culture, of working class

86

culture and especially its central domain: cultural relations/ struggles/forms at the point of production. Culture is not simply a *response* to imposition which blinds or blunts a 'proper' understanding, nor is it merely a compensation, an adjustment to defect – these are essentially mechanized, reactive, models. Cultural forms occupy precisely those same spaces and human potentialities which are fought over by capital to continue valorization and capital accumulation. There are different logics possible in the direct experience of production than are posed in the capital relation itself, for itself. Merely because capital would like to treat workers as robots does not mean they are robots. The direct experiences of production are worked through and over in the praxis of different cultural discourses. To be sure, these discourses do not arise purely on the basis of production, and many of their important contents and inner relationships arise from or in articulation with external forces and institutions: the family, state, labour organizations, etc. It is also clear that in this society, for the moment, the material consequences of these cultural forms are for continued production in the capitalist mode. But none of this should blind us to the complexities, struggles, and tensions on the shop floor even if they do not always call their name in a way we can recognize. There are forms of praxis arising from definite human agency at the site of production which, in the very same moment, provide the conditions for capitalist relations and also partially penetrate and variably challenge these relationships.[49]

EDUCATIONAL ACTION

These arguments may seem a long way from the reality of class-room practice and curricular activity. After all, the academic debate about the conceptual issues and the empirical justification surrounding the hidden curriculum is, in part, just that – an academic debate about how we are to interpret what goes on in schools. However, besides the comparison between what happens in schools and its supposed effect on (or correspondence to) what occurs outside these institutions, a number of things need to be realized about this discussion. As I maintained previously, there are very real ties between conception and action. As I argued, a vision of the successful degradation of work unwittingly accepts on a conceptual level a management ideology, one that on a political level can lead to a cynicism or pessimism about the possibilities of any successful action in both the socio-economic arena and in the school. Or, it can cause us to wait for some cataclysmic event that will suddenly alter everything. Either one can ultimately lead to inactivity.

With this in mind, let us return to the pessimistic posture I pointed to earlier in this chapter. The position has it that schools can be no more than reproductive mirrors. Therefore, any action within them is doomed to failure. If I have been correct in my analysis here – that in nearly every real work situation, there will be elements of contradiction, of resistance, of relative autonomy, that have transformative potential, then the same should be true in schools. If we ignore these institutions we ignore something to which I shall return to in Chapter 5, the elemental fact that millions of people *work* in them. Because of their structural position as state employees, the conditions of their work can lead them to the beginnings of a serious appraisal of power and control in society. As the fiscal crisis of the state deepens, as the conditions of state employees become less secure because of the 'crisis of accumulation,' as educational work enters more and more into the political and economic arena as I predict it will, this increases the possibility of self-conscious organized action.[50] Even on the level of informal work, the work culture of teachers (which undoubtedly exists as I know from personal experience) can be used for educative purposes. It can be employed in a process of political education by using elements of it as exemplars of the very possibility of regaining at least partial control over the conditions of one's work and for clarifying the structural determinations that set limits on progressive pedagogic activity.[51]

But action can be taken not only in the long slow process of enabling teachers to understand their situation. There is a great need for curricular action as well. Here I will not say much beyond what has been said by others who have struggled long and hard to introduce honest, controversial, and racially, sexually, and economically progressive material into schools.[52] If resistances are found, if even only on an informal level we find men and women in our businesses, factories, and elsewhere struggling to maintain their knowledge, humanity, and pride, then curricular action may

be *more* important than we realize. For students need to see the
history and legitimacy of these struggles. The teaching of serious
labor history, organized around the countervailing norms generated
by men and women who have resisted living out the hidden curriculum, could be one effective strategy for educational action
here. As Raymond Williams reminds us, the overcoming of what
he has called the 'selective tradition' is essential for current
emancipatory practice.[53]

How much we have lost due to this selective tradition is
partially seen in the following quote from Montgomery.

> Not only did workers doggedly resist the employers' efforts
> to introduce stopwatches and incentive pay, *they also*
> *frequently formulated their own counter-proposals* for
> industrial reorganization. On one level these included
> standard pay classifications, union control over reductions in
> the work force, the 8-hour day, and above all, management's
> consent to treat with the workers' elected delegates on all
> questions affecting the operation of the works. On another
> level, the unions of coal miners and railway workers, speaking
> from positions of unprecedented strength, demanded public
> ownership of their industries with a large managerial role for
> the employees, and conventions of the Amalgamated
> Clothing Workers openly debated ways to assume the
> management of the men's clothing industry.[54]

A recognition of what we have lost, however, requires not
only theoretical and historical analysis, but the ongoing production of viable curricular materials and teaching strategies that can
be used in classrooms and elsewhere.[55] Local political and organizational activity to provide the conditions necessary for even
attempting to use new or previously prepared documented
material obviously needs to be considered. The selective tradition
has operated in such a way that the most widely employed curriculum materials now provide a less than significant sense of the
heritage of a sizeable portion of the population. Significant
aspects of the labor movement are often systematically neglected,
defined as outside the boundaries of 'responsible' labor activity, or
subject to editorial commentary that manages to disparage them.[56]
It is evident that concrete educational and political work could be
done here. This educational and political work should not be

limited to our formal educational system. Political education at the workplace − in our stores, offices, factories, and elsewhere − can be (and is) going on. Since these active elements of a work culture exist, and since cultural processes of resistance, mediation, and transformation can be found, then they can be worked with. Politically progressive educators, union organizers, informally and formally organized groups of women, men, black, hispanic, and other workers, and others can work together in finding non-elitist forms of engaging in such overt action. This politicization is a perfect complement to the 'democratization' of technical/administrative knowledge that I argued for in Chapter 2.

But what about our understanding of the hidden, not the overt, curriculum? If simple models of reproduction and correspondence cannot adequately account for the complexity of day to day life in either schools or where people work, this has important implications for future research on the hidden curriculum. Again being careful about romanticizing the resistance to ideological and economic 'determinations,' we should want to see if patterns of mediation, resistance, and partial transformation similar to those found in the workplace are found in the school. With the increasing encroachment of procedures for rationalization and management ideologies into schools (e.g., systems management, management by objectives, competency-based instruction, the growth of national testing, and so on), do teachers respond in ways like those of the workers I have examined here? Do students, like those found in the study by Willis that I mentioned previously in Chapter 1, also act against, partially transform, or somehow engage in activity that goes beyond mere socialization to and reproduction of the norms and values considered legitimate in the hidden curriculum? Does this ultimately turn back against them at a deeper ideological level? Which students − by race, sex, and class − do what?[57] These are the questions to which we shall now turn.

We may find that much more is going on than meets the eye or than some of the more deterministic hidden curriculum theorists would have us believe. If determinations are seen not as producing mirror images, but as setting contradictory limits,[58] limits that at the level of practice are often mediated by (and can *potentially* transform) the informal (and sometimes conscious) action of groups of people, then we can explore ways these limits are now being contested. In the process, we might find spaces where limits dissolve. There are few things more worthy of effort.

RESISTANCE AND CONTRADICTIONS IN CLASS, CULTURE, AND THE STATE: CULTURE AS LIVED-II

I

INTRODUCTION[1]

Let us now turn our attention from the workplace back to the school itself. So far I have critically examined claims about both the school's function as what Althusser has called an ideological state apparatus — one that produces agents (with the 'appropriate' dispositions, values, and ideologies taught through a hidden curriculum) to fill the needs of the social division of labor in society — and the place of our educational institutions in producing the particular knowledge and cultural forms 'required' by an unequal society — that is, as a site for the production of cultural commodities (technical/administrative knowledge) that are important to an economy and to increasingly powerful class segments. My examination of the workplace documented the necessity of seeing culture as a lived process as well as a commodity. There, class cultures both mediated and transformed the sets of structural 'determinations' of which corporate cultural capital is a part in significant ways. Just as the relatively autonomous nature of culture offered the key to that analysis, so too will the notion that one cannot reduce the cultural sphere to an epiphenomenal 'reflection' of the economic sphere offer the key for my discussion of the way class cultures are lived out in schools in this chapter. The question of relative autonomy will emerge from this chapter's discussion in another way as well, when I examine the school's response to the lived culture of students and to the pressures from the economic and political spheres later on in this chapter.

As in former chapters, I shall argue that social reproduction is by its very nature a contradictory process, not something that

91

simply happens without a struggle.[2] In order to do this, I shall have to examine in some empirical detail the nature of the contradictions present both at the cultural level in the school and go further in my discussion of the 'needs' of the state. In so doing, I shall show how the very contradictions that students live out in their day to day lives may end up supporting the institutions and ideologies that they seem to oppose yet offer a terrain for action at the same time. Finally, I shall analyze some of the major proposals for school reform that are the result of state intervention to 'solve' the problems generated by these struggles and contradictions – proposals such as vouchers, tax credits, and the like – in the light of my examination of contradictions within culture, economy, and the state. This will enable us to assess the extent to which such proposals can serve the purposes intended or whether they too may ultimately serve dominant interests in the economy and the state rather than those disaffected groups for whom they are intended.

As we shall see, both aspects of Althusser's phrase, 'ideological state apparatuses' – ideology and the state – will be needed to unpack schooling and the current proposals being made to reform it. However, here too the analysis presented will require us to think about ideology, class, and the issue of relative autonomy differently than the dominant, more functionalist and mechanistic traditions (and even Althusser). The perspective employed here reinstitutes class (*and* its accompanying conflict) as a fundamental dynamic to the issue of reproduction. Here class connotes not just 'how much money you make' or 'what kind of job you have' – the way most American social stratification researchers and many leftist political and economic theorists usually employ it – but one's relationship to the control and production of cultural and economic capital. Most importantly, it connotes a complex and creative cultural process as well, including language, style, intimate social relations, wishes, desires, and so on. Class is something that is both a structural position (where you stand in the unequal processes of power, control, and reproduction) *and* something lived, not an abstract entity or set of structural determinations somewhere 'out there' in an equally abstracted and totally separate economic sector of society.[3] And the ideologies that are lived out are not merely reflections of what is functional for reproduction.

IDEOLOGY AND LIVED CULTURE

In Chapter 3, I demonstrated that no assemblage of ideological practices and meanings and no set of social and institutional arrangements can be totally monolithic. As Gramsci, Wright and others have been adamant in pointing out, there will be counter-vailing tendencies and oppositional practices going on as well. These tendencies and practices may not be as powerful as the ideological and material forces of determination which aim towards reproduction; they may in fact be inherently contradictory and relatively disorganized. But, they will exist. To ignore them is to ignore the fact that in any real situation there will be elements of resistance, of struggle and contradiction, all of which will act against the abstract determination of the real life experiences of human actors. As I documented earlier, social and cultural life is simply too complex to be caught by totally deterministic models.[4]

As Richard Johnson notes, this is the case in part because the array of commonsense practices and meanings that constitute dominant ideologies may be internally inconsistent. These commonsense practices and meanings are often 'deeply contra-dictory, shot through with [both] ideological elements [and] with elements of good sense.'[5] Thus, side by side with beliefs and actions that maintain the dominance of powerful classes and groups, there will be elements of serious (though perhaps incom-plete) understanding, elements that see the differential benefits and penetrate close to the core of an unequal reality. Johnson is again helpful when he argues that:

> There is no doubt that there are ideological conditions for
> the existence of a given [mode of production] , but this
> does not, in any concrete society, exhaust all that belongs to
> the ideological instance. There are cultural elements to
> which capital is *relatively* indifferent and many which it has
> great difficulty in changing and which remain massively and
> residually present.[6]

This is clearly an anti-reductive program, one increasingly shared by a number of leftist scholars. Gramsci, Wright, and Johnson's arguments document how much we still have to learn from those who argue against mechanistic theories of economic and cultural reproduction. Even a relatively surface recognition of

93

their points would have us interrogate complex social processes and institutions like the school, and evaluate their efficacy in the following ways. What does our mode of production look like? What are its most significant characteristics? Which groups of people and classes benefit most and least from these characteristics? How do these *patterns* of class reproduction and differential benefit work themselves out in our day to day lives, for instance in the actual curricular, pedagogical, and evaluative activity in which we participate, and to which students respond, in schools? Yet they would add something else. If cultural/ideological and political forms are really dialectically related to material forces (they often act back and mediate some determinations and are not reducible to them) how does this operate in these same schools? If determinations are at times contested, if reproduction is filled with conflict, filled with elements of good and bad sense that are struggled over, what are the actual grounds of these struggles (e.g., where are they found, what are they over, etc.)?

These are not easy matters to deal with as you would imagine, for our appraisal of all this has to do two things. Not only does it need to be structural — that is, it must, at the level of theory, be general enough to provide fruitful explanations of how the social order is both organized and controlled so that the differential benefits are largely accounted for — but, at the same time, it should not be so general as to be unable to account for the everyday actions, struggles, and experiences of real actors in their day to day lives in and out of schools. It must account, hence, for where, how, and why people are caught, and where they may not be totally so. This requires a particularly sensitive perspective, a combination of what might be called a socio-economic approach to catch the structural phenomena and what might be called a cultural program of analysis to catch the level of everydayness.[7] Nothing less than this kind of dual program, one that looks for the series of connections and interpenetrations, not the one-way determination, of the economic, political, and cultural 'arenas' can overcome the previously noted problems of straightforwad base/ superstructure models. In essence, what is called for is a Marxist ethnography of life in and around our dominant institutions.

In the next part of my discussion, then, I want to provide an analysis of ways of integrating these elements together into a coherent approach that continues to go beyond theories of mechanistic determination. I shall draw upon a number of interesting studies, in particular Paul Willis's research reported in his volume *Learning to Labour*,[8] Robert Everhart's analysis of an American junior high school in his *The In-Between Years*,[9] and Angela McRobbie's research on working-class girls in schools.[10] These investigations provide an important base from which we can interrogate the relationship among the internal qualities of schools, the lived culture of students within them, and the needs of accumulation and legitimation to which schools must respond. They help us understand what actually happens in schools and what the actual experiences of students are. And at the same time, once again they provide important correctives to the overly deterministic appraisals that some of us on the left have been too apt to embrace.

DETERMINATIONS AND CONTRADICTIONS

Anyone familiar with recent scholarship on schooling and inequality is undoubtedly also familiar with the rapid growth of evidence on how schools act as agents in the economic and cultural reproduction of an unequal society.[11] Nor is there any lack of evidence that a hidden curriculum in schools exists, one that tacitly attempts to teach norms and values to students that are related to working in this unequal society.[12] Yet, my argument in the prior section of this chapter implies that we must contest a particular assumption – that of passivity. This assumption tends to overlook the fact that students, like the workers I previously examined, are creatively acting in ways that often contradict these expected norms and dispositions which pervade the school and the workplace. In more analytic terms, the institutions of our society are characterized by *contradiction* as well as by simple reproduction.[13]

As I showed in the previous chapter, workers at all levels attempt to create informal conditions to gain some measure of control over their labor, to establish some serious sense of informal power over time, pacing, and the employment of their skills. At the same time that they are controlled, they also continuously attempt – often through cultural, not political ways – to articulate challenges to that control. These studies provided empirical support for the general theoretical position I argued for earlier, that economic form does not totally prefigure cultural form. The cultural sphere has some degree of relative autonomy. I shall have more to say about this in a moment.

Similar things hold true for students, especially for some of those who are destined to become workers in these very same industries; and any evaluation of schooling must take this into account or risk failure. Students become quite adept at 'working the system.' Large numbers of them in inner-city and working-class schools, to say nothing of other areas, creatively adapt their environments so that they can smoke, get out of class, inject humor into the routines, informally control the pacing of classroom life, and generally try to make it through the day. In these same schools, many students go even further. They simply reject the overt and hidden curricula of the school. The teacher who is teaching about mathematics, science, history, careers, etc. is ignored as much as possible. Also, the covert teaching of punctuality, neatness, compliance, and other more economically rooted norms and values is simply dismissed as far as possible. The real task of the students is to last until the bell rings.[14]

Thus, just like in the workplace, any theory of the school's role in economic and cultural reproduction must account for the rejection by many students of the norms that guide school life. In fact, this very rejection of the hidden and overt curriculum gives us one of the major principles from which we can analyze the role of our educational institutions in helping to reproduce the social division of labor and inequality in corporate societies. For, much of the way our schools function in roughly producing knowledge and agents for a labor market is related not so much to a strong and unyielding correspondence between the characteristics companies think they want in their workers and what values schools teach, but, at least in certain segments of the working class, to a rejection of the messages of schooling and even our most creatively designed curricula by the students themselves. Analyses of this rejection can provide insights that can help us go a long way in seeing part of both the social 'functions' of and the values promoted by the school. Only with a more complex understanding of what schools actually do can we begin to grapple with the range of suggested reforms being proposed currently. But how are we to find this out? We must enter the school and see it first hand. We need to find out what meanings, norms, and values students, teachers, and others really act on in schools. Only then can we begin to see the layers of mediation that exist 'between' the economic sector of a society and its other institutions. In essence, the school becomes a fundamental institution for seeing the dialectical relationships and tensions between the economic, political, and cultural spheres. And the school is the arena for working out these relationships and tensions that Willis, Everhart, McRobbie, and others have chosen to focus upon.

CLASS, CULTURE AND GENERALIZED LABOR

Let us examine Paul Willis's provocative study first. His primary questions involve how major aspects of a working-class ideology are formed and how it is that hegemony is recreated. In short, he begins with an issue very much like that concerning us here. How do ideology and class operate in schools today? Whose ideologies are dominant and in what ways? Is only reproduction going on? Unlike a number of recent theorists of reproduction who argue that the ideological forms of capitalistic society are so powerful as to be total, Willis suggests something slightly more optimistic. He argues that even though the cultural and economic apparatus of an unequal society does have immense power to control the actions and consciousness of people, there are 'deep disjunctions and desparate tensions within social and cultural reproduction.' As he says, 'Social agents are not passive bearers of ideology, but active appropriators who reproduce existing structures only through struggle, contestation and a partial penetration of these structures.'[15]

Learning to Labour is an ethnographic account of a cohesive group of working-class boys in an all-male comprehensive secondary school in an industrial area of England. The 'lads,' as they are called, constitute a group of students who, like many of the students I mentioned earlier, spend a good deal of their time in school trying to maintain their collective identity and get through the day. They skillfully work the system to gain some measure of control over the way they spend their time in school, to have some free time and space, and to 'have a laff.' Most importantly, they reject a large portion of the intellectual and social messages of the school, even though the institution tries to be 'progressive.'

The lads are contrasted to another group of students – the 'ear'oles' (or earholes, so named because they seem simply to sit and listen). These are the students who have accepted the importance of compliance to educational authority, technical knowledge, qualifications, and credentials. Nearly everything about the ear'oles provides a symbol to be rejected by the lads. The ear'oles' clothes, haircuts, conformity to both the values and curricula of the school, the teaching staff's more easy relationship with them, all of these are attributes of inclusion in a world the lads must reject. It is not real; it bears little resemblance to the familiar world of work, to making one's way economically in an industrial community, to the street. Instead, 'the adult world, specifically the adult male working-class world, is turned to as a source of material for resistance and exclusion.'[16] For the lads, 'real life' needs to be contrasted to the 'oppressive adolescence' which is represented by the behavior of both the teachers and the ear'oles.[17] Whether it be the accepted social relations of the school, the formal teaching of what the school considers legitimate curricular knowledge, or the rules governing the physical facility of the school building itself, these are interpreted as both opportunities and challenges to increase one's personal mobility within the building, to meet each other, or basically to 'have a laff.'

But what about those aspects of the formal curriculum that attempt to be directly 'relevant'? Even something like career education and associated curricula fare no better. In fact, such programs may even fare worse. While the school curriculum attempts to portray jobs as offering opportunities for mobility, for personal gratification, for choice, the lads will have none of this. They have already experienced the world of work from their parents, their acquaintances, and in their own part-time jobs. This experience clearly contradicts the messages of the school which are viewed cynically. Though only dimly conscious of it, the lads already 'know' that they are being committed to a future of generalized labor. Thus, work is not something one really has a choice about (this is in essence a construct of middle-class consciousness). Rather, most semi-skilled and manual jobs are the same. Choice is relatively meaningless. In the minds of the lads, nearly all work is 'equilibrated by the overwhelming need for instant money, the assumption that all work is unpleasant, and that what really matters is the potential work situations hold for self and particularly masculine expression, diversions, and "laffs" '.[18] These are all learned creatively in the informal culture – what Willis labels the counter-school culture – of the school.

In this way, physicality, masculinity, and manual labor all

provide opportunities for confronting not the 'false world' of the school but the real day to day existence the lads affirm. This process of affirmation and rejection illuminates one of the more important insights into the social reproductive role of the school.

By rejecting the world of the school, by rejecting what the ear'oles do, the lads also reject mental labor. They see it as effeminate, as not physical enough. *The seeds of reproduction lie in this very rejection.* The distinctions made and acted upon by the lads imply a strong dichotomy between mental and manual labor. The seeing of strength in the physical, the dismissing of mental 'book learning,' provides an important element in the recreation of the ideological hegemony of the dominant classes.

How is this done? Consider this. In general, as we saw, one of the principles guiding the articulation of social relations in our economy is the progressive divorce of mental from physical labor.[19] There are laborers who run machines, who work with their hands, or do menial paper work, and there are those who plan it and think it through. Planning is to be separated from execution whenever possible so that each process can be better standardized and controlled. In rejecting mental labor, hence, the lads are enhancing a distinction that lies at the roots of the social relations of production. Yet this is not a one-way operation. There is strength as well as weakness — paradox and contradiction — in the lads' action on this distinction.

Along with Willis, we can employ two major categories for analyzing the contradictions and paradoxes of life for these students, and the economic class they represent: *penetration* and *limitation*.[20] Penetration refers to those instances where students have developed responses to schools and work that see the unequal reality they will face. Their rejection of so much of the content and form of day to day educational life bears on the almost unconscious realization that, as a class, schooling will not enable them to go much further than they already are. The culture the lads create inside and outside their school actually constitutes a rather realistic assessment of the rewards of the obedience and conformism which the school seeks to extract from working-class youths. Along with scholars like Bernstein and Bourdieu, Willis argues that the cultural capital employed in schools ensures the success of the children of dominant groups in society.[21] The repudiation of ideas of qualifications, diplomas, and compliance by the lads penetrates close to the core of this reality. Conformism may help the individual (but again not the working class in general); but the lads focus on their own informal group and not conformism to the model of individual achievement represented by the school. They, therefore, penetrate the ideology of individualism and competition that supports the economy.

Of course, this penetration is not a conscious option, an overt choice that represents the ideological solidarity of a working-class movement. Instead, it is a response to lived conditions both inside and outside of the school, ones experienced by the lads at home, on the shop-floor, within the counter-school culture, and elsewhere. It is an informal cultural response to the ideological and economic conditions and tensions they confront. And while it holds out the possibility of economic and political awareness, it remains relatively disorganized and unguided.

The conflict between the working-class culture of the lads and that of the school has another side, however, one that is properly called limitations. The cultural penetrations of the lads are repressed and prevented from going further (and in fact often paradoxically link the lads more fully to an unequal economy) by the contradictions built into their actions. For instance, as I noted, by dismissing mental labor, they heighten the division between the mental and the physical. Another instance is the way students like the lads tend to treat girls and women. Mental labor is effeminate; therefore, by preferring manual labor, and through it affirming their own subjectivity, they also affirm a sexual division of labor, as well.

In Willis's words:

> We can see here the profound, unintended and contradictory importance of the institution of the school. Aspects of the dominant ideology are informally defeated there, but that defeat passes a larger structure more unconsciously and more naturalized for its furnacing in (pyrrhic) victory. Capitalism can afford to yield individualism amongst the working class but not division. Individualism is penetrated by the counter-school culture but it actually produces division.[22]

In short, the ideology of individualism is 'defeated,' but at the expense of increasing the power of more subtle and important economic and sexual divisions. Notice that no simple model of economic determinism or correspondence will do as an explanatory framework here. Reproduction is carried out as much through contradiction, through the relative autonomy of the lads at a cultural level.

Is this what the school consciously wants? Probably not. Nor does it want what else the institution latently brings out. The educational beliefs and pedagogic practices of many educators also act in a paradoxical way here. For example, we tend to picture certain elements of progressive pedagogy as being effective in 'reaching' students who have been 'unsuccessful' in more traditional classroom environments. More and more varied curricular materials, guest speakers, films, more personal and caring teachers, greater student autonomy, and so on are often seen as answers in making education both more palatable and more rewarding to these students. If we could get students like the lads to listen and learn through better designed programs, then we could help large numbers of them get rewarding jobs, and increase the chances of mobility for a large portion of them (and legitimate both the economy and the educational apparatus in the process). However, the tacit values that underlie the schools are wholly at odds with those of the lads.

What actually seems to happen is that the somewhat more progressive setting sets limits on and enables students to develop within their own day to day lives in school an array of working-class themes and attitudes which give them strength and can act against the ideological values represented by the school. Resistance, subversion of authority, working the system, creating diversions and enjoyment, building an informal group to counter the official activities of the school, all of these are specifically brought out by the school, though all of these are the exact opposite of what the administrators and teachers want. Hence, if workers are interchangeable and work itself is undifferentiated and generalized, thereby looking about the same from job to job, the school plays an important part in enabling the lads to develop penetrations into it. At the same time, however, the limitations are clearly there, limitations that just as clearly end up tying such working-class youths to a labor market and preparing them for generalized and standardized work.

This is an essential point and needs to be gone into just a bit more. As Harry Braverman notes in his exceptionally important investigation of the role of the technical and administrative approaches capital uses in economic production, the use of labor in the modern corporation is increasingly guided by a number of needs.[23] First, the labor process itself must be focused, intensified, and made more speedy. Second, the control of this process needs to be removed from the workers themselves. And third, to create an even more efficient mode of production, complex skills and crafts need to be broken down into less complex components, and then standardized. Thus, in general (though this varies by industry and 'level of occupation' within the workplace), as control becomes centralized and more rationalized and as the scope and speed of production increases, a different kind of worker is required. Less skilled workers who are open to a greater degree of systematization become essential. Groups of people who can deal with a more intense working pace and who are flexible enough to allow for interchange between standardized labor processes also become more important. What is not needed is a craft ideology with its sense of personal control of one's job, pride in one's work, or personal meaning in work activity.[24]

Here one can see how segments of such a labor force may be produced in a *non-mechanistic way*. For, as we have seen, there is not necessarily a mirror-image correspondence between the economic and social needs of corporate production and the imposition of these needs on students in schools. Rather, the cultural response of these students is complex and both gives strength and yet prepares them to work in a job setting that can give them little sense of pride or craft.

This side of the argument, that involving the role of both the school and the informal culture which certain working-class students create within it in reproducing the social division of labor, can be seen in this quote.

> The cultural and institutional processes [of schools] — taken as a whole — tend to produce large numbers of workers approaching this type. The nature of the 'partial penetrations' we have looked at are precisely to devalue and discredit older attitudes towards work, feelings of control, and meaning at work. In certain respects these developments are progressive with respect to monopoly capital and are likely to supply the instrumental, flexible, un-illusioned, 'sharp,' unskilled but well socialized workers needed to take part in its increasingly socialized processes.[25]

102

There is a real social contradiction operating here, as we have seen. The rejection of both the older attitudes toward work and the old skills must not go too far if a corporate economy is to maintain itself. If workers reject modern work, or have a complete understanding of the meaninglessness of so much of the labor they are called upon to do, then this could easily degenerate into a lack of loyalty and an erosion of the motivation to work in these increasingly centralized and rationalized industries. The modern monopoly's need for a less job-bound and less skilled work-force could also result in a group of workers who are 'susceptible to mass critical political perspectives,' especially in times of an economic crisis. How is this critical sense of the reality of the workplace held by some workers prevented from becoming a sense of solidarity, from becoming a political and economic perspective on their own lack of power? It is *here* where the school plays such an essential role. For, while the informal culture of students like the lads allows them to penetrate almost to the heart of this reality, this same counter-school culture that they engender somehow acts against them as well. They ultimately become the workers needed by an unequal economy, workers who are better able to cope with and have some semblance of power on the shop-floor, but workers who ultimately employ categories and distinctions that are at root aspects of the ideological hegemony required by the economy they started out penetrating.

CLASS, CULTURE, AND WORKING-CLASS MOBILITY

So far I have focused on students, students whose backgrounds in a particular industrial community and from a particular segment of the working class resonate throughout their experience. Yet, clearly the lads are not the only students in schools. In working-class areas, as Willis admits, a large portion of the students are members of that amorphous group the lads call the ear'oles. These may be the children of parents who are slightly 'higher up' on the economic ladder within the working class, but still they constitute a large portion of working-class people.

What of students like the ear'oles? Do working-class students who, unlike the lads, seemingly generally accept the forms of knowledge, the credentialing process, and the ethnic of mobility simply sit still and listen? Is there a complex cultural form at work here as well, one that is also contradictory? Recent research seems to point to just this possibility. For like the lads in Willis's English high school, similar things hold true for students in the United States, though the specifics of class reproduction are somewhat more muted due to a different history and a more complex articulation among the state, education, and an economy. Here again students participate in the contested reproduction of the ideological and material system of which they are a part. As Robert Everhart shows in his investigation of a predominantly working-class junior high school, the cultural world of these youths, youths like the ear'oles, also recreates, defends, and contests the hegemonic forms that dominate the larger society, but again not in any mechanistic way.[26]

Let us examine this more closely. While one might get the impression that such working-class youths sit passively by and both accept and act on the formal ideological messages of the school, what one finds is decidedly more complex. And, like the lads, the complexity is filled with both penetrations and limitations. The vision we may have of these 'kids' (as Everhart calls them) as doing their work, attending to school matters, and basically being taught the norms of compliance and relative docility that will equip them well for their particular rung on the labor market, is not quite as accurate as we might have thought.

As many other studies have shown, most of the time these students are in school is spent not on 'work' (what teachers think school is for) but on regenerating a specific lived culture – talking about sports, discussing and planning outside activities done with friends, talking about the 'non-academic' things they do in school.[27] Like the lads, a large amount of time was spent finding ways to 'goof off,' to make class more interesting, to gain some measure of control over the pattern of day to day interaction that was so standard in school. In fact, as Everhart shows, nearly half of the time spent in school was not over 'work' but in these other activities.

Unlike the lads, though, most of these groups of kids *did* meet the requirements of the school. They did this 'despite a consuming interest in their own activities and the seemingly ambivalent manner in which they treated anything having to do with academics.' However, because of its size and bureaucratic nature and because of the large numbers of students the school had to deal with, it actually demanded relatively little from these students. In fact, many of them could complete the required work in very little time (or could and did easily copy it from others), thus leaving a good deal of time for their own collective cultural activity. The students gave the school what relatively little was required, but certainly no more.[28]

This was true at the level of conduct as well. There were few serious instances of disrespect to a teacher or to an administrator, and little evidence of maliciousness or vandalism.[29] Overt violations of the codes of the school were only acceptable if they did not put you in too much danger. While skipping classes, goofing off, and such things as fighting, swearing, drinking, and drugs, were part of the cultural world of many of the kids, most of them maintained adequate or better grades. However, this does not imply that they had all totally accepted the formal ideology of the school, or its hidden curriculum. Rather, it just as often seems to signify that a significant portion of these youths put up with this formal set of beliefs and practices 'as a price to pay for their own activity to be generated.'[30]

Even for those students whose social class membership and expectations of the family created a sense that one should and would do well in school, having friends and having a good time were often more important than a very high average in their grades in school.[31]

The message seemed to be the following. In the daily routine of the school, one met the minimal demands of the institution — and tried to keep these demands as minimal as possible — and at the same time one's group structured its own agenda as well. This agenda centered around resistance to the regularities of organized school life and creating oppositional forms that often contradicted the emphases of formal educational practice. Again, where individualistic achievement, technical competencies, and the ideology of individualism pervades the organizational properties of the institution, this is countered by the cultural life of the students where constant attempts at group humor, 'bugging the teacher,' sharing answers, and maintaining a cohesiveness in the face of the individuating practices of the school were the dynamic elements guiding the kids' lives.

For the students in this junior high school, since the school defines what is legitimate knowledge, what the appropriate strategies for gaining it are, how decisions should be made within the school itself, and so on, and this definition is pervasive throughout the institution, one has two alternatives (though of course these will not really be conscious decisions). As a student, you can either accept it and remain relatively bored a good deal of the time. Or you can find the cracks in the organizational control and exploit them to maintain some sense of power over your daily life. If overt rejection of the ideological messages of the school and of its knowledge and authority is too threatening, then the cracks are still there to be used, expanded when possible, or even created.

In fact, those students who were most successful at mediating the demands of minimal work and exploiting the cracks were the ones who emerged as models for the others. Thus, most of the students who were highly regarded by other students were those who combined two attributes, attributes that are important for seeing ideology and its contradictions at work in this setting. 'Kids who were "smart" (that is, who could get good grades *and* who goofed off)' seemed to be the ones who fared best in the eyes of their peers. If you could do fairly well with minimum effort and still have time to goof off you did fine.[32] Hence, the ideal student seemed to accept on one level the goals and procedures of the school, but at the same time was able to use them for his or her own purposes, purposes that were often quite opposite to those of the institution.

Notice what is happening here. While the kids clearly exercise a fair amount of informal power in the school setting — by goofing off, bugging teachers, and so on — like the lads they both participate in and at least partially reproduce hegemonic ideologies that may be less than helpful. In Everhart's words:

> As a form of knowledge, as a cultural system not unlike
> similar patterns in other settings, the exercise of power in
> this manner indicates how cultural forms are [often]
> reproductive and how participants, through opposition,
> actually participate in that reproductive practice.[33]

Not all of these kids are the same of course. For some students in this junior high school, the oppositional practices are massive. They spend all their time goofing off, 'smoking dope,' or simply skipping classes. Like the lads, these students are recreating the conditions of their own futures as generalized laborers. On another level, however, while the culture has a differential impact on students, *everyone's* future is partly 'determined' by the culture

106

the students create. As Everhart goes on to say, the creation and emergence of these cultural forms tends to affect all students:

> and serves to reinforce the interpretation that systems of social relations are not meant to be confronted and critically analyzed, but rather resisted through these oppositional forms. And in the rise of the forms themselves, indeed the meaning attached to them, the basic system of social relations . . . remains unaffected, unexamined. . . . It seems then that the [actual cultural knowledge forms generated by the kids] , while they are present in the forms of resistance, are also present as reproductive of that very system they oppose. As participants, as creators of those cultural forms, students are reproducing forms that will damn them to expressions of reaction but will not foster critical opposition. In this building of culture, students participate in the building of reproductive processes that make it likely they will suffer the same fate elsewhere, especially in the workplace.[34]

Yes there will be mobility for some of them, but not for all that many. Any real overt resistance is a threat to this possibility; but it is just this, only a possibility. This is already prefigured, 'known,' in the cultural sphere. It penetrates to the heart of the myth of the economy, yet clearly limits many of these youths to the blue-collar and low-level white-collar jobs in which they will ultimately find themselves.

In essence, when a majority of American workers report that they would not work in the same job if given the choice again, yet continue to work in these conditions – while attempting to make them more liveable through humor and the formation of an informal group culture – the ideological conditions that may foster this are produced out of the student culture in contradictory and complex ways in schools such as these.[35]

In ways that may be more masked than those of the lads, these 'ear'oles' already 'know' the norms of systematic 'soldiering' on the job, looking for ways of generating fun and collectivity, and working the system to expand one's control of a situation. At the same time, they are also caught in the contradictions, the limitations, of their own lived cultural response. For the maintenance of some power and autonomy on the shop-floor or in an office does not necessarily challenge the needs of capital *if the minimum requirements of production are usually met*. Thus, though many of these working-class students will go on to more skilled or higher status jobs than the lads, they also are actively involved in the recreation of the social relations that dominate the corporate production process.

Work need not be meaningful in this production process. It *is* just there to satisfy one's other needs, needs that are met when the work is done. One does it for money, and because it provides opportunities for a collective lived cultural response when it is engaged in. The seeds of ideological reproduction are laid. It will be a reproduction filled with contradictions, one that will be continually contested by the cultural response of these kids as they find their ways into jobs, but it too will remain relatively unproductive as long as the penetrations into the nature of work and control generated by these working-class youths and their parents are unorganized and unpoliticized.

CLASS AND PATRIARCHY: THE CULTURE OF FEMININITY

Perhaps because many of the investigators have been male, girls' cultural forms have been seen as marginal. However, as McRobbie and others have argued, girls seem more marginal because they are often 'pushed by male dominance to the periphery of social activity' though they struggle against this and act in culturally creative ways, ways which, like the lads and the kids, also limit them and give them power in one and the same historical moment.

The conditions under which many working-class girls live can be significantly different from those of boys like the lads and the kids, though. Their free time is controlled by parents more closely. They 'assume an apprenticeship for domestic labour which begins at home.' In fact, a major way girls earn the money they may need is by helping out with domestic tasks (and through 'baby sitting,' of course).[36] Though the traditional definitions of women's occupational roles are being broken because of a continual process of contestation by women and men, the fact that nearly all women are being prepared for both workplace *and* domesticity[37] means that in a time of economic crisis — when decent jobs are so scarce — particular themes and cultural forms will be heightened within the lived culture of working-class girls.

Angela McRobbie's research among a group of girls in a primarily working-class area is exceptionally helpful in enabling us to go further here. Like Willis and Everhart, she set out to map the ways these working-class girls lived out class and gender as a 'distinctive way of life,' one that was filled with elements of good and bad sense, if you will. In this case, the community provided employment for their fathers in an auto plant and for their mothers in shift or part-time labor such as waitressing, bar tending, office work, or cleaning. Thus, we are describing here another particular segment of the working class.

Underpinning McRobbie's concern with culture is an awareness that the culture of these girls is both partly 'determined' by their economic and sexual position and embodies sets of meanings and practices that are relatively autonomous. It is involved in both reproduction and contestation. In her words, we must see this as an issue of *relative* autonomy because, regardless of its form, the girls' culture:

> [is] in no sense a free floating configuration. Instead it [is] linked to and partly determined by, though not mechanically so, the material position occupied by the girls in society; their social class, their future role in production, their present and future role in domestic production and their economic dependence on their parents. And because cultures, though referring to the essentially expressive capacities of the group in question, are not created from scratch by the group but instead embody 'the trajectory of group life through history, always under conditions and with raw materials which cannot wholly be of its own making,' then it [is] important to situate the girls from the start within a pre-existent culture of femininity which they, as females in a patriarchal society, are born into and which is continuously transmitted to them over the years by their mothers, sisters, aunts, grandmothers, neighbors, and so on.[38]

In essence, what McRobbie found was that the girls' actions ultimately constituted an endorsement of traditional female roles and of 'femininity,' not because it is always 'imposed' upon them (though this does in fact happen) but as a creative response to the objective and ideological conditions in which they live. Housework, marriage, and children were the three irreducible facts of

109

life that stood behind their experience and that provided the horizon against which their activity in and out of school was coded. What 'saved' them, from what they 'knew' from their mothers, sisters, aunts, neighbors, etc. was an unexciting and all too real future, were two things. They formed intense friendships, based on gender and class similarities. And, of great significance, they tended to immerse themselves in an 'ideology of romance' and to act in ways that accentuated both their femininity and sexuality.[39]

In contradistinction to the working-class girls, there was also a group of middle-class girls whose parents tended to be members of the new petty bourgeoisie and to be in management positions at the factory, in government, or professional work, etc. These girls had a decidedly different experience and had a different way of coding their feminine and class experiences. Many of them spent time at art centers, playing games, engaging in dramatics and dancing, and doing school work. Because their 'material horizons are so much broader,' even though boys and romance may well play an important part in their consciousness, they 'know' that there will be opportunities beyond marriage, housework, childcare, and low-paid drudgery. Even with a crisis in the economy, both the residual cultural forms of mobility among the middle class — of *careers*, not only jobs — and the emergent cultural forms of mobility among women — careers for *women* as well as men — will be acted upon in their day to day lives.[40] Though both groups of girls may be directed toward the home, middle-class girls are directed toward a different kind of labor outside of it.[41]

This is unlike the working-class girls in many ways. For as these working-class girls get closer to adolescence, achievement drops markedly. Pressures to conform to the feminine ideal increase, as do pressures to think more and more about boys and about accompanying concerns with their own attractiveness, popularity, and so on.[42] When these pressures are *articulated with the fact of the girls' class position*, they act in ways that are quite powerful.

In ways similar to the lads and the kids, the girls gauged a good deal of their 'success' by their ability to work the organizational and curricular system of the school to their own ends. In asserting their opposition to middle-class behavior, language, dress, and norms, these working-class girls sought to transform the school into an arena for expanding their social life, 'fancying boys,' teaching each other the latest dances, 'playing up the teachers,' getting together to have a cigarette, discuss music and rock stars, and so on. In this set of oppositional practices, their very femininity enabled them to stand even farther apart from what they saw as the 'snobs,' those middle-class girls who were more materially advantaged. In their view, the snobs from the middle class, by accepting the official ideology and knowledge of the school, were clearly more valued by the teachers. However, even though these working-class girls may have felt a bit like they were 'failures' in school, they felt equally as contentious of the snobs' conscientiousness and hard work. Class antagonisms were lived out in their feelings that the middle-class girls lacked 'style,' had little taste in boys, 'sucked up' to their teachers, and kept their language 'clean.'[43]

McRobbie describes these oppositional practices in this way.

One way in which the girls combat the class based and oppressive features of the school is to assert their 'femaleness,' to introduce into the classroom their sexuality and their physical maturity in such a way as to force the teachers to take notice. A class instinct then finds its expression at the level of jettisoning the official ideology for girls in the school (neatness, diligence, appliance, femininity, passivity, etc.) and replacing it with a *more* feminine, even sexual one. Thus the girls took great pleasure in wearing make-up to school, spent vast amounts of time discussing boyfriends in loud voices in class and used these interests to disrupt the class . . .

Marriage, family life, fashion, and beauty all contribute massively to this feminine anti-school culture and, in doing so, nicely illustrate the contradictions inherent in so-called oppositional activities. Are the girls in the end not doing exactly what is required of them — and if this *is* the case, then could it not be convincingly argued that it is their own culture which itself is the most effective agent of social control for the girls, pushing them into compliance with that role which a whole range of institutions in capitalist society also, but less effectively, directs them towards? At the same time, they are expressing a class relation, in albeit traditionally feminine terms.[44]

111

The paradox is striking. The girls develop cultural forms that give them power. They can control boys' actions (and their own futures) to some extent by enhancing their own sexuality. They can form groups that recreate their solidarity as working-class girls and that enable them to develop and play out themes of resistance and class struggle. Yet the contradictions within the cultural sphere are intense. They are sexually exploited by the boys. Their realistic appraisal of their future lives as wives and mothers — that marriage is an economic necessity given the political economy of that geographic area — leads them to rely on a culture of femininity that is exploitative and reproduces many of the conditions on which the social and sexual divisions of labor are based. This dual ideological performance of their lived culture speaks to both the determined and creative and autonomous qualities of culture. The cultural meanings and practices that grow out of the interaction of gender and class both penetrate to the heart of patriarchal power and class relations, and limit the possibilities for action, if they are once again left unorganized.

Thus, the dynamics of class and sex work together in such a way as to 'force' these girls into a contradictory position, one that they live out in their day to day lives. Their antagonistic relationship to both middle-class girls and the school is expressed largely in 'feminine' terms. Yet their experience in their own families also teaches them that romanticism and femininity are not necessarily to be found or to remain for long, given the reality of the role of wife, mother, or woman worker. In short, 'the code of romance doesn't deliver the goods.' Caught in this situation, they still cannot see themselves except ultimately as wives and mothers.[45]

Working-class girls and women are not duped here. They are often very conscious about the restrictions of marriage and the 'traditional' roles this may entail. However, they are also rather realistic about it. The economic position and the conditions of gender oppression in which they find themselves mean that a rejection of marriage can bring high emotional and economic costs should they reject it. The cult of romance protects one from these costs, and *does* give one real power in the family, while partially reproducing the restrictions of traditional gender and economic roles.[46]

Mike Brake's discussion summarizes some of these arguments and points to the continued dominance of 'femininity' as a self-selecting cultural form.

Subcultures arise as attempts to resolve collectively
experienced problems arising from contradictions in the
social structure. [They] generate a form of collective identity
from which an individual identity can be achieved outside
that ascribed by class, education, and occupation. This is
nearly always a temporary solution, and in no sense is a real
material solution, but one which is solved at the cultural
level. Youth cultures interact with manufactured popular
cultures and their artifacts [but not in any] deterministic
[way]. . . . On the whole, youth cultures tend to be some
form of exploration of masculinity. These are therefore
masculinist and [we must] consider their effect on girls. . . .
[One] distinct sign of the emancipation of young girls from
the cult of romance, and marriage as their true vocation,
will be the development of subcultures exploring a new form
of femininity. Given the material place of women in society
today this is likely to take some time.[47]

Clearly the development of such 'new forms of femininity' is
occurring as class and gender actors struggle in the home, school,
and workplace. Yet the general import of Brake's points and of
my discussion of the girls studied by McRobbie is to raise a critical
issue about *how* one studies reproduction and contradiction in
schooling, class, and culture. The issue here is not just to acknow-
ledge the importance of a feminist perspective in unpacking all of
this; nor is it to mention women occasionally in one's analysis of,
say, the role of education in the reproduction of class relations.
Rather, a social formation needs to be understood as being constituted – that is, as being actively reconstructed – on the grounds
of both gender and class relations. The two, gender and class, are
not separate but are articulated together.[48] This is clear in the
creative cultural elements of the lads and the girls, for instance.

In many ways, we need to recognize that the sexual division
of labor of which the lads and the girls partake did not come
about 'as a sexual division from capital's own structures.' Instead,
'capital has built its own divisions on to already existing sexual
divisions.' In this way, while patriarchal gender relations and
capitalist social relations are very difficult to separate, they are not
reducible to each other. Bland *et al.* put it this way: 'The sexual
division of labour structured in male dominance is "colonized,"
"taken over" by the structures of capital.'[49] Thus, the ideological

meanings and practices we see in the girls, with all of their contradictions that both limit them and give them strength, can only be
understood by seeing how the economics of capital, the ideology
of patriarchy, and the cultural forms of working-class life reproduce
and contradict each other.

BEING BROWN, BLACK, AND POOR

The groups of students I have discussed so far have been from
different segments of the working class, but they have all been
white. Similar patterns of cultural penetration and limitation
occur among brown and black working class and poor groups as
well. Among the cultural patterns that dominate working-class,
especially male, youth is a celebration of masculinity, of playing
the 'heavy man.' This was evident in the patterns of cultural
resistance of the lads, and was partly mirrored in the creation and
recreation of a culture of femininity by the girls. Another form,
and one that is quite visible in schools in urban areas on both sides
of the Atlantic, is the practice of 'being cool.' This involves
abstracting oneself from one's ascribed class position by a sophisticated process of distancing in dress, posture, walk, and now more
and more, speech.[50] This creative cultural process provides important grounds for contesting dominant patterns of gender, class,
and racial domination and exploitation.

For example, among black youth in, say, England, patterns
of contestation and struggle are found in the development of a
specifically Afro-Caribbean culture of resistance, one that is
similar in many ways to those found in the ghettos of America's
inner cities. The lived culture of these youths speaks to a subtle
'awareness' that the culture of the school and the formal knowledge in the curriculum is not responsive to black history or
experience. Because of this, many students have readopted Creole
as their language as both a sign of exclusion and as a mechanism of
solidarity. Since the kind of education these non-white students
actually receive 'leads to a depression of the general opportunities
for employment and educational advancement' — an education
that 'reproduces the young non-white worker at the lower end of
education and skill' — Creole is spoken as part of a complex
process of contestation and affirmation at a cultural level. The
school's more individualistic culture, now rejected, acts as a

114

cultural background against which linguistic resistance is developed.[51]

However, again a paradoxical situation similar to the lads, kids, and girls emerges. Creole acts as a 'living index' of the extent of black alienation from the norms, values, and goals of those groups of people who occupy the higher positions in society. Yet at the same time that this is a clear 'recognition' of what the future holds for these black and brown youths, and will in fact provide the grounds for solidarity on the job, it condemns them to similar low paying and exploitative positions to those they would have gotten through their schooling. Given this, many of these youths simply reject these kinds of economic positions themselves. However, no matter how this is construed by the political right, this is *not* a rejection of work itself, but a refusal to accept the kinds of work and the accompanying working conditions that are offered. In their lived awareness of what schools may offer them as a group with a dual oppression – black or brown (or red in the USA) and poor – their resistance to school and the development of their own cultural forms also show an awareness of how schools and jobs help to define a person's identity. Because of this, black and brown youths like these often seek a 'dignified identity in a world which has shown oppression, rejection, and humiliation.'[52] Strength and weakness are lived out every day in this way.

Though I shall not go into it in detail, among brown and black working-class girls the objective conditions under which they live assist in the creation of contradictory ideologies similar to those of the girls that I have just discussed. Elements of working-class culture, of specifically gender cultures, and of ethnic traditions will blend together in a complex process of cultural creation and determination, little of which can be directly related to economic forces in the abstract.[53] All three – gender, class, and race – will constitute the girls' culture. Here, too, the culture of femininity, a culture that has its roots in the experience of patriarchal relations upon which the logics and social relations of capital have built and partly transformed, will still be found playing an important part.

Brake shows the extent to which the economic aspects of the current structural crisis impact on these girls, and especially on 'minority' girls. Speaking of England, though the figures are not that dissimilar in the United States, Canada, and elsewhere, he notes the following.

115

[It is important to remember] women's relationship to production. . . . For working class youth, work has been hard to find. Minorities in particular have found difficulties in obtaining work, and especially girls. Manpower Services Commission report a rise of 120 per cent in unemployment among young people for the five years up to 1977 as against 45 per cent among the population as a whole, especially for black youth (350 per cent). Female unemployment rose fast for the 18-24 age group for both black and white, but there was an increase of 30 per cent for black females as opposed to 22 per cent for all females. Given these figures, one begins to see the importance that the cult of femininity (that is of non-work dominated identity) has for [many] girls.[54]

Girls' activity in dealing with all of this, and that of the lads and the kids I have analyzed here, speaks eloquently to the utter complexity of the cultural sphere. Good and bad sense coexist. Ideological hegemony is part of a contested terrain, one that is contested at the cultural level itself. Yes, schools may be sites where the distinction between mental and manual labor is recreated, where divisions by race, sex, and class are reproduced; but, clearly much more is going on. Though schools may do this as part of their action in 'producing students' according to the categories of deviance that are in large part naturally generated by their functions in the production of technical cultural capital and the reproduction of the division of labor, to lose sight of the role of the students in this is to miss entirely the power and limitations existing in the cultural sphere.

UNDERSTANDING REPRODUCTION

I have gone on at length here to document something of no small importance to our understanding of schools as sites of economic and cultural reproduction. Notice what is gained by entering into the debates over the social role of the school and, especially, by combining an analysis of the connections schools may have to other powerful social agencies with an attempt again to go beyond correspondence theories to work out the intricate interconnections among schools, economy, and culture. A key here, obviously,

116

is culture. The potency of the studies I have analyzed is their status as Marxist ethnographies. That is, they attempt to comprehend a concrete setting and do it by placing that setting within a larger framework of class and ideological and material forces, forces that set limits on, and actually help produce, the meanings and practices that one finds. At the same time that they go a long way in providing possible social explanations about why and how these conditions are produced, these studies do not lose the richness and variability of the experience of students of this class. They each have a rather strong commitment to the idea that, in the analysis of the social totality lived through in these microcosms, class conflict is essential to the study of culture and institutions of economic and cultural organization, selection, and transmission such as schools. What makes this work so significant to an investigation of schooling and reproduction is the clearly articulated focus on class not as an abstract category but instead as a lived experience.[55]

Furthermore, and what must not be forgotten, they show that the real problem is not only to interrogate the social reality of schools to find out where institutions are related, and how these sets of relations are constituted, but also where there are contradictory elements, and finally, where these elements are partly progressive and not totally reproductive. In essence, any analysis of the role of schooling in reproduction and any evaluation of the processes and results of schooling must remember that reproduction is hard and often resisted work.[56] Thus, the overriding concern with the economic outcomes of institutions, even those like schools — with their contributions to inequality and their role in reproduction — tends to suppress 'the fact that these conditions [for "successful" reproduction] have continually to be won — or lost — in particular conflicts and struggles.'[57]

The students to which I directed our attention embodied these points. They helped produce the inherently contradictory outcomes of the institution, but only through struggle. They lived out class as an active force, one that is both creative and limiting at the same time.

The notion of consent, of self-creation if you will, is critical in this account. For, as Willis, Everhart, and McRobbie all show, there is a moment of active appropriation at work in processes like these. We can see ideological hegemony in all its power and contradictions in the way, say, the working-class boys in Willis's study

117

literally nearly celebrate their future entry into manual labor.[58] Only by understanding this can we fully comprehend the outcomes of the school.

This point is quite important. One could claim that my analysis here documents the process through which students like the lads, the girls, and the kids ultimately lose, the process through which they are subtly determined, the way 'the economy controls culture.' Yet we must not forget the importance of the very nature of the determinations and contradictions I have sought to illuminate here, using Willis's, Everhart's, and McRobbie's work. For the hegemonic ideology of our society is 'deeply and essentially conflicted' in a number of ways, ways that will continue to generate conflicts that may be difficult to resolve within existing institutional power relations and boundaries. As Todd Gitlin has pointed out, for instance, the ideological forms that dominate economies like our own urge people to work hard; yet at the same time these forms propose that real satisfaction is to be found not in work but in leisure, an area 'which ostensibly embodies values opposed to work.'[59] This conflict is clear in the lads and the kids, for example, and is what might best be called a structurally generated contradiction. It will create tensions and conflicts that, when they are lived through by large groups of people, will provide for the possibility of penetrations into social reality similar to those 'seen' by the lads and the kids. Conflicts and contradictions within patriarchy, and between patriarchy and capitalism, may lead to similar things. Whether these tensions and conflicts will ultimately turn back upon those experiencing them, thereby linking them more fully to a corporate economy and ultimately benefiting those who control economic and cultural capital is, of course, not an uninteresting question given my arguments here.

But the realization that these tensions and conflicts are worked out in nearly every institution, especially the school as we have seen, has given us an essential insight into the reality we as educators are called upon to face every day. Ignoring them or neglecting the socio-economic and cultural sophistication needed to understand them will unfortunately not make them go away.

Actually we couldn't ignore them even if we wanted to, for these cultural and economic contradictions are now causing an immense amount of reevaluation of the structure and control of education. Indeed, there are a number of educators and policymakers who are proposing ways of 'solving' these conflicts and tensions today. And it is to a number of proposals for reforming the institutional arrangements in schools that they think cause them that we shall now turn. How are we to understand these reforms? Where should we stand on them? Will they be effective in helping the lads, kids, and girls?

II

REPRODUCTION AND REFORM

The question of where one stands is not inconsequential since educational reforms are being currently proposed that would, it is argued, eliminate some of the economic and cultural conditions that we have seen were 'reproduced' in the day to day life of the high school and junior high school students I analyzed. And a person must make sense out of these reforms if he or she is to decide whether to support or reject them.

One doesn't need to be a participant in the analysis of the school's role in the economic and cultural reproduction of the class, race, and gender structures in which the lads, girls, and kids find themselves to realize that there is intense conflict among other groups over schools today. Industrialists and state bureaucrats wish to make schools efficient, to enable them to meet the ideological and 'manpower' requirements of the economy. The tax problems generated by the economic crisis contribute a good deal to the attempts of the same people to make education more efficient.[60] At the same time, because of a crisis in legitimacy there is pressure from 'below,' from many of the parents of students from racial, sexual, class, and interest groups to make schools responsive to the often competing needs that each of these groups have identified.

One could go on almost indefinitely, listing the claims upon school time, policies, and resources. And a similar amount of paper could be used to list the proposals for altering the way schools operate today to bring them into closer correspondence to these conflicting claims. Among the most prominent of these proposals, however, ones that are generating a good deal of discussion at the governmental level, are things like programs for voucher plans and tax credits.[61] If schools do all these social things people like Althusser, Bowles and Gintis, Apple, McRobbie, Willis,

Everhart, and others say that they do, and if they are not responsive to our competing economic and ideological interests, then the
market should be opened up, it is claimed. If schools do act as
important sites of the production and reproduction of culture and
an economy then give control back to, say, the parents. Reduce
the control of the state by giving parents vouchers to pay for the
kind of education they want for their children. In this way we can
perhaps reduce the size and bureaucratic nature of the institution
and make it more 'relevant' to larger groups of children and
parents. Here parents would basically be free to choose among
nearly any educational and curricular arrangement (with some
limits, of course) by paying public or private schools directly. The
educational system would become a market, one regulated by the
state but still open to all comers. This would eliminate many of
the problems I focused upon in the previous sections of this
chapter. Or would it?

UNDERSTANDING LEGITIMATION, ACCUMULATION AND THE STATE

In the introduction to this chapter I noted that many investigators
into the relationship between education and the larger society see
the school as an ideological state apparatus. In my prior sections I
focused primarily on one element of that phrase – ideological. Yet
just as critical is the other element – the fact that it is a *state*
apparatus. This is so commonsensical we are apt to forget it. As
the recent literature on the role of the state in social reproduction
argues, however, to forget this means that we neglect the important functions the state itself performs in maintaining the relations
of domination and exploitation in our society. Just as when we
saw that if we wanted to unpack the daily lives of students in
schools we had to relate those lives to class, culture, and economy
'outside' of the institutions, so do we need to do that here. Without that we cannot fully appreciate the larger framework that
reforms like voucher plans fit into.

Remember that, as an aspect of the state, schools seem to
engage, among others, in two fundamental activities. They assist in
both legitimation and establishing some of the prior conditions
necessary for capital accumulation. While the school 'produces'
these outcomes in contradictory, unintended, and contested ways,

it is important now to focus more directly on these elements as they relate to the state, especially since the reforms being discussed are generated within it.

An example I used in Chapter 1 should help us also remember that these two functions of the state are often in conflict. As Randall Collins argues, for instance, the state's role in accumulation has led to a situation in which more and more workers have gotten more and more credentials. In the process, the credentials themselves are devalued.[62] Because of this, the legitimacy of part of the state, here the school itself, is cast into doubt. Thus, the schools' role in accumulation may lead to an overproduction of credentialed workers and challenge the legitimacy of the way schools operate. One function of the state is almost necessarily in conflict with the other. These contradictions will be especially evident in times of crisis, like right now, in an economy. An economy plagued by inflation, unemployment, and recurrent recessions requires fewer credentialed workers. Like the girls, the lads, and the kids, the school is caught in a structurally generated contradiction.

It is out of this conflict that we can begin to understand the current cry for tax credits and voucher plans. With a crisis in the economy and in many of its major institutions the state itself begins to lose legitimacy. It cannot control the economy without entering more and more directly into that economy; nor under current fiscal conditions can it maintain these other institutions without entering more directly into their day to day operations as well. [63] This is a paradoxical, almost no-win situation. The state does not require merely control of what goes on; it needs consent as well. Without such consent, it loses its legitimacy in the process. Here, then, is the paradox. By directly intervening, the state itself becomes blamed for the general structural crisis. Since it cannot control enough of the variables — to do so would require an enormous amount of power vested within the state, something the American population would probably not stand for and something therefore that would create its own crisis in consent — it loses some of its legitimacy. This provides a very real crisis. While the state, as we saw in Chapter 2, must intervene more and more into the productive and allocative policies of the economy and become even more active in all social arenas, it must sometimes back away from such active intervention in education to preserve its legitimacy.

Given these contradictory functions, pressures, and para-doxes, how is the state to cope with this? It can generate consent and legitimacy by expanding the market of capitalist social rela-tions and individual consumption and then regulating this mar-ket to ensure that the function of accumulation will be met. This is a prime element in comprehending the role of many state reforms.

This is very complex, but let me try briefly to lay out what it means. My first points will be somewhat economistic, but I shall then deepen the explanation of how certain ideologies may function considerably. In order for the economy to continue generating profits and employment and in order for capital accumulation to go on, the consumer must be stimulated to purchase more goods *individually*. This is a primary way markets expand. That is, the ideology of what might be called possessive individualism needs to be strengthened. However, ideologies are not merely abstract ideas that remain in our economic rela-tions. They tend to permeate all of our experience, sets of social relations, and expectations. And it is exactly here that we can see contradictions operating. By stimulating an ideology of possessive individualism, the economy 'creates' a crisis in the school. The school, which under current financial and ideological conditions cannot meet the stimulated needs of competing individuals and interest groups, loses its legitimacy. The state, in order to maintain its own legitimacy, hence, must respond in a way that both continues to expand capitalist social relations *and* an individualistic market at one and the same time. This is exactly the place of voucher plans and tax credit systems.

The contradiction is relatively clear. A crisis is caused in part by the fact that the economy needs to sponsor an ideology of consumption on an individual not a collective level. In this way, more goods are produced and consumed. At the same time, however, this sets loose social forces that impact on nearly every sphere of social life. Individual groups will then focus on the consumption of *all* goods and services, including education, in a less collective way. General collective needs over, say, education will be seen in the light of what it can do for my own specific group, family, or self, as an individual right. To the extent that schools cannot meet these needs — and they really can't in many ways — the state apparatus will be caught in a crisis of legitimacy.

This makes any evaluation of 'where should I stand?,' and of the progressive potential of these kinds of proposals to reform schools, difficult indeed. They are largely determined by the contradictory role of the state. They open up an area to capitalist social and market relations that once — even given many of the problems of existing schools — had been somewhat less open. They contribute to a relatively unchecked ideology of individual consumption. Yet as we shall see soon, they do in fact present the possibility of interesting interventions to create those alternative 'institutional arrangements and values' that I mentioned in Chapter 2.

A NOTE ON THE POLITICAL SPHERE AND LIBERAL DISCOURSE

That these reforms may offer possibilities means that we need to be careful of interpreting them as only reflections of the economic needs surrounding individualism, as merely the result of economic contradictions working themselves out in 'superstructural' institutions which ultimately can do nothing but lend economic and ideological support to the bourgeoisie. In fact, I do not want to imply that the notion of the individual is purely an economic category. It is a political category as well. The growth of the discourse of individual rights in the political sphere itself has had a major impact in the economic sphere. It helps us explain why proposals for voucher plans and tax credits arise and why such plans might be backed by many groups, including the parents of students like the kids, girls, and lads.

In examining the historical place the idea of individual rights (what he calls liberal discourse) has had in class conflict, Gintis offers a rather provocative thesis.

> Class struggle in advanced capitalism in the twentieth century has been waged using the tools of discourse of liberalism — the discourse of natural rights. These tools, while appropriated from the bourgeoisie, have been transformed in the course of struggles into effective and potentially revolutionary political weapons. This transformation has predominantly taken the form of expanding the range over which *person* rights are to hold sway, and restricting

the range over which *property* rights are to operate. As a
result, we may say that liberal discourse itself, far from being
'bourgeois,' is the product of class struggle. In particular,
liberal discourse does not correspond to any integrated
world view and has been used by both capital and labor
for distinct ends. Yet liberal discourse is not neutral: the
content of class demands has been shaped by these tools
of discourse and their transformation over time.[64]

Gintis goes on to argue that the turning of person rights
against property rights actually represents one of the most characteristic stances of the popular classes. The clear and insistent
demands of workers for the vote based on being a person, not on
owning property, is one example of this stance. Another includes
the fight for the right of workers to organize against their
employers. A third, 'and manifestly unrealizable under capitalism,'
is the right to employment. Others can also be found: the demand
that equal treatment and due process apply to market transactions;
the struggle by the women's movement for equal treatment, 'in
an attempt to weaken the free exercise of property rights on the
part of discriminatory employers;' worker's action in support of
decent occupational and health conditions which have been aimed
at using the state to regulate and restrict property rights of
employers; and, finally, the goal of equality of opportunity,
a goal that is 'simply the application of the liberal concept of
equality before the law, but now applied to the capitalist
economy itself.'[65]

Thus, the increasing dominance of person rights over property
rights has involved a struggle over and the demand for '*the extension of political and economic life governed by formally democratic practices.*'[66] In essence, class struggle has both transformed
and been transformed by person oriented, liberal discourse. To
quote from Gintis again, quite often 'the political advances of the
left have been expressed, justified and organized not in terms
of [traditional Marxist categories], but in terms of *extensions of
liberal discourse.*'[67]

As he goes on to say,

> [The] *content* of class struggle flows in part from its *form*;
> that is, from the tools of communicative discourse —
> language and other types of symbolic expression —

available in society for the framing of projects and the creation of solidarity and unity of direction within a collectivity. Tools of communicative discourse do not reflect consciousness; on the contrary, the consciousness of individuals and groups is framed by the forms of discourse they appropriate and use in their struggles. . . . Thus a critical aspect of class struggle involves the reproduction and transformation of the very tools of discourse through which class struggle is waged. Modern liberal discourse, the idiom of rights, then, is not an expression of the 'hegemony' of the bourgeoisie. Rather, it is a product of class struggle, substantially different in distinct historical periods, and internally contradictory due to the infusion of discrepant elements into it in the course of specific class confrontations. Whence its emancipatory possibilities.[68]

Now this goes a long way in enabling us to understand how extending 'freedom of individual choice' to the very selection and organization of schools might strike such a responsive chord among particular class segments and racial groups. Since liberal discourse has been one of the primary tools both for channeling *and* expressing the conflict between classes and races, and since it has its own relatively autonomous dynamic that impinges on both the political and economic spheres, it can be and has been used by both sides in the struggle for power and control. As we shall see here, this is exactly what can give it its possible emancipatory potential. As we shall also see, however, given the current imbalance of forces within the state and given the emerging economic crisis in which the state needs to cut a large portion of its expenditures, the employment of liberal discourse in this case may lead to more gains going to the most advantaged groups in our society.

EXPORTING THE CRISIS IN THE STATE

So far I have outlined an argument concerning how we might interpret proposals to alter school and curricular control based on the fact that schools are part of the state. I have claimed that the contradictory pressures on the state and the requirements of the political sphere itself create needs within it to propose reforms such as voucher plans which would enable it to deal more easily with its own internal and external needs. These proposals document something quite interesting. When there is a serious crisis in the state, as there now seems to be, one very effective strategy is for the state to attempt to export its crisis *outside* of itself. Thus, by reducing overt state control and turning over schooling to a market, one deflects criticism.

This performs an interesting function. By deflecting criticism away from the state and seemingly establishing a more pluralistic market, the crucial question of the differential benefits of our social formation may also be deflected. The symbolic benefit of choosing one's school may tend to be exactly that, symbolic. The material benefits may continue to recapitulate the structure of inequality.[69] In this regard we need to again consistently keep in mind Navarro's previously mentioned finding that in almost every social arena from health care to anti-inflation policies, the actual impact of state policies has shown a consistent pattern in which the top 20 per cent of the population consistently benefit much more than the other 80 per cent.[70] The question of such a pattern and the differential benefits that seem to arise from a pluralist or market solution to school problems need to be seriously considered.

The negative possibility of this is clear enough if we see reforms of this type within the current resurgence of the right in the United States and elsewhere. One of the reasons the right is enjoying an advantage in arguments about how we should cope with the problems of the schools, the state in general, and the economy is partly because of the 'skillful populist translation of its key themes into grievances about taxes, strikes, and bureaucracies.' It has been able to restate the case for the expansion of capitalist social and market relations in a particular form, 'as a market order which maximizes individual freedom and choice.'[71] Its incorporation of liberal discourse is rather interesting here. Thus, it is quite possible that supporting such things as voucher plans and tax credits — while enabling more, and more interesting, choices for the lads, the kids, and others to evolve — will do something else that is less satisfying on the more general ideological and structural level. It may assist in the legitimation through the state of the 'bourgeois ideal of the market,' a model of all social relations based on 'individual calculation and the pursuit of self-interest, and the accommodation and adjustment of interests

126

through competition,'[72] thus partially reproducing the patterns of differential benefits Navarro describes.

In saying this, however, I do not want to contradict my earlier arguments against seeing the state, like hegemonic ideologies, as monolithic internally. In fact, exactly the opposite is often the case. This presents another aspect that once again makes a cut and dried evaluation of state sponsored reforms no easy matter, since the state is a site of conflict as well as domination. The fact that the state apparatus might wish to export its crisis and reestablish market power over schools is indicative of the partial success of some groups – race, class, and gender groups who have not historically been helped as much by schools – in challenging the legitimacy of routine operations within the state. It actually points to a partial breakdown of hegemonic control.[73]

TOWARDS POLITICAL AND EDUCATIONAL ACTION

Up till now, I have been rather negative about reforms such as voucher plans, tax credits, and the like. However, I do not want to dismiss the possibility that such proposals do signify a partial breaking in the power of the state, a different balance of contending forces within the state apparatus itself, and hence can be used for progressive ends. Such a plan could in fact be employed to create models of socialist education. That is, it could create schools that would be laboratories for the development of socialist alternatives to our dominant educational models. This is not unimportant. We have lost our own history of socialist education and, in essence, are faced with starting anew. Alternative pedagogies and curricular models need to be developed in an atmosphere that fosters such a process. Voucher plans might actually provide some of these conditions if used carefully by committed groups of people.

I want to stress this point. The articulation and construction of serious democratic socialist alternatives is not to be taken lightly. As long as such a clear alternative does not exist, each segment of the working population will remain unlinked to the others in terms of its vision of education and will propose disparate plans and demands. These individual corporate demands (as Gramsci would call them) will not be effective in generating pressure for the restructuring of economic and cultural institutions and their control. Sassoon makes this point rather well.

127

The working-class movement has not often been able to suggest a programme adequate to the needs of the mass of the population going beyond the corporate demands of various sectors. Because of this lack of objective unity around an alternative political proposal, various governments are able to play off one group against the corporate demands of another.[74]

As part of this development of a concrete alternative political proposal, the building of a clear pedagogic and curricular model that could be worked from and argued over by, say, parents, progressive unions, and others could be an important starting point in articulating a collective program.

Voucher plans might help in yet another way. Structural changes in our society need to be prefigured in local experiments. That is, the skills and norms of democratic control of one's institutions and the reorganization of them so that they benefit the majority of the population need to be learned and tested out in practice. The creation of tax credits and vouchers could provide a limited step in this direction *if* they enable people to become more deeply involved in the democratic day to day planning and operation of the institutions that surround them.

These are probably the most positive possibilities for the progressive use of such reforms. In many ways, though, they are rather Utopian and, I think, may not outweigh the differential power in the way our existing institutions are controlled and the patterns of unequal benefits that exist. Organizational change, no matter how interesting, may not be sufficient in the face of these conditions. Because of this, while we may and should explore the potential within these reforms, I think we need to be both honest about the other possible long-term negative consequences of these state-sponsored proposals, and search for coherent alternative strategies for building a more powerful base from which to act.

Appropriate strategies include building allies, concrete political action, and altering curricular practice within schools. We need, for instance, to continue the slow and painstaking work of political education of teachers and other workers within the state as it is currently organized. I do not mean this as a Utopian vision. The budgetary problems of school systems in places like Chicago, Cleveland, and elsewhere where teachers are denied pay for their work or must work in increasingly underfunded facilities have important implications here. These conditions can allow for a more sophisticated politico-economic analysis among these state workers and can provide important opportunities for struggle at a local level.

However, it is possible that the voucher plan's fragmentation of schools could also lead to a fragmentation of teachers. That is, there may be less space for political education among teachers. The importance of winning teachers — many of whom are becoming disillusioned by the over-all results and conditions of their work and the effect of their teaching — over to a more progressive political perspective is minimized here. That some of the conditions under which teachers work could lead to the possibility of such political education is something I will take up in the next chapter.

If I am correct that inroads can be made with state employees like teachers, then another idea becomes vitally important — linkages. These local struggles in schools and state agencies need to be connected with struggles for economic and political justice by other organized groups such as workers on the shop-floor and in offices, women who are beginning to organize in offices and stores, minority parents, and so on. These linkages are essential to provide a basis of both legitimacy and strength. They are a critical part of the development of the collective program mentioned by Mouffe earlier. Since teachers are being treated increasingly like the employees in industry and the service sector of our economy, such conditions may be more attainable in the future.

Voucher plans and tax credits could hamper this strategy. If, as I want to argue, the hard political labor at the level of one's local institutions — in particular the school, welfare institutions, health care, the workplace, and so on — is essential for socialist politics, then proposals for opening schools to market relations could defuse this kind of struggle. One must ask, therefore, whether these reforms will make it that much more difficult to make linkages between, say, politically committed teachers and organized groups of workers and parents. Can they lead to a more collective appraisal? If not, are they worth our support?

So far I have talked about teachers, parents, and other organized groups and the potential of building coalitions among sets of class actors. But what of the students themselves? The investigations of Willis, Everhart, and McRobbie that I analyzed earlier pose some rather significant issues and strategies that need to be taken seriously. The first concerns the level of content in schools and makes even more important the arguments about teaching the history of workers' struggles and visions that I made in Chapter 3.

The issue is not just to consider proposed reforms in organizational arrangements, but what is and is not actually taught as well. Whole segments of the American population are cut off from their past. Their own current conditions remain relatively unanalyzed, in part because the ideological perspectives they are offered (and the critical tools not made available) defuse both the political and economic history and the conceptual apparatus required for a thorough appraisal of their position. The possibility of concerted action is forgotten. This again points to the importance of concerted efforts at engaging in curricular change to make this history and the many *current* programs of, say, worker control available to students like the lads and the kids,[75] as well as making socialist feminist programs available to the girls (and boys).

Obviously, we need to be realistic here. Simply getting more or different knowledge into schools is not enough (nor may it even be possible at times). However, again we must conceive of a socialist strategy as being based on a broad front with both cultural and politico-economic action being necessary at one and the same time. Isolated attempts at curriculum reform will remain relatively inconsequential probably. But, again, if they can be linked with other struggles and with other groups, their chances are undoubtedly increased. As I argued before, no institution and no dominant ideology is totally monolithic. There will be 'spaces' that can be worked in that will at least offer the chance of partial success, even if this success concerns learning more about both the politics of organizing and the conditions necessary for further concrete work.

Held up to this light, to the extent that voucher plans and the like will have schools controlled by an individualistic market, it will be harder to exert pressure on school systems as a whole to remedy this imbalance in curricular content. Just as seriously, this may effectively remove a potent point around which a number of groups could organize. Thus, such plans may make it less easy to create the conditions for large-scale future work.

One final point needs to be made about the content and the students themselves, a point that is of considerable moment given my arguments about the constitutive elements of the lived culture of students from those segments of the working class we examined. It is essential that we remember that the reproductive process in which these students in schools — and their parents in the work-place — participate is not all powerful. It *is* contested. There *are* elements of good sense within it. There are alternative collective practices generated out of it on what I have called the cultural level. Given that this is the case, it directs our attention to the potential of ongoing political education of both the students and their parents (and I think to the potential of their educating the educators as well). It may be possible to use these elements of class resistance for both pedagogical purposes (in reorienting our teaching practices so that they are more in line with the vital elements of working class culture),[76] and for the purpose of focusing this discontent on the unequal structural conditions that dominate this society.

That there is this resistance means that the lived culture of the students themselves may offer potent areas for political work. Their own attempts to have physical areas of their own — ball fields, basketball courts, discos, etc. — can be developed into exercises in political power. Their demands for decent jobs within their local communities can also be helped and defended. A growing group of progressive youth workers and social workers in the United States, England, and Latin America have a long history of engaging in this kind of action. In the process they have developed skills of organizing black, brown, and white youth and stimulating the growth of politically sensitive leadership among these youths.[77] Educators have a good deal to learn from them.

Contestation at the cultural level, and the elements of good sense within it, provide other opportunities as well. Themes of feminist consciousness that will begin to emerge in some working-class girls' culture also can be focused on and used. McRobbie makes an interesting point here. Since teaching has often been a career open to women, it may also be possible that at the same moment that traditional models of occupations may be presented to students, the notion that an independent identity outside the home and marriage may also be presented may contradict some of these ideological messages. Furthermore, since so many teachers *are* women, messages of struggle and resistance, even if they are unpoliticized, may be being given as well. As she puts it, 'the possibility which the school offers for the introduction of feminist critiques in the classroom should not be underestimated, a

131

potential which is now being explored by groups of feminist teachers.'[78]

Once again, the importance of coalitions among committed people is apparent here. Groups of activists in the black, hispanic, Native American, and in the legal and health communities, as well as in a number of our more progressive unions and feminist groups, have begun to take all this seriously. Clearly, a significant amount of collaborative work needs to be done on both the educational and political levels. Given the varying forms of resistances that are building up at workplaces currently, it may be somewhat easier for such coalitions to be formed. (However, we must also remember how effective the right has been in bringing these groups under its own interests. Clearly, progressive action is not guaranteed in any way and must be worked for, not waited for as if it will arise in some naturally preordained way.)

CONCLUSIONS

In this final section I have briefly outlined some major criticisms of proposed reforms and what I perceive to be some of the strategies that need to be engaged in. I have noted that reforms such as tax credits and voucher systems are contradictory. Because they may be transformed, as historically all liberal discourse has, in the course of their use by the 'popular classes,' they may lead to the growth of alternative institutions, ones that may help the development of interesting and workable socialist models of pedagogical and curricular arrangements. This is not to be dismissed lightly.

In saying this, I have also claimed that the actual planning, building, and running of such an institution can be important in enabling people to learn the economic, political, and organizational skills and norms that are required for more democratically run institutions. However, and this is of great significance, this presupposes that these progressive groups can actually control and organize the programs they desire. Hence, these groups should be extremely wary if they are not able to control the program that is being proposed.

If in fact voucher plans fragment specific movements rather than unite them, acceptance should be strongly reconsidered. Furthermore, the issue of *how* these groups will gain more power through the use of voucher plans is a critical issue. For instance, in the proposals being considered in California and elsewhere, too much is left open. The actual mechanisms for giving disenfranchised groups control *and* ensuring it are unspecified. Given what Navarro and others have shown about the way lobbying and unequal power and benefits work in the state and local governmental arenas, such plans may lead to a recreation of inequality, not the opposite. Again one should be very skeptical unless shown otherwise.

On a larger scale, I have noted that these proposals may enable the state to export its crisis of legitimacy and may open up a large area of our lives even more to reorganization around the principles of capitalist social relations. Because of this I have also argued that, by enabling the state to export its crisis and by isolating small groups of teachers and 'community' groups from similar class actors, such proposed reforms may make it much more difficult for political organization and action to go on. Finally, I have urged that organized political and pedagogical action, beginning at a local level but connected across various progressive groups involved in the struggle for a less exploitative set of institutional arrangements, is a prior condition for serious action.

In saying this, I am implying that there are no general principles, no easy answers, to the question of when and where one should support or oppose reforms of this type. *It is decidedly dependent on the balance of forces within a specific arena.* Only by analyzing the specificity of each individual location can one make a decision on appropriate strategies. In some locations, the 'liberal discourse' of such reforms may in fact provide the first real opportunity for oppressed groups to organize and control their own institutions, and to develop the organizational skills to transfer these principles and practices to other institutions within their community. In other locations, it may very well be the case that, say, tax credits or vouchers will have exactly the opposite effect. They may in the long run fragment progressive groups and make concerted and coordinated efforts that much more difficult. Only within the context of an analysis of the objective and ideological conditions and forces that actually exist in each location, and in the state in general, can one come up with a viable approach. In general, I would argue against supporting such reforms. On a less general level, there are times I could envision them as allowing progressive action to be initiated, but only if the prior conditions of guaranteeing real power and control are met.

Thus, a very real skepticism should guide our appraisals.

Because of this, certain questions need always to be asked in evaluating state reforms. What reforms can we genuinely call *non-reformist* reforms, that is, reforms that both alter and better present conditions and can lead to serious structural changes? What reforms should be supported because of their possible contribution to the political education of a large group of people or to their learning strategies that may ultimately enable them to reassert control of their economic and cultural institutions? Which reforms contribute to coalitions that may alter the balance of forces? What kinds of coalitions will tend to be progressive in the long run? Are there elements within students and parents themselves, in their lived culture, that penetrate into the reality of dominant social relations? How can these be employed?[79]

These questions will not be easy to answer. They require a sense of history, a framework that points to the class configuration and relations of economic, political, and cultural domination of local schools and communities (and then beyond that community), and finally, probably a lived experience within that location.

Not only will answers not be easy, but action based on them will be 'hard and contested' as well. As I argued earlier, we need to see the struggle to create more just economic and cultural institutions as a war of position, as a struggle on a variety of fronts.[80] One of these fronts is certainly education. If the state — because of our economic crisis and its own crisis of legitimacy, the competing forces within it, and the reality of what is in store for the lads, the girls, and the kids — offers possibilities for democratic socialist interventions then they should be taken up. But, as I have tried to demonstrate in the last section of this chapter, taking them up is not all that simple. This may be one of the times we should look a gift horse in the mouth.

CHAPTER 5

CURRICULAR FORM AND THE LOGIC OF TECHNICAL CONTROL: COMMODIFICATION RETURNS

Exporting its major problems is not the only, or even the primary, way the state can respond to the crisis of accumulation and legitimation in which it finds itself. Given the size of its internal bureaucracy and given the intense pressures being placed upon it by economic forces at the present time, the state (and schools) can and must deal with the crisis by refocusing inwards as well. It can attempt to tighten the reins on its production of 'useful' knowledge and agents for the labor force, and also on its *own* workforce, in ways that embody the technical and administrative knowledge and procedures employed in the advanced industrial sector of the economy. As I shall demonstrate in this chapter, the impact of this on teachers can be immense.

In the last two chapters I analyzed how workers and students create and recreate lived cultures that provide the grounds for resistances to the ideologies of rationalization, technical and administrative procedures, and 'needs' for control in the workplace and the school. Workers do not accept it without a struggle. Children of these workers often live out a contradictory culture in the school that 'mirrors' the contradictions within the culture their parents have creatively evolved in their own experiences with both the commodification and labor processes of capital. Yet the fact that resistances have historically evolved does not mean that the fruits of these ideologies, knowledge forms, and procedures are forgotten or are not used. Instead, they are *transformed*. Thus, worker resistance to Taylorism and similar techniques led both to research on and the development of managerial approaches embodying human relations and to using the increased stock of technical/administrative knowledge to build control into jobs in more subtle ways.

This very same history has transformed the kinds of ideologies

135

and techniques that are now impacting on education. For given the perceived legitimacy of these managerial approaches in the economy (remember, this is where Taylorism actually succeeded in many ways) and given the fact that the state cannot escape its own current crisis in legitimacy and the larger economic crisis, the fruits of this same technical/administrative knowledge that has been transformed in the offices, factories, and businesses surrounding education will return to the school as part of the way the state perceives it must cope with these difficult problems. The production of this knowledge earlier, in part by the higher reaches of the educational apparatus, has finally led to its reintroduction to all levels of schooling later on.

As we shall see here, at the same time that the state attempts to export some of its problems outside itself, it tries to deal with them in other ways by combining technical and industrial models with liberal discourse in its day to day operations. The combination of the languages and procedures of capital with that of the liberal discourse of person rights is even more important to education now since the pressures from the economy, from other aspects of the government, and from elsewhere will be very intense. Shifts in power within the state apparatus itself will become quite visible. Those groups within education favoring a closer alignment between schools and the needs of industry for economic and cultural capital will become increasingly powerful. At the same time, capitalists themselves will become more outspoken in their own moves to employ schools for the needs of legitimation and accumulation in the economic sphere. These kinds of shifts are occurring at the present time. Schools cannot easily ignore all this. However, and this is quite important, once again these very pressures will open up spaces for action.

CORPORATE IDEOLOGIES: REACHING THE TEACHER

It does not require an exceptional amount of insight to see the current attempts by the state and industry to bring schools more closely into line with 'economic needs.' Neither side of the Atlantic has been immune to these pressures. In the United Kingdom, the Great Debate and the Green Paper stand as remarkable statements to the ability of capital to marshall its forces in times of economic crisis. As the Green Paper notes: 'There is a wide gap between the world of education and the world of work. Boys and girls are not sufficiently aware of the importance of industry to our society, and they are not taught much about it.'[1]

It goes on, making the criterion of functional efficiency the prime element in educational policy.

> The total resources which will be available for education and the social services in the future will depend largely on the success of the Industrial Strategy. It is vital to Britain's economic recovery and standard of living that the performance of manufacturing industry is improved and that the whole range of Government policies, including education, contribute as much as possible to improving industrial performance and thereby increasing the national wealth.[2]

In the United States, where governmental policies are more highly mediated by a different articulation between the state, the economy, and schools, this kind of pressure exists in powerful ways as well. Often the workings of industry are even more visible. Chairs of Free Enterprise devoted to economic education are springing up at universities throughout the country. Teaching the message of industry has become a real force. Let me give one example taken from what is known as the Ryerson Plan, a corporate plan to have teachers spend their summers working mainly with management in industry so that they can teach their students 'real knowledge' about corporate needs and benefits.

> The anti-business, anti-free-enterprise bias prevalent in many parts of our American society today is very real and is growing. Unless we quit just talking about it — and do something about it now — it will prosper and thrive in the fertile minds of our youth. It will be nurtured and fed by many teachers who have good intentions but no real knowledge of how a free market operates in a free society.
>
> American business has a very positive story to tell and one of the most important places to start is with the youth of our country. The last 4,000 years of recorded history proves the interdependence of economic freedom and personal freedoms of all civilizations, countries and societies. We have a perfect example in a present day test tube. Take a look at Great

Britain's decline over the last 30 years.

Our response is simple and effective. Reach the high
school teachers of America with the true story of American
business and they will carry the message to their students and
their fellow teachers. The message, coming directly from the
teacher, rather than books, pamphlets or films, will have a far
more telling and lasting effect. Convince one teacher of the
vital importance of our free enterprise system and you're
well on your way to convincing hundreds of students over a
period of years. It's the ripple effect that anti-business
factions have been capitalizing on for years.[3]

It is an interesting statement to say the least, one that is
being echoed throughout advanced corporate economies. While it
seems rather blatant, to say nothing of being historically inaccurate,
we should be careful of dismissing this kind of program as overt
propaganda that is easily dismissed by teachers. As one teacher
said after completing it,

My experience with the steel industry this summer has given
me a positive and practical introduction to the business
world that I might never had had, had it not been for the
initiative of Ryerson management. Now I can pass a more
positive portrayal of the industry on to my students; students
who are usually very critical, very distrustful, and basically
ignorant of the operation of big industry today.[4]

This is, of course, only one of many plans for getting the
ideological message across. In fact, though there has been serious
resistance to this kind of material by progressive forces in the
United States, the movement to 'teach for the needs of industry' is
growing rapidly enough so that a clearinghouse, appropriately
named The Institute for Constructive Capitalism, has been established at the University of Texas to make the material more
available.[5]

Now I do not want to minimize the importance of such overt
attempts at influencing teachers and students. To do so would be
the height of folly. However, by keeping our focus only on these
overt attempts at bringing school policy and curriculum into closer
correspondence with industrial needs, we may neglect what is
happening that may be just as powerful at the level of day to day

school practice. One could fight the battles against capital's overt encroachments (and perhaps win some of them) and still lose within the school itself. For as I shall argue here, for teachers and students some of the ideological and material influences of our kind of social formation are not most importantly found at the level of these kinds of documents or plans, but at the level of social practice *within* the routine activities of schools.[6]

In essence, as I pointed out earlier, I want to argue that ideologies are not only global sets of interests, things imposed by one group on another. They are embodied by our commonsense meanings and practices.[7] Thus, if you want to understand ideology at work in schools, look as much at the concreta of day to day curricular and pedagogic life as you would at the statements made by spokespersons of the state or industry. To quote from Finn, Grant, and Johnson, we need to look not only at ideologies 'about' education but ideologies 'in' it as well.[8]

I am not implying that the level of practice in schools is fundamentally controlled in some mechanistic way by private enterprise. As an aspect of the state, the school mediates and transforms an array of economic, political, and cultural pressures from competing classes and class segments. Yet we tend to forget that this does not mean that the logics, discourses, or modes of control of capital will not have an increasing impact on everyday life in our educational institutions, especially in times of 'the fiscal crisis of the state.'[9] This impact, clearly visible in the United States (though it is becoming more prevalent in Europe and Latin America as well), is especially evident in curriculum, in essence in some very important aspects of the actual stuff that students and teachers interact with.

In this chapter, I shall be particularly interested in curricular *form*, not curricular content. That is, my focus will not be on what is actually taught, but on the manner in which it is organized. As a number of Marxist cultural analysts have argued, the workings of ideology can be seen most impressively at the level of form as well as what the form has in it.[10] As I shall argue here, this is a key to uncovering the role of ideology 'in' education.

In order to understand part of what is occurring in the school and the ideological and economic pressures being placed upon and which work their way through it, as we did in Chapters 2, 3, and 4, we need to situate it within certain long-term trends in the capital accumulation process and see its relation to changes in the labor process. Recently these trends have intensified and have had a rather major impact on a variety of areas of social life. Among these trends we can identify certain tendencies such as:

> the concentration and centralization of capitals; the expansion of labour processes that are based on production-line technologies and forms of control; the continuing decline of 'heavy industry' and the movement of capital into modern 'lighter' forms of production, most notably the production of consumer durables; and major shifts in the composition of labour power — the secular tendency to 'de-skilling,' the separation of 'conception' from 'execution' and the creation of new technical and control skills, the shift of labour out of direct production and into circulation and distribution, and the expansion of labour within the state.[11]

As we shall see, the development of new forms of control, the process of deskilling, the separation of conception from execution, are not limited to factories and offices. These tendencies intrude more and more into institutions like the school. In order to unpack this, we shall have to go even further than we did in earlier chapters in our examination of the very nature of the logic of corporate deskilling and control.

DESKILLING AND RESKILLING

At first, let me speak very generally about the nature of this kind of control. In corporate production, firms purchase labor power. That is, they buy the capacity one has to do work and, obviously, will often seek to expand the use of the labor to make it more productive. There is an opposite side to this. With the purchase of labor power goes the 'right' to stipulate (within certain limits) how it is to be used, without too much interference or participation by workers in the conception and planning of the work.[12] How this has been accomplished has not stayed the same, of course. Empirically, there has been a changing logic of control that has sought to accomplish these ends.

Given this history, it is helpful to differentiate the kinds of control that have been used. I shall simplify these around basic ideal types for ease of understanding.

We can distinguish three kinds of control that can be employed to help extract more work — simple, technical, and bureaucratic. Simple control is exactly that, simply telling someone that you have decided what should go on and they should follow or else. Technical controls are less obvious. They are controls embedded in the physical structure of your job. A good example again is the use of numerical control technology in the machine industry where a worker inserts a card into a machine and it directs the pace and skill level of the operation. Thus, the worker is meant to be simply an attendant to the machine itself. And, finally, bureaucratic control signifies a social structure where control is less visible since the principles of control are embodied within the *hierarchical* social relations of the workplace. Impersonal and bureaucratic rules concerning the direction of one's work, the procedures for evaluating performance, and sanctions and rewards are dictated by officially approved policy.[13] Each of these modes of control has grown in sophistication over the years, though simple control has tended to become less important as the size and complexity of production has increased.

The long period of experimentation by industry on the most successful modes of controlling production led to a number of conclusions. Rather than simple control where control is openly exercised by supervisors or persons in authority (and hence could possibly be subverted by blue- or white-collar workers), power could be 'made invisible' by incorporating it into the very structure of the work itself. This meant the following things. The control must come from what seems to be a legitimate overall structure. It must be concerned with the actual work, not based on features extraneous to it (like favoritism and so on). Perhaps most importantly, the job, the process, and the product should be defined as precisely as possible on the basis of management's, not the worker's, control over the specialized knowledge needed to carry it out.[14] This often entailed the development of technical control.

Technical control and deskilling tend to go hand in hand. As we saw in Chapter 3, deskilling is part of a long process in which labor is divided and then redivided to increase productivity, to reduce 'inefficiency,' and to control both the cost and the impact of labor. It usually has involved taking relatively complex jobs (most jobs are much more complex and require more decision-making than people give them credit for), jobs that require no small amount of skill and decision-making, and breaking them down into specified actions with specified results so that less skilled and costly personnel can be used, or so that the control of work pace and outcome is enhanced. The assembly line is, of course, one of the archetypical examples of this process. At its beginnings, deskilling tended to involve techniques such as Taylorism and various time and motion studies. Though these strategies for the division and control of labor were less than totally successful (and in fact often generated a significant amount of resistance and conflict),[15] they did succeed in helping to legitimate a style of control based in large part on deskilling.

One of the more effective strategies has been the incorporation of control into the actual productive process itself. Thus, machinery in factories is now often designed so that the machinist is called upon to do little more than load and unload the machine. In offices, word-processing technology is employed to reduce labor costs and deskill women workers. Thus, management attempts to control both the pace of the work and the skills required, to increase more effectively their profit margins or productivity. Once again, as the history of formal and informal labor resistance documents, this kind of strategy — the building of controls into the very warp and weft of the production process — has been contested.[16] However, the growing sophistication by management and the state bureaucrats in the use of technical control procedures is apparent.[17]

I have mentioned that deskilling is a complex process as it works its way through a variety of economic and cultural institutions. Yet it really is not that hard to grasp one of its other important aspects. When jobs are deskilled, the knowledge that once accompanied it, knowledge that was controlled and used by workers in carrying out their day to day lives on their jobs, goes somewhere. As I demonstrated in Chapter 3, management attempts (with varying degrees of success) to accumulate and control this assemblage of skills and knowledge. It attempts, in other words, to separate conception from execution. The control of knowledge enables management to plan; ideally, the worker should merely carry these plans out to the specifications, and at the pace, set by people away from the actual point of production.

But deskilling is accompanied by something else, what might be called reskilling. New techniques are required to run new machines; new occupations are created as the redivision of labor goes on. Fewer skilled craftspersons are needed and their previous large numbers are replaced by a smaller number of technicians with different skills who oversee the machinery.[18] This process of deskilling and reskilling is usually spread out over the landscape of an economy so it is rather difficult to trace out the relationships. It is not very usual that you can see it going on at a level of specificity that makes it clear, since while one group is being deskilled another group, often separated by time and geography, is being reskilled. However, one particular institution — the school — provides an exceptional microcosm for seeing these kinds of mechanisms of control in operation.

In examining this we should remember that capitalist production has developed unevenly, so that certain areas of our social institutions will vary in the kind of control being used. Some institutions will be more resistant than others to the logic of corporate rationalization. Given the relatively autonomous nature of teaching (one can usually close one's door and not be disturbed) and given the internal history of the kinds of control in the institution (paternalistic styles of administration, often in the USA based on gender relations), the school has been partly resistant to technical and bureaucratic control, *at the level of actual practice*, until relatively recently. This 'relative autonomy' may be breaking down today.[19] For just as the everyday discourse and patterns of interaction in the family and in, say, the media are increasingly being subtly transformed by the logic and contradictions of dominant ideologies,[20] so too is the school a site where these subtle ideological transformations occur. I shall claim that this goes on through a process of technical control. As we shall now see, these logics of control can have a rather profound impact on schools.

CONTROLLING CURRICULAR FORM

The best examples of the encroachment of technical control procedures are found in the exceptionally rapid growth in the use of prepackaged sets of curricular materials. It is nearly impossible now to walk into an American classroom, for instance, without seeing boxes upon boxes of science, social studies, mathematics, and reading materials ('systems,' as they are sometimes called) lining the shelves and in use.[21] Here, a school system usually purchases a total set of standardized material, one that includes statements of objectives, all of the curricular content and material needed, prespecified teacher actions and appropriate student responses, and diagnostic and achievement tests coordinated with the system. Usually, these tests have the curricular knowledge 'reduced' to 'appropriate' behaviors and skills. This emphasis on skills will become rather significant later on in my discussion.

Let me give one example, actually taken from one of the better of the widely used curricular systems, of the numerous sets of materials that are becoming the standard fare in American elementary schools. It is taken from *Module One* of *Science: A Process Approach*. The notion of module is important here. The material is prepackaged into cardboard boxes with attractive colors. It is divided into 105 separate modules, each of which includes a set of pregiven concepts to teach. The material specifies all of the goals. It includes everything a teacher 'needs' to teach, has the pedagogical steps a teacher must take to reach these goals already built in, and has the evaluation mechanisms built into it as well. But that is not all. Not only does it prespecify nearly all a teacher should know, say, and do, but it often lays out the appropriate student responses to these elements as well.

To make this clear, here is one sequence taken from the material that lays out the instructional procedure, student response, and evaluative activity. It concerns colors.

> As each child arrives at school, fasten a red, yellow, or blue paper rectangle on the child's shirt or dress. . . . Comment on the color of the paper and ask the child to say the name of the color he or she is wearing. . . .
> Put thirty yellow, red, and blue paper squares in a large bag or small box. Show the children three paper plates: one marked red, one yellow, and one blue. (See *Materials* for suggestions on marking.) These colors should closely match those in the bag. Ask the children to come forward, a few at a time, and let each child take one square from the bag and place it on the plate marked with the matching color. [A picture of this with a child picking out paper from a box and

144

putting it on a plate is inserted here in the material so that no teacher will get the procedure wrong.] As each child takes a colored square, ask him to name the color of that square. If the child hesitates, name it for him.[22]

In the curricular material, everything except the bag or box is included — all the plates and colored paper. (The cost, by the way, is $14.00 for the plan and the paper.)

I noted that not only were the curricular and pedagogical elements prespecified, but all other aspects of teachers' actions were included as well. Thus, in the 'Appraisal' of this module, the teacher is asked to:

Ask each of six children to bring a box of crayons and sit together. . . . Ask each child to point to his red crayon when you say the word red. Repeat this for all six colors. Ask each child to match one crayon with one article of clothing that someone else is wearing. . . . Before each group of children leaves the activity, ask each child individually to name and point to the red, blue, and yellow crayon.[23]

Even with this amount of guidance, it is still 'essential' that we know for each child whether he or she has reached the appropriate skill level. Thus, as the final element, the material has competency measures built into it. Here the specification reaches its most exact point, giving the teacher the exact words he or she should use:

Task 1: Show the child a yellow cube and ask, What is the color of this cube?

This is done for each color. Then, after arranging orange, green, and purple cubes in front of a child, the material goes on.

Task 4: Say, Put your finger on the orange cube.
Task 5: Say, Put your finger on the green cube.
Task 6: Say, Put your finger on the purple cube.[24]

I have gone on at length here so that you can get a picture of the extent to which technical control enters into the life of the school. Little in what might be metaphorically called the 'production process' is left to chance. In many ways, it can be considered a picture of deskilling. Let us look at this somewhat more closely.

My point is not to argue against the specific curricular or pedagogical content of this kind of material, though an analysis of this certainly would be interesting.[25] Rather, it is to have us focus on the form itself. What is *this* doing? For notice what has happened here. The goals, the process, the outcome, and the evaluative criteria for assessing them are defined as precisely as possible by people external to the situation. In the competency measure at the end of the module, this extends to the specification of even the exact words the teacher is to say.

Notice as well the process of deskilling at work here. Skills that teachers used to need, that were deemed essential to the craft of working with children — such as curriculum deliberation and planning, designing teaching and curricular strategies for specific groups and individuals based on intimate knowledge of these people — are no longer as necessary. With the large-scale influx of prepackaged material, planning is separated from execution. The planning is done at the level of the production of both the rules for use of the material and the material itself. The execution is carried out by the teacher. In the process, what were previously considered valuable skills slowly atrophy because they are less often required.[26]

But what about the element of reskilling that I mentioned earlier was essential to understand how ideological forms can penetrate to the heart of institutions like the school? Unlike the economy where deskilling and reskilling are not usually found operating at one and the same moment with one and the same people, in the school this seems to be exactly the case. As the procedures of technical control enter into the school in the guise of predesigned curricular/teaching/evaluation 'systems,' teachers are being deskilled. Yet they are also being reskilled in a way that is quite consequential. We can see signs of this at both teacher training institutions, in in-service workshops and courses, in the journals devoted to teachers, in funding and enrollment patterns, and not least in the actual curricular materials themselves. While the deskilling involves the loss of craft, the ongoing atrophication of educational skills, the reskilling involves the substitution of the skills and ideological visions of management. The growth of behavior modification techniques and classroom management strategies and their incorporation within both curricular material and teachers' repertoires signifies these kinds of alterations. That is, as teachers lose control of the curricular and pedagogic skills to large publishing houses, these skills are replaced by techniques for better controlling students.

This is not insignificant in its consequences for both teachers and students. Since the material is often organized around and employs specified outcomes and procedures and these are built into this kind of material itself (with its many worksheets and frequent tests), it is 'individualized' in many ways. Students can engage in it themselves with little overt interaction on the part of the teacher or each other as they become more used to the procedures, which are usually highly standardized. The students' progress through the system can be individualized, at least according to speed; and this focus on individualizing the speed (usually through worksheets and the like) at which a student proceeds through the system is becoming even more pronounced in newer curricular systems. Since the control is technical — that is, management strategies are incorporated into it as a major aspect of the pedagogical/curricular/evaluative 'machinery' itself — the teacher becomes something of a manager. This is occurring *at the same time* that the objective conditions of his or her work are becoming increasingly 'proletarianized' due to the curricular form's logic of technical control. This is a unique situation and certainly needs further thought. The possible effect of these forms of technical control on the students is just as serious and is something to which I shall return shortly.

Yet there are important consequences besides the deskilling and reskilling that are occurring. As the literature on the labor process reminds us, the progressive division and control of labor also has an impact at the level of social relations, on how the people involved interact. While this has had a momentous effect in factories and offices, its effects will undoubtedly be felt in the school too. And as in the workplace, the impact may have contradictory results.

Let me be more specific here. With the increasing employment of prepackaged curricular systems as the basic curricular form, virtually no interaction between teachers is required. If nearly everything is rationalized and specified before execution, then contact among teachers about actual curricular matters is minimized.[27]

If such technical control is effective, that is, if teachers actually respond in ways that accept the separation of planning from execution, then one would expect results that go beyond this 'mere' separation. One would expect, at the level of classroom practice, that it will be more difficult for teachers jointly to gain informal control over curricular decisions because of their increasing isolation. In essence, if everything is predetermined, there is no longer any pressing need for teacher interaction. Teachers become unattached individuals, divorced from both colleagues and the actual stuff of their work. However, and here is part of what I mean by a contradictory effect, while this may be an accurate estimation of one of the results of technical control on one level, it forgets that most systems of control embody contradictions within themselves. For instance, while deskilling, forms of technical control, and the rationalization of work have created isolated individuals in, say, factories, historically they have often generated contradictory pressures as well. The use of technical control has often brought unionization in its wake.[28] Even given the ideology of professionalism (an ideology that might make it difficult for collective struggles to evolve), which tends to dominate certain sectors of the teaching force, other state employees who in the past have thought of themselves as professionals have gained a greater collective sense in response to similar modes of control. Thus, the loss of control and knowledge in one arena may generate countervailing tendencies in another.

We cannot know yet how this will turn out. These contradictory results only emerge over long periods of time. In industry, it took decades for such an impact to be felt. The same will no doubt be true in schools.

ACCEPTING TECHNICAL CONTROL

So far in this chapter, I have looked at teachers as if they were workers. That is, I have argued that the processes that act on blue- and white-collar workers in the larger social arena will and are entering into the *cultural forms* that are considered legitimate in schools. Yet schools, because of their internal history, are different in some very important ways from factories and offices, and teachers are still very different from other workers in terms of the conditions of their work. Products are not as visible (except much

148

later on in the rough reproduction of a labor force, in the production and reproduction of ideologies, and in the production of the technical/administrative knowledge 'required' by an economy)[29] as in offices and factories. Teachers have what Erik Olin Wright has called a 'contradictory class location' and hence cannot be expected to react in the same ways as the workers and employees of large corporations.[30] Furthermore, there are children who act back on teachers in ways an automobile on an assembly line or a paper on a desk cannot.[31] Finally, teaching does not take place on a line, but goes on in separate rooms more often than not.

All of these conditions do not mean that schools are immune or autonomous from the logic of capital. The logic will be mediated (in part due to the school as a *state* apparatus); it will enter where it can in partial, distorted, or coded ways. Given the specific differences of schools from other workplaces, a prime moment in its entry can be found less at the level of overt or simple controls (do this because I say so) or at the level of bureaucratic form (because individual teachers can still be relatively free from those kinds of encroachments).[32] These controls will go on, of course; but they may be less consequential than *the encoding of technical control into the very basis of the curricular form itself*. The level of curricular, pedagogic, and evaluative practice within the classroom can be controlled by the forms into which culture is commodified in schools. If my arguments are correct, then how are we to understand the acceptance and growth of this process of control?

These forms enter into schools not because of any conspiracy on the part of industrialists to make our educational institutions serve the needs of capital, as in the earlier quotes from the Green Paper and the Ryerson Plan. It occurs in large part because schools are a rather lucrative market. These sets of material are published by firms who aggressively market where there is a need, or where they can create needs. It is simply good business practice in terms of profit margins to market material of this type, especially since the original purchase of the 'system' or set of modules means increasing purchases over the years. Let me explain this by comparing it to another arena where similar techniques are employed to increase capital accumulation. Think of shaving. Large razorblade manufacturers sell razors at below cost, or even sometimes give them away as promotional 'gimmicks,' because they believe that once you buy the razor you will continue to buy their blades

149

and their upgraded version year after year. In the curricular systems we are considering here, the purchase of the modules (though certainly not cheap by any stretch of the imagination) with their sets of standardized disposable material means the same thing. One 'needs' to continue to purchase the work and test sheets, the chemicals, the correctly colored and shaped paper, the publishers' replacements of outmoded material and lessons, etc. Profits are heightened with every replacement that is bought. Since replacement purchases are often bureaucratically centralized, because of budget control, in the office of the administrator, the additional material is usually bought from the producer (often at exorbitant costs) not gotten from one's local store.

Thus, as with other industries, this 'good business sense' means that high volume, the standardization of each of the elements of one's product and of its form, product upgrading, and then the stimulation of replacement purchasing are essential to maintain profits.[33]

Yet the notion of aggressive marketing and good business sense is but a partial explanation of this growth. In order to comprehend fully the acceptance of technical control procedures embodied in curricular form, we need to know something of the history of why these kinds of materials evolved in the first place. Let me note these briefly.

The original introduction of prepackaged material was stimulated by a specific network of political, cultural, and economic forces, originally in the 1950s and 1960s in the United States. The views of academics that teachers were unsophisticated in major curriculum areas 'necessitated' the creation of what was called teacher-proof material. The cold war climate (created and stimulated by the state in large part) led to a focus on the efficient production of scientists and technicians as well as a relatively stable work-force; thus, the 'guaranteeing' of this production through the school curriculum became of increasing import.[34] On top of this was the decision of the educational apparatus of the state, under the National Defense Education Act, to provide the equivalent of cash credits to local school districts for the purchase of new curricula created by the 'private sector' to increase this efficiency. At the same time, the internal dynamics within education played a part since behavioral and learning psychology — on whose principles so much of these systems rely — gained increasing prestige in a field like education where being seen as a science was critically important both for funding and to deflect criticism,[35] thereby enhancing its legitimacy within the state apparatus and to the public. In the more recent past, the increasing influence of industrial capital within the executive and legislative branches of government, as well as in the attendant bureaucracy,[36] no doubt is an essential element here since there is recent evidence that the federal government has backed away from the widespread production and distribution of large-scale curricula, preferring to stimulate the 'private sector' to enter even more deeply into such production.[37]

This gives us a brief sense of history, but why the continued movement toward this today? A key element here is seeing the school as an aspect of the state apparatus. For the state's need for *consent* as well as control means that the forms of control in school will be encoded in particular ways.[38]

The strategic import of the logic of technical control in schools lies in its ability to integrate into one discourse what are often seen as competing ideological movements, and, hence, to generate consent from each of them. The need for accountability and control by administrative managers, the real needs of teachers for something that is 'practical' to use with their students, the interest of the state in efficient production and cost savings,[39] the concerns of parents for 'quality education' that 'works' (a concern that will be coded differently by different classes and class segments), industrial capital's own requirements for efficient production and so on, can be joined. It is here again that one can see how two important functions of the state can be accomplished. The state can assist in capital *accumulation* by attempting to provide a more efficient 'production process' in schools. At the same time, it can *legitimate* its own activity by couching its discourse in language that is broad enough to be meaningful to each of what it perceives to be important constituencies, yet specific enough to give some practical answers to those who, like teachers, 'require' it. The fact that the form taken by these curricular systems is tightly controlled and more easily made 'accountable,' that it *is* usually individualized (an important ideological element in the culture of the new petty bourgeoisie), that it focuses on skills in a time of perceived crisis in the teaching of 'basic skills,' etc., nearly guarantees its acceptability to a wide array of classes and interest groups.

Thus, the logic of control is both mediated and reinforced by the needs of state bureaucrats for accountable and rational procedures and by the specific nexus of forces acting on the state itself. The curriculum form will take on the aspects that are necessary to accomplish both accumulation and legitimation.[40] As Clarke puts it:

> Even where institutions meet a logic required by capital, their form and direction are never the outcome of a simple unidirectional imposition by capital. They involve a complex political work of concession and compromise, if only to secure the legitimacy of the state in popular opinion.[41]

This is exactly what has occurred in the use of this kind of curricular form.

THE POSSESSIVE INDIVIDUAL

So far I have examined the encroachment into the work of teachers of the technical control systems embodied in curricular form. Yet, teachers are not the only actors in the setting where we find this material. There are the students as well.

A number of writers have noted that each kind of social formation 'requires' a particular kind of individual. Williams and others, for instance, have helped us trace the growth of the abstract individual as it developed within the theoretic, cultural, and economic practices of capitalism.[42] These are not simply changes in definition of the individual, but imply changes in our actual modes of material and cultural producing, reproducing, and consuming. To be an individual in our society signifies a complex interconnection between our day to day meanings and practices and an 'external' mode of production. While I do not mean to imply a simple base/superstructure model here, it is clear that in some very important ways there is a dialectical relationship between economic and ideological form. As Gramsci and others would put it, ideological hegemony sustains class domination; subjectivities cannot be seen as unrelated to structure. Yet the questions remain: How are they related? Where are the sites where this relationship is worked out? The school provides a critical point at which one can see these things working out. As Richard Johnson notes, 'It is not so much a question that schools . . . *are* ideology, more that they are the sites where ideologies are produced in the form of subjectivities.'[43]

But what kind of subjectivity, what kind of ideology, what kind of individual may be produced here? The characteristics embodied in the modes of technical control built into the curricular form itself are ideally suited to reproduce the possessive individual, a vision of oneself that lies at the ideological heart of corporate economies.

The conception of individualism located in the material we have been examining is quite similar to those found in other analyses of aspects of the cultural apparatus in our society. As Will Wright has demonstrated, for example, in his recent investigation of the role of cultural artifacts like film as carriers and legitimators of ideological changes, important aspects of our cultural apparatus represent a world in which the society recognizes each member as an individual; but that recognition is dependent almost entirely upon technical skills. At the same time, while heightening the value of technical competence, these films direct the individual to reject the importance of ethical and political values through their form. They portray an individualism, situated in the context of a corporate economy, in which 'respect and companionship are to be achieved only by becoming a skilled technician.' The individual accepts and does any technical job that is offered and has loyalty to only those with similar technical competence not primarily 'to any competing social and community values.'[44]

An examination of these curricular 'systems' illuminates the extent to which this kind of ideological movement is occurring in increasingly dominant curricular forms. Here, the *rate* at which a student proceeds is individualized; however, the actual product as well as the process to be accomplished are specified by the material itself.[45] Thus, it is not 'just' the teacher who faces the encroachment of technical control and deskilling. The students' responses are largely prespecified as well. Much of this growing arsenal of material attempts as precisely as possible to specify appropriate student language and action as well, often reducing it to the mastery of sets of competencies or skills. Here Wright seems correct.

The notion of reducing curriculum to a set of skills is not unimportant in this regard since it is part of the larger process by which the logic of capital helps build identities and transforms cultural meanings and practices into commodities.[46] That is, if

153

knowledge in all its aspects (of the logical type of that, how, or to — i.e., information, processes, and dispositions or propensities) is broken down and commodified, like economic capital it can be accumulated. The mark of a good pupil is the possession and accumulation of vast quantities of skills in the service of technical interests. As an ideological mechanism in the maintenance of hegemony this is rather interesting. In the larger society, people consume as isolated individuals. Their worth is determined by the possession of material goods or, as Will Wright noted, of technical skills. The accumulation of such goods or of the 'cultural capital' of technical competence — here atomistic bits of knowledge and skills measured on pre-tests and post-tests — is a technical procedure, one that requires only the mastery of the prior necessary technical skills and enough time to follow the rules, at one's own pace, to their conclusion. It is the message of the new petty bourgeoisie writ large on the ideological terrain of the school, one that may actually lead to its rejection by students from other classes and class segments in the day to day life of students in school.

In fact, one might hypothesize just this, that this kind of movement speaks to the increasing importance in the cultural apparatus of the ideologies of class segments with contradictory class locations, in particular what I have called the new petty bourgeoisie — those groups who make up middle management and technical occupations.[47] The particular kind of individualism we are witnessing here is an interesting shift from an ideology of individual autonomy, where a person is his or her own boss and controls his or her destiny, to a careerist individualism. Here the individualism is geared towards organizational mobility and advancement by following technical rules. As Erik Olin Wright puts it, for the new petty bourgeoisie 'individualism is structured around the requirements of bureaucratic advancement.'[48] It may also be a coded 'reflection' of the increasing proletarianization of white-collar work. For, while previously individualism signified some serious sense of autonomy over how one worked and what one produced, for a large portion of white-collar employees autonomy has been trivialized.[49] The rate at which one works may be individualized, but the work itself, how it is accomplished, and what the exact specifications of the final product will be, are increasingly being specified.

At this stage, we are left with many questions. When technical control means that the form that the curriculum takes is highly specified, that it is individualized to such an extent that there is little required interaction among the students so that each activity is by necessity viewed as an individual intellectual act of skill, that answers often take the form of simple physical activities (as we saw in the module I discussed earlier), that answers are either correct or incorrect based on the application of technical rules, and this kind of form is what one follows throughout one's elementary school life, what impact does it have on the teachers and students who interact with it at the level of practice each day?

We do have evidence to suggest what procedures of this type do to workers in industry and in offices.

In many cases, even given the development of a work culture that provides a grounding for cultural forms of resistance, increasing rationalization and a more sophisticated level of control over a long period of time tends to encourage people to manifest an interesting array of traits: a 'rules orientation' — that is, an awareness of rules and procedures and a habit of following them; greater dependability — that is, performing a job at a relatively consistent level, being reliable, and getting the job done even when rules have to be modified a bit to meet changing day to day conditions; and, the 'internalization of the enterprise's goals and values' — that is, conflict is minimized and slowly but surely, there tends to be a homogenization of overt interests between management and employees.[50]

Will this happen in schools as well? This clearly points to the significance of engaging in analyses of what actually happens within the black box of the school. Do teachers and students accept this? Will the gradual introduction of the logic of technical control generate resistances, if only on a cultural level? Will class and work cultures similar to these we examined in Chapters 3 and 4 contradict, mediate, or even transform the expected outcomes? It is to this that we shall now turn.

RESISTANCES

I have not presented an optimistic appraisal here. As the activities of students are increasingly specified, as the rules, processes, and standard outcomes are integrated through and rationalized by the materials themselves, so too are teachers deskilled, reskilled, and anonymized. Students work on material whose form both isolates individuals from each other and establishes the conditions of existence for the possessive individual; the form of the material and the embedded nature of the technical control process does nearly the same for the teacher. Surrounded by a specific logic of control, the objective force of the social relations embodied in the form itself tends to be quite powerful.

Yet I am not arguing for a crude kind of functionalist perspective, where everything is measured by, or is aimed toward, its ability to reproduce an existing static society. The creation of the kind of ideological hegemony 'caused' by the increasing introduction of technical control is not 'naturally' pre-ordained. It is something that is won or lost in particular conflicts and struggles.[51]

On the one hand, teachers will be controlled. As one teacher said about a set of popular material even more integrated and rationalized than the ones I have pointed to here, 'Look, I have no choice. I personally don't like this material, but everyone in the district has to use this series. I'll try to do other things as well, but basically our curriculum will be based on this.'

On the other hand, resistances will be there. This same teacher who disagreed with the curriculum but used it, also was partially subverting it in interesting ways. It was employed only three days a week instead of the five days that were specified. As the teacher put it, 'Listen, if we worked hard we'd finish this stuff in two or three months and besides it's sometimes confusing and boring. So I try to go beyond it as often as possible, *as long as I do not teach what is in the material to be covered by this series next year.*' Thus, as we can see from this last part of her comment, internal conditions make such overt resistances more difficult.

Yet these internal conditions need not preclude teachers from also making these commodified cultural forms their own, to generate their own creative responses to dominant ideologies, in a manner similar to what the counter-cultural groups studies by Marxist ethnographers have done to commodified culture. These groups transformed and reinterpreted the products they bought and used so that they became tools for the creation of alternative pockets of resistance.[52] Students and teachers may also find methods of creatively using these systems in ways undreamed of by state bureaucrats or corporate publishing. (I must admit, however, that my repeated observations in classrooms over the last years make me less than totally optimistic that this will always or even very often be the case.)

Other elements in the environment may provide the site for different meanings and practices to evolve, though, even within the curricular form itself. For we should remember that there may be progressive elements within the *content* of the curriculum that contradict the messages of the form.[53] The very fact that industrialists *are* interested in content, speaks to the import of content as a contested area. And it is in the interaction between the content, the form, and the lived culture of the students that subjectivities are formed. No element in this set of relations can be ignored.

While I have focused on the form of the material here, it is important to specify in somewhat more detail what is entailed in analyzing the possible contradictions between form and content. An ideological 'reading' of any material is not a simple matter. Such a reading in fact cannot be limited to content analysis, to what a 'text' simply and openly 'says,' especially if we are interested in the grounds upon which resistance may be generated. In this regard, our analyses could profit immensely from the incorporation of the work of people such as Barthes, Macherey, Derrida, and other investigators of the process of signification and impact of ideology on cultural production. Thus, to complete our analyses of content, we would need to engage in a semiological reading of the cultural artifact to 'extract the structure of significations within the object which provides the parameter' for possible readings of it.[54] This is not to imply that all possible readings can be specified. One must still be aware, as Derrida argues for instance, that reading a text is an active process of signification. As one commentator puts it, this active process 'decentres the orthodox, customary meaning of the discourse by its invocation of other, less orthodox, private meanings and references.'[55] Thus, every discourse, all content, may have a 'surplus of meaning.' This surplus can create a 'play' in the process of signification, so that while each element in the text may have 'normal' ways in which it is used, it also refers to other possible meanings at the same time.

I want to stress this point. Interrogation of the content itself is important not just to see what ideologies are 'expressed' or 'represented' in the material itself (the notion of representation being an inherently complex and difficult one in the first place), but so that we can begin to both unpack the way any content 'is itself part of an active process of signification through which meaning is produced'[56] and understand the possible contradictions within the content, the text, itself.

In his discussion of the lack of analyses of contradiction in studies of the content of cultural products like the media, Hill makes a similar point.

> If the media do not merely express ideologies, they must then be considered as actively constitutive of ideologies. That is to say, ideologies are not merely ingredients to be detected in the media, but also its products. And again, as active productions, ideologies are not merely to be seen as sets of positivities but also as processes of exclusion — with these 'exclusions' potentially being able to feed back to disturb or deform their progenitive system (and thereby furnishing our analysis with a notion of 'contradiction' retrieved from both a reductionism which would merely place it as a reflection of contradictions determined at the level of the economic and the homeostasis of a reproduction-oriented Marxist functionalism).[57]

As Hill implies in the above quote, the 'meaning' of the content is not only to be found in the text or cultural product itself, in its codes and regularities (though such a reading is an essential part of a complete analysis). The meaning is also constituted 'in the interaction between the text and its users,'[58] in our own case between curriculum content and student.

This still is incomplete, though. As Hill also states, a key is the notion of exclusion. Cultural products not only 'say,' but they 'don't say' as well. The fact that one needs to investigate not only 'what material says' and its surplus of meaning, contradictions, and structures of signification but also what it excludes is brought home by people such as Macherey and Eagleton. As both have noted, any text is not necessarily constituted by readily evident meanings — those positivities that Hill talked about in the prior quote from him — that are easily seen by an observer. Rather, a text 'bears inscribed within it the marks of certain determinate absences which twist its significations into conflict and contradiction.' The *not said* of a work is as important as the said since 'ideology is present in the text in the form of its eloquent silences.'[59]

In brief, then, to examine adequately the possible contradictions between form and content in these curricular materials we would be required to unpack what is present and missing within the content itself, what structures provide the parameters for possible readings of it, what 'dissonances' and contradictions exist within it that provide for alternate readings, and finally the interactions between content and the lived culture of the reader.[60]

This last point about the lived culture of the actors, the students themselves, needs to be stressed, for we must remember their lived cultures that were described earlier. One would expect resistances to the ideological practices I have discussed in this chapter on the part of the students as well as teachers, resistances that may be *specific by race, gender, and class*. My earlier quote from Johnson is correct here. The formation of ideologies — even those of the kind of individualism I have examined in this analysis — is not a simple act of imposition. It is produced by concrete actors and embodied in lived experiences that may resist, alter, or mediate these social messages.[61] As I demonstrated in the previous chapter's analysis of the lived culture of particular segments of the working class, for instance, working-class youth partly defeat the ideology of individualism. The same was true for many women and 'minority' students. While we can and must focus on these resistances, though, their actual meaning may be unclear. Do they, like those of the aforementioned lads, kids, and girls, also reproduce at an even deeper level ideological meanings and practices that provide quite powerful supports to relations of domination? This requires much more study.

Take teachers, for example. While technical controls could possibly lead to unionization, within the school most resistances that occur will be, by necessity, on an individual not a collective level because of the very social relations generated by the curricular form itself.[62] The effects, hence, can be rather contradictory.

We must remember as well that, as I mentioned earlier, these more 'invisible' modes of control may be accepted if they are perceived as coming from a legitimate over-all structure. The fact that curriculum selection committees give teachers a say in the curriculum they will employ means that some of the prior conditions for the consent necessary for this kind of control to be successful have already been laid. The choice is made, in part, by the teachers themselves. It is hard to argue in the face of that. This affects the level of content once again. While the ideology of

159

choice remains, teachers and even parent advisory groups are usually limited in their choices to sets of textual or prepackaged curricular material published by the relatively few major corporate publishing concerns which aggressively market their products. While numerically one's choices may be high, often there will be little difference among the curricular materials from which one can choose. At the level of content, especially in elementary schools, perceived ideological differences over race, sex, and class in the communities in which publishers want to sell their products will provide substantial limits on what is considered 'legitimate' (or safe) knowledge. After all, the production of these curricular materials *is* a business. In the United States, as well, most texts and predesigned curricular materials are produced with state adoption policies in mind. That is, a number of states maintain approved lists of material. Those districts purchasing from the approved list will have their costs partly reimbursed by the state. Getting one's products on that list is quite important, therefore, since a substantial profit is nearly guaranteed.

Conspiracies to eliminate provocative or honest material are not necessary here. The internal working of an educational apparatus, in conjunction with both the political economy of publishing and the fiscal crisis of the state, is sufficient to homogenize the core of the curriculum. This is not to deny the power of industry in making its case the fundamental problem schools are to face or to deny capital's power in comparison to other groups. Rather, it is to claim that this power is highly mediated and works its way through schooling in ways that are not always identical to its original intent. The effect may be relative ideological homogenization, but to say that this is ultimately what industry wants is to substitute a logic of cause and effect for what is, instead, a particular conjuncture of ideological, cultural, political, and economic forces and conflicts which 'creates' the conditions of existence of the material.

Yet this very process of determination can be contradictory, in part because of the fiscal crisis faced by school systems. Once the curriculum is in place, the original subsidized costs become fixed costs assumed by the local school district. As school budgets are voted down more and more, money is not made available to purchase new material or replace outdated ones. Any 'surplus' money tends to go into the ongoing purchase of the consumable material required by the prepackaged curriculum. One is slowly

160

left with expensive 'dinosaurs.' The economics of this are essential if we are to see the contradictory pressures this will evoke. Since the state apparatus has expanded the range of participation in curriculum decision-making by creating selection committees (which sometimes now include parents as well as teachers), yet the selected material can often not be replaced because of its expense later on, the state opens up new spaces of opposition.[63] The growth of the discourse of rights of selection (a right that now cannot be acted upon in any significant way) is objectively at odds with the economic context in which the state currently finds itself. It thereby transforms the issue into a potentially volatile one, in much the same way as was shown by my discussion in Chapter 4 of the contradictory relationship between the liberal discourse of rights and the 'needs' of advanced capitalism.[64]

These potential conflicts, however, may be mitigated by rather powerful economic and ideological conditions that may seem all too real to many of the individuals employed within the state. And the very same pressures may have important and similar implications for those teachers who may in fact recognize the impact that rationalization and control are having on them.

It is easy to forget something: that this is not a good time, ideologically or economically, for teachers who engage in overt resistances. Given a difficult ideological climate and given the employment situation among teachers today — with thousands having either been laid off or living under the threat of it — the loss of control can progress in a relatively unthreatened way. Deskilling and reskilling, progressive anonymization and rationalization, the transformation of educational work, somehow seem less consequential than such economic concerns as job security, salary, etc., even though they may seem to us to be clearly part of the same dynamic.

When all this is said, though, we must recognize that these powerful social messages, while embedded in the actual experiences of teachers and students as they go about their day to day lives in classrooms, *are* highly mediated by other elements. The fact that individual teachers like most other workers may develop patterns of resistance to these patterns of technical control at the informal cultural level alters these messages. The contradictory ideologies of individualism and cooperativeness that are naturally generated out of the crowded conditions of

161

many classrooms (you can't be an isolated individual all the time when there are twenty or thirty other people around with whom one teacher must cope) also provide countervailing possibilities. And lastly, just as blue- and white-collar workers have constantly found ways to retain their humanity and continually struggle to integrate conception and execution in their work (if only to relieve boredom) so too will teachers and students find ways, in the cracks, so to speak, to do the same things. The real question is not whether such resistances exist — as I have shown throughout this volume they are never far from the surface — but whether they are contradictory themselves, whether they lead anywhere beyond the reproduction of the ideological hegemony of the most powerful classes in our society, whether they can be employed for political education and intervention.

Our task is first to find them. We need somehow to give life to the resistances, the struggles. What I have done here is to point to the terrain within the school (the transformation of work, the deskilling and reskilling, the technical control, and so on) over which these struggles will be fought. The resistances may be informal, not fully organized or even conscious; yet this does not mean that they will have no impact. For as Gramsci and Johnson[65] remind us, hegemony is always contested. Our own work should help in this contestation and point to places for active engagement.

My analysis of the process through which technical/adminis- trative knowledge reenters the school through dominant curricular forms highlights some of the strategies for action that I discussed in earlier chapters. As I noted, the expansion of particular logics of control of the labor process creates contradictory effects and provides a potential for successful political work. With the loss of control, one should expect increasing unionization of teachers. This provides an important context. While the history of unioniza- tion has in part been the history of economistic demands (and this is *not* always wrong, by the way), at the same time it is not naturally preordained that salaries and so on are the only things that can be placed on the agenda. Thus, this makes more significant my earlier suggestion that the growing 'proletarianiza- tion' of state workers and the rapid decrease in their objec- tive standard of living and job stability may, in fact, make it easier for the formation of coalitions between teachers and other workers in similar conditions. If Castells's argument is correct — that ultimately the conditions will worsen — then cuts in public services, welfare, education, health, unemployment benefits, and so on will become increasingly extensive in the forseeable future. This will have a tendency to place the interests of school employees in the maintenance of their programs and jobs on the same side as the large number of people who will have to fight to retain the programs, services, and rights they have won after years of struggle.

This tendency is coupled with something else. The rapidity of the pace in which procedures are introduced to rationalize teachers' work and to control as many aspects of education as possible is having an impact similar to what happened when Taylorism was introduced in industry. Its ultimate effect may not be totally successful control, though one should not dismiss its power and sophistication. Rather, in the long run, it may discredit teachers' organization of their own work so that the activities necessary for serious education to go on, activities that teachers have developed out of their own experiences and work culture, will be labeled with the educational equivalent of 'soldiering' when they are not expressly linked to the production of the knowledge and agents needed by an economy. Needless to say this would have a truly destructive effect on any system of education worth its name.

Enabling teachers to see the implications of this and having both them and other blue-, pink-, and white-collar workers recognize the similarities of their collective predicament is an important political step. If they do in fact occupy a contradictory class location, then a significant path towards political education can be traveled. This, of course, is something that progressive elements within teacher unions in the United States, Canada, Latin America, and England and elsewhere in Europe have recognized and on which they are acting now.

Within the school itself, there are areas that need to be stressed as well, even if only briefly. The question of curriculum content that I have raised before is still a serious issue. I have maintained in this chapter that, while it is no simple process to read the ideological elements in or effects of content, the fact that it is a contested area for industry proves the importance of continued attempts both to maintain the democratic elements that currently exist within the content itself and to continue to fight the overt and covert intrusion of business and rightist interests into the selection of appropriate curricular knowledge.

Yet my arguments here have also pointed out the necessity of acting on more than content. At the level of form, clearly the emphasis on individualized, rationalized material makes it quite difficult for collective learning experiences to go on. Altering that emphasis as much as is possible, focusing on joint activity – even if only on such simple things as reports, papers, inquiry, collectively produced drama, art, and so on – is not insignificant. This can and should be made an overt element in the content as well, where the demystification of the 'great man' theory of history, science, etc. is so necessary. One can stress the contributions of groups of real working people acting together as an organizing principle here.[66]

Of course, much more could be said. Again, my claim is *not* that it will be easy to establish such progressive coalitions or to engage in either political education among state workers or curriculum reform. Given current economic conditions and given the right's skillful integration of popular democratic and corporate claims and their incorporation of populist themes into the rhetoric of an increasing sphere of capitalist social relations, the implications are exactly the opposite. It is possible, not easy. However, it is on the terrain that I have identified in this chapter that a good deal of the struggle will be worked out. The terrain offers not just increasing incorporation, rationalization, and control, but opportunities as well.

CHAPTER 6

EDUCATIONAL AND POLITICAL WORK: IS SUCCESS POSSIBLE?

RECONSTRUCTING THE TRADITION

I have tried to do a number of things in this volume. A good deal of my argument has involved a conceptual and empirical critique of mechanistic theories of reproduction, without denying the very real 'determinations' that exist. I have claimed that it is no simple matter merely to reduce all aspects of the form and content of the hidden and overt curriculum in schools to direct expressions of economic needs. Even when education does 'function' to support the maintenance of our current mode of production, the reasons for this are highly mediated and *always* embody more than a simple functionality. In large part, this is due to the fact that one cannot read culture and politics as mirror-like images which passively reflect dominant class interests. To do so is to be inherently undialectical, as well as to ignore the crucial significance and dynamics of patriarchy.

Of course, there are serious connections among the cultural, political, and economic spheres, with the latter being quite powerful. And just as surely, there are material and ideological conditions that provide the conditions of existence for a good deal of our social formation. Yet, at the same time, the *relatively* autonomous nature of these spheres, the contradictions within *and* among them, and their complex interpenetrations are lost if we do not challenge the overly deterministic theories that dominate current analyses of education. Of equal import, by ignoring the contradictions we unrealistically reduce the arenas in which effective educational and political action can and must go on.

On the other hand, if we see culture and politics as providing sites of struggles, then counter-hegemonic work within these spheres becomes important. If cultural form and content and the state (as well as the economy) are inherently contradictory, and if these contradictions are lived out in the school itself by students and teachers, then the range of possible actions is expanded considerably.

One caveat is in order here, however. What I have not been about in this volume is a thorough-going refutation or dismissal of the work of the political economists of education or the theorists of cultural reproduction. As my arguments have shown, some of their claims, and even part of their conceptual apparatus, need to be questioned. Yet to do this in some wholesale fashion would be to ignore the critical importance of how far they have taken us and the debt we owe them for that. Rather, we need to build on their work, reject what now seems too simplistic or incorrect, and expand our analysis into areas that they were unprepared to travel.

Thus, a particular kind of discipline has been required here, one that is critical of the overly reductionistic and economistic categories that have proven in the long run to be damaging to the Marxist tradition, and one which — at the same time — interrogates the school with an interest in uncovering the roots of domination and exploitation which undoubtedly exist. This is a difficult path to take. It involves criticizing a tradition and using it in the same moment. However, it really isn't that difficult, since — as any reading of current leftist literature quickly documents — this is a period of intense theoretic and political debate within the tradition. These debates have helped create (recreate, actually) much more flexibility and openness and have repeatedly informed the analyses offered in this book.[1]

As Finn, Grant, and Johnson note, one of the major conceptual and political weaknesses of many theories of reproduction (Althusser is a prime example) is that 'they appear to have little place for that capacity for resistance which may be exercised by children and teachers in schools.'[2] Thus, while it is important to realize that schools do help reproduce gender relations and the social relations of production, ' "behind their backs," they also reproduce historically specific forms of resistance.'[3] These points are not limited only to our discussions of schools, obviously, but to the workplace, the family, and so forth.

Philip Wexler has made a similar argument in his own inquiry into the limitations of a significant portion of leftist scholarship. As he puts it, many of the conceptual models now in use 'surrender in advance the human capacity for appropriation and transformation to the needs of a system for which individuals are merely structural supports.'[4]

Obviously, there will be correspondences between the 'internal' characteristics of schools and 'external' institutions.[5] Indeed, one would be surprised if they did not exist. However, these correspondences when found are not the result of a guiding principle that works its way from outside to inside in some mechanistic fashion. Rather, they are constructed by the internal interactions of real actors within a lived culture, actors who struggle, contest, and act in ways that may contradict the 'needed' correspondence.[6]

Because of these issues, and because of the state's own needs to try to support the process of capital accumulation and to legitimate both this process and itself, I have argued here that the school is a site for reproduction and production. But this is not simply reproduction and production of agents, knowledge, and ideologies, but of contradictory tendencies in a number of spheres, each of which can have a significant impact on the other.[7] Based on this, I have suggested strategies and action on a variety of fronts: within schools and universities involving curriculum, democratizing technical knowledge, using and politicizing the lived culture of students and teachers, etc.; and outside the school involving both educational practices in progressive labor unions, political and feminist groups, and so on, and in political action to build a mass socialist and democratic movement in the United States.

Thus, in large part my inquiry has been designed to answer what to me is one of the most significant questions we can ask. Is there anything that can be done now? For surely, if education is but a mere reflection of the economy and the ideological requirements of the bourgeoisie and new petty bourgeoisie, then the economy is where one must place all one's marbles, so to speak. By interrogating schools in a number of ways in this volume — focusing on class conflict, on cultural forms of resistance, on the workplace, on the school as a contradictory state apparatus, on the role of the formal educational system not only in reproduction and distribution but production as well — I am convinced even more strongly that such an analysis of education reveals how significant education is as both a process and a set of institutions. In a war of position, we ignore it at our own peril.

Yet even if I am partly wrong, even if economic struggles

offer the only answer to the conditions (and so many others) I described in Chapter 1, we could not ignore education. For even if, say, struggles over our mode of production, and at the workplace and point of production, were the major answer, this would not reduce the significance of the school. As was shown in Chapter 5, the school *is* a workplace. The state itself employs millions of people — many of whom are women — whose day to day conditions and their position in society are being transformed by the emerging crisis confronting us.

Of course, this is not an either/or choice. 'Educational work' needs to be done at the workplace; 'economic work' needs to be done in education. The structures of class, race, and gender exploitation and domination are not 'out there' in the abstract, somewhere in a thing called the economy. They surround us. We live them in our day to day discourse and practices in the families, schools, and jobs that make them up. Therefore, one starts at that level. But as I have maintained repeatedly, building alternative meanings and practices in our daily institutions does not stand alone. It must be organized, connected to the work of other progressive individuals and groups. Only then can we make a difference at a structural level.

As we saw, part of this structural level is defined by the commodification process, by the contradictory interrelationships between knowledge as a commodity and economic form. This set of relationships itself is both reproductive and can exacerbate tensions. Hence, my focus on the role of technical knowledge in the economy, state, and culture.

More and more, technical knowledge defines our conceptions of self and competence. While this tendency is more advanced in the United States than elsewhere — in part because of the relative lack of an aristocratic lineage as in, say, England — its incorporation throughout advanced industrial countries is marked. This has important implications at the cultural and ideological level everywhere as, increasingly, what Habermas calls the 'public sphere' is reduced to expressions of technical values, rules, procedures, and concerns.[8] On an economic level, the uses to which this knowledge is put in our economy are part of the larger processes of accumulation and legitimation, as well as part of changing patterns of class relations. That this dynamic has remained relatively undertheorized is one of the major weaknesses in previous examinations of schools.

An investigation of the connections between commodified

and lived culture, connections that impact on the school and actually help construct it as a site of class, race, and gender conflict, has provided some of the framework of this volume. While the 'circulation' of technical/administrative knowledge as a form of capital (and as a set of complex exploitative social relationships) is *not linear*, I have found it helpful to think of it by employing the metaphor of circulation itself. In summary, as we saw, the educational apparatus is partly organized in such a way that it ultimately provides a major site for the production of technical/ administrative knowledge through its agents, research programs, and commitments. This is not 'forced' on the educational apparatus, but is due largely to the contradictory 'functions' in which these institutions are engaged. This knowledge is commodified and accumulated as a form of cultural capital by the most powerful interests in the economy and the state. The control techniques and forms of social relations generated out of it are employed in an ever growing portion of the workplaces within the society, in advertising and human control, in communications, the family, and culture.[9] It is mediated, resisted, and sometimes transformed. New forms of it are developed, becoming somewhat more sophisticated and 'humane' in the process.

Yet its very use gives it increased legitimacy, thereby enhancing its further spread into institutions of the state such as the school. This condition is furthered and the pace speeded up because of the crisis in accumulation and legitimation as a whole. As it spreads throughout society as a set of techniques and an ideology of accountability and control, this cultural capital becomes embodied in the new petty bourgeoisie who are employed as middle-level bureaucrats, engineers, technicians, supervisors, managers, and professionals in industry, the service sector, and the state.[10] The form such cultural capital takes and its use provide both for continued employment and advancement of the new petty bourgeoisie and for its ultimate control by capital.[11] However, when it finally reaches the school it is again mediated and transformed by teachers and children of those very same workers and employees who have historically confronted technical/ administrative knowledge in their own workplaces. It is accepted only in part as peer cultures and lived class, race, and gender cultures enable students (and again many teachers) to reject and/ or mediate its logic and social relations. This very process of resistance, mediation, and transformation (part of which currently

169

goes by the name of declining test scores and lowered standards, discipline problems, lack of motivation, and the like) causes new forms of technical knowledge to be employed (in curricular form and so on), just as in the offices and factories. And it is off the grounds of these altered forms of control and social relations that new technical/administrative knowledge and new ideologies are ultimately produced in and by the educational apparatus.

Yet this production need *not* always be 'functional' for capital. For instance, while there are times that the development of the productive forces of society also makes necessary a 'transformation' of both the labor process and human labor, we should remember that such transformations may also demand social and technological conditions that may ultimately be less than totally compatible with capitalist logic.

> For instance the development of scientific research requires a massive investment in education which is only profitable in the long term. So too the introduction of information as a productive force requires a good deal of autonomy in decision-making and produces a situation that is entirely contradictory to the discipline capital imposes on workers.[12]

As this example demonstrates, the production and use of technical/administrative knowledge is both reproductive and non-reproductive at the same time. Thus, again we can see that our society is not 'a system of structural self-reproduction.' Instead, it is an unstable and contradictory structure of 'asymmetrical multidimensional relationships.'[13]

POLITICAL ACTION, DEMOCRACY, AND EDUCATION

Certain structural trends are apparent that will exacerbate the contradictions within and among the economic, political, and cultural spheres. These trends point to arenas into which a number of the actions and strategies that I have suggested in this book fit.

Capital will undoubtedly attempt to discipline labor by both directly controlling the labor process in all sectors of the economy and, indirectly, controlling the state more, and by maintaining a relatively high level of unemployment. Social services will be substantially reduced because 'they are too costly.' (This, of course, will also lead to a reduction of jobs within the state, where most of these social services are provided.) Workers in the traditional working class and in what has been called the 'new working class' such as service workers, therefore, will find pressure for their jobs to be more rationalized, divided, and redivided to increase 'productivity' and 'efficiency.' Furthermore, many of them will be forced to accept much lower real wages and less desirable working conditions. This will hit black, brown, and women workers in the competitive sector quite hard.[14]

These pressures will generate tensions in the political sphere and at a cultural level that can be rather powerful, especially given Gintis's earlier arguments about the dynamics of the discourse of person rights and the contradictory tendencies in the extension of formal democratic procedures. In its quest for efficiency, expert authority, rationalization, and increased discipline, capital may undermine the substance of democracy. As the Trilateral Commission document, *The Crisis of Democracy*, warned, there are all too many social dangers from an 'excess of democracy.' Extending the substance of democracy to the economic and cultural spheres, extending it beyond the formal mechanisms of politics like voting, does not necessarily serve capital. Capitalism and democracy, hence, may increasingly come into conflict.[15]

This means that the defense of democracy, and its expansion into important aspects of our lives, is quite important both substantively and strategically. It can help unify the bulk of the population by uniting them around an historically pivotal theme in the United States and elsewhere. And it can begin to overcome, in the *political* sphere, the division of the working class into class fractions brought about by the productive arrangements in society.[16]

Richard Edwards summarizes a number of these arguments in his own discussion of the importance of developing a program that is both 'democratic and thoroughly socialist.' As he puts it, the renewed interest in industrial and political democracy by rank and file groups to open up the Steelworkers Union, to 'reclaim the Teamsters,' to institute a program of local initiative in the United Mine Workers, and so on, all of these attempts to return power to the members suggest that in their day to day activity at the workplace, a growing segment of the working class is already participating in 'the emerging struggle for democratic rule.'[17]

As Edwards goes on to say,

171

The defense of democracy thus entails a demand for its application at all levels and in all spheres of society. This is a crucial point, for here emerges the central theme of all socialist programs: the defense of political democracy is simply the logical corollary to the demand for democracy at the workplace and social control of the production process. Once workers raise a challenge to the existing system of control in the firm, they will through their experience be led to see the common content of these struggles. The defense and extension of democracy may ultimately rest, then, on the working class's effort to [reorganize and democratize] the means of production and to organize, through democratic rule, society's material resources for the benefit of all in society. Democracy thus becomes the rallying cry not only to unite various fractions of the working class, but also to unite the political and economic struggles of that class.[18]

In a time when capital and the state, hence, can no longer 'afford' substantive democracy, we need to reappropriate democracy as a discourse and a set of practices back from the right. Here neither Edwards nor I mean democracy as merely a formal assemblage of mechanisms. For too long that has served a bit too much to legitimate exploitation. Rather, we mean a practice that is based in the control of decisions about production, distribution, and consumption in the hands of the majority of working people in this country, one that is not limited to the political sphere but to, say, economics and, critically, gender relations. As part of a transitional program and as a goal in itself, this becomes quite consequential.

Given the resurgence of the right, this may seem Utopian. However, there are grounds for optimism. In a recent survey of public attitudes on the economy, for example, we find results like these.

. . . 66 percent of those surveyed agreed that people do not work as hard as they could 'because they aren't given enough say in decisions which affect their jobs.' Seventy-four percent would support a plan whereby consumers in local communities 'are represented on the boards of companies that operate in their local region.' Fifty-two percent would support a plan 'in which employees determine broad company policy.' Sixty-six percent would favor working for a company that is employee owned and controlled.[19]

This does not sound like a straightforward endorsement of either the logic or the policies of capital.

Rachel Sharp extends this argument to the schools, arguing that a democratization of decision-making procedures there needs to be continually fought for if it is to be maintained.[20] The increasingly organized attempts by groups of teachers — such as Rank and File in England, Women's Educational Press in Canada, and the Boston Women's Teachers' Group in the United States — to combine actions against patriarchal relations, against racism and the intrusion of rightist ideological techniques and interests, against anti-democratic decision-making in social services, toward the building of real and workable alternatives to current educational content and methods, and for the continued movement toward affiliations with other groups, points to the sensitivity of many educators to these issues in their day to day lives.

Supporting such trends is very significant as a counter to opposite tendencies in education. For instance, in England, state sponsored educational reforms over the past three decades have 'tended to distance ... teachers from a popular and especially a working class constituency.'[21] Many teachers already recognize this. If my analysis in this volume is correct, this can be and needs to be criticized and worked against.

Criticism of the way our system works is not enough, however. It needs to be accompanied by specific 'proposals for an alternative social model (which we may call socialist if we like).' These proposals should not be borrowed whole from other countries, but need to be both adapted to the current conditions of, in my case, the American people and contrary to the interests of capital. Without this, again, little in the way of serious and progressive structural change can be expected.[22]

As a number of people have documented, there *are* alternatives being built now and they are growing. These counter-hegemonic examples can and must be employed to reinstill a sense of imaginative possibility in people. They provide significant points of reference for demonstrating what can be done now in the way of concrete work.[23] Yet these successful struggles are not as helpful as they might be if they are not communicated. If we are to overcome apathy and cynicism, as well as the workings of the selective tradition, the non-reformist reforms that people throughout society are putting in place can be put on the agenda only if others are aware of them. Labor activists, university teachers, and others do have an important role to play in this regard. This is part of accomplishing what Gramsci urged, building a group of 'intellectuals' who are organic members of the 'subordinate classes.'

In part, this is an issue of political pedagogy, of appropriate teaching. Thus, as Peter Dreier suggests:

> Teachers help to shape the assumptions, values and choices of their students, by what they say as well as by what they don't say. The existence of Marxist, socialist, and radical scholarship, now available in monographs, texts, anthologies, journals, and films, is an important antidote to mainstream analyses of society. But however receptive students may be, analyses that offer a radical critique of the current problems of capitalism will only reinforce their cynicism unless they are accompanied by an analysis of the possibilities for transforming the situation into something better. . . . In the past two decades, many radicals have shifted from false hopes . . . to no hopes at all. We must now learn, as teachers, scholars, and activists, to walk the tightrope between romanticism and cynicism. The lessons of our own radical scholarship are clear: building a popular mass movement requires a critique of the present, a vision of the future, and a strategy. Yet neither vision nor strategy is possible, on a mass basis, unless the cynicism about social change that now pervades American politics and culture can be overcome.[24]

Part of our task, hence, is educative in the fullest sense of that word. We can help labor recapture its partially lost traditions. While important parts of these traditions are still being lived out in cultural ways in our offices, stores, factories, and mines[25] — something that was documented in my discussion of the work culture of men's and women's day to day lives — the history of what people strived for, of the visions of a more equitable society, and of the demands for and struggles over them, all of this needs to be made visible and legitimate once again.

Internal education of the membership of unions, feminist

174

collectives, 'rank and file' educational groups, and so on on the issues of increasing corporate control, cultural, political, and economic democracy, and, especially, alternatives to existing forms of economic and political organization are, therefore, an essential first step.[26] This is *not* a one-way street. The impressive socialist feminist arguments about how one should organize and engage in counter-hegemonic activity can teach us all a good deal, as can rank and file and environmental movements elsewhere.[27]

It is not just at the level of political or educational action that work needs to be done. Scholarship is necessary as well in a number of vital areas. For instance, the real histories of socialist and oppositional educational practices has yet to be told.[28] Thoughtful discussions and analyses of the principles of socialist models of curriculum and teaching need to be developed, ones that, for example, reduce the division between conception and execution and mental and manual labor. This is clearly a practical matter as well. We cannot wait for the state somehow magically to open up its doors — such as in the voucher plan with all its contradictions — to the development of socialist principles, content, and methods. Working models are necessary right now.[29] This requires us to communicate what we are doing with each other in both formal and informal ways.

Yet only communicating with other educators is not enough. Working-class parents and youth, organized groups of workers, and others should be involved in the articulation and criticism of these proposals. In the process, educators can educate these groups, at the same time that they (the educators) are being educated themselves. After all, it is somewhat silly to deny the fact that teachers do know things that tend to work in classrooms. In this way, by working in concert with others, the practice of developing our methods and content will also embody the social commitments we articulate.[30]

The point that educational activity becomes more, not less, important is reiterated by the members of the Education Group at the Centre for Contemporary Cultural Studies. As they put it: 'Reproduction is only secured after considerable ideological work and is thus susceptible to educational work of an oppositional or counter-hegemonic kind.'[31] A key here is the articulation of a dual focus on *both* socialist and feminist activity. The transformation of our culture, politics, and mode of production rests on a recognition of the importance of gender (and race, as well) determinacy.

175

This means that 'the older forms of socialist populism which conflated the particular experiences of girls, young women and mothers with those of an undifferentiated populace, or working class, will no longer suffice as a starting point.'[32] Intellectuals can help here, by highlighting the experiences of women, by making it an integral part of one's analyses and action,[33] and by fully integrating it into any alternative program.

If the development of clear alternative programs is essential, these alternatives need to be based on the democratic strength that actually exists in the United States. Without clear programs *that seem to provide for at least partial solutions to local and national problems*, 'most people will accept the dominant view, which is inherently undemocratic and anti-egalitarian.' Thus, these programs need to be sensible not only to hard-core activists but to working people with families and jobs.[34]

Carnoy and Shearer again are helpful in specifying the characteristics of a transitional program that would both build a long-term structurally oriented movement and embody what in Chapter 4 I called non-reformist reforms.

> It is possible for a movement to lose many times in the conventional sense — in elections, [etc.] — and yet win in the long run, in the construction of a more democratic society.
>
> A movement must define political progress more broadly than do conventional politicians — and it must fit a notion of political progress into the over-all framework of a transitional program and a long-term strategy.
>
> Such a transitional program would have the following characteristics: it should, as enacted, increase the power people have over their lives and reduce the power of corporations and those with money; it should be easily explainable to people and embodied in clear measures such as bills, initiatives, or organizing demands; it should have a simple identifier (such as EPIC — End Poverty in California — in the 1930s); elements of it should, in theory, be realized at the level of political struggle in which people are engaged — state government, county government, and city government; as much as possible, it should *relate to the needs of people in their daily lives*; and, finally, the program should reflect the constituency that can make up a *majority* movement for change.[35]

176

Though they are speaking primarily to the issue of economic democracy, the italicized portion of the above quote is consequential to a broader set of issues as well. It stresses the importance of something I have noted earlier. It is at the level of our daily lives where the cultural, political, and economic spheres are lived out in all their complexity and contradictions, not just in the more removed areas of high finance, federal government, and the like (though these cannot be ignored).[36] Theoretic analysis, though essential, cannot substitute for concrete work in all three spheres at that level.

What then are the possibilities of success? Here we need to be honest. We simply cannot know. What we can do is ensure that, as researchers and intellectuals, on a theoretical level our investigations illuminate both the reproduction *and* non-reproduction that is going on. We can see how the emerging structural crisis will 'determine' our own and others' actions and offer possibilities. The issue is not only theoretic, of course. How are we to know what non-reproductive activity is occurring *if we do not participate in it ourselves*? If we do have agency — as I have insisted throughout this book and as the activity of vast numbers of people in their productive labor documents — then transformation is possible. As we become less reductive and less mechanistic, important changes in our theories are indeed going on. Logically and politically, however, these changes entail a practice. The socio-economic and cultural realities with which I began this book can only be altered if we take that practice seriously.

177

NOTES

CHAPTER 1
REPRODUCTION, CONTESTATION, AND CURRICULUM

1. Manuel Castells, *The Economic Crisis and American Society* (Princeton: Princeton University Press, 1980), p. 3.
2. *Ibid.*, p. 12. Compare here, also, the arguments made by Althusser about the relative autonomy of the cultural, political, and economic spheres. Louis Althusser, *Lenin and Philosophy and Other Essays* (London: New Left Books, 1971).
3. Castells, *The Economic Crisis and American Society*, pp. 179-81.
4. David Featherman and Robert Hauser, 'Sexual Inequalities and Socio-Economic Achievement in the U.S., 1962-1973,' *American Sociological Review* XLI (June 1976), 462. See also Erik Olin Wright, *Class Structure and Income Determination* (New York: Academic Press, 1979).
5. Michael Olneck, personal communication. See also Castells, *The Economic Crisis and American Society*, p. 192.
6. Castells, *The Economic Crisis and American Society*, p. 187, and Wright, *Class Structure and Income Determination*, especially Chapters 6-9.
7. Martin Carnoy and Derek Shearer, *Economic Democracy* (White Plains, New York: M.E. Sharpe, 1980), p. 24.
8. See Francis Fox Piven and Richard Cloward, *Poor People's Movements* (New York: Vintage, 1977).
9. Castells, *The Economic Crisis and American Society*, pp. 178-85. See also James O'Connor, *The Fiscal Crisis of the State* (New York: St Martin's Press, 1973).
10. Carnoy and Shearer, *Economic Democracy*, p. 51.
11. There is a countervailing tendency toward granting workers some semblance of control, if only to increase production and decrease worker resistance. See, for example, Richard Edwards, *Contested Terrain* (New York: Basic Books, 1979).
12. Castells, *The Economic Crisis and American Society*, pp. 161-85.
13. O'Connor, *The Fiscal Crisis of the State*, pp. 13-15. There have been attempts to organize women workers of course, ones that continue today. See Roslyn L. Feldberg, 'Union Fever: Organizing Among Clerical Workers, 1900-1930,' *Radical America* XIV (May-June 1980), 53-67, and

Jean Tepperman, 'Organizing Office Workers,' *Radical America* X (January-February 1976), 3-20.

14. Lillian Rubin, *Worlds of Pain* (New York: Basic Books, 1976).
15. Todd Gitlin, 'Hegemony in Transition: Television's Screens,' in *Cultural and Economic Reproduction in Education*, Michael W. Apple, ed. (London: Routledge & Kegan Paul, 1982).
16. Castells, *The Economic Crisis and American Society*, pp. 144-5, and Michael Useem, 'Corporations and the Corporate Elite,' *Annual Review of Sociology* VI (1980), 41-77.
17. Carnoy and Shearer, *Economic Democracy*, p. 17.
18. Castells, *The Economic Crisis and American Society*, p. 66.
19. Useem, 'Corporations and the Corporate Elite,' 53.
20. Edwards, *Contested Terrain*. This is not to imply that all plans for worker 'input' are necessarily progressive. For an interesting argument that most current plans for job enrichment and increasing worker participation actually increase the efficiency of capitalist production and reproduce management's capacity to dominate the labor process, see James W. Rinehart, 'Job Enrichment and the Labor Process,' paper presented at a conference on New Directions in the Labor Process sponsored by the Department of Sociology, State University of New York at Binghamton, Binghamton, New York, May 5-7, 1978.
21. Christopher Jencks *et al.*, *Who Gets Ahead?* (New York: Basic Books, 1979). See also Wright, *Class Structure and Income Determination*.
22. Herbert Kliebard, 'Bureaucracy and Curriculum Theory,' in *Freedom, Bureaucracy and Schooling*, Vernon Haubrich, ed. (Washington, D.C.: Association for Supervision and Curriculum Development, 1971), pp. 74-93.
23. Michael W. Apple, *Ideology and Curriculum* (London: Routledge & Kegan Paul, 1979). See also, Steven Selden, 'Conservative Ideologies and Curriculum,' *Educational Theory* XXVII (Summer 1977), 205-22, Harry Braverman, *Labor and Monopoly Capital* (New York: Monthly Review Press, 1974), and Randall Collins, *The Credential Society* (New York: Academic Press, 1979).
24. Paul DiMaggio, 'Review Essay: On Pierre Bourdieu,' *American Journal of Sociology* LXXXIV (May 1979), 1461.
25. *Ibid.*, 1461-2.
26. The debate over the relationship between base and superstructure is exceptionally intense at present. See, e.g., Raymond Williams, *Marxism and Literature* (New York: Oxford University Press, 1977), Michele Barrett *et al.* eds, *Ideology and Cultural Production* (New York: St Martin's Press, 1979), Paul Hirst, *On Law and Ideology* (London: Macmillan, 1979), Colin Sumner, *Reading Ideologies* (New York: Academic Press, 1979), and John Clarke, Chas Critcher, and Richard Johnson, eds, *Working Class Culture* (London: Hutchinson, 1979).
27. Stuart Hall, 'The Schooling-Society Relationship: Parallels, Fits, Correspondences, Homologies,' mimeo, p. 6.
28. O'Connor, *The Fiscal Crisis of the State*.
29. I have argued that there are three functions of the state — legitimation,

accumulation, and production. See Michael W. Apple and Joel Taxel, 'Ideology and the Curriculum,' in *Educational Studies and Social Science,* Anthony Hartnett, ed. (London: Heinemann, 1981).

30. See Pierre Bourdieu and Jean-Claude Passeron, *The Inheritors* (Chicago: University of Chicago Press, 1979), p. 81, and Collins, *The Credential Society.*

31. Ron Aminzade, personal communication. The literature on what is implied by the school's role as a state apparatus is increasing rapidly. It does, however, tend toward a functionalism that may not do justice to the contradictions and competing class interests both within the state and between the state and the economic and cultural spheres of a society. See Roger Dale, 'Education and the Capitalist State: Contributions and Contradictions,' in *Cultural and Economic Reproduction in Education,* Apple, ed.

32. Richard Johnson, 'Histories of Culture/Theories of Ideology: Notes on an Impasse,' in *Ideology and Cultural Production*, Michelle Barrett *et al.*, eds, p. 73.

33. Chantal Mouffe, 'Hegemony and Ideology in Gramsci,' in *Gramsci and Marxist Theory,* Chantal Mouffe, ed. (London: Routledge & Kegan Paul, 1979), p. 187.

34. See Jerome Karabel and A.H. Halsey, eds, *Power and Ideology in Education* (New York: Oxford University Press, 1977) and Caroline Hodges Persell, *Education and Inequality* (New York: Free Press, 1977).

35. On the debate engendered by these differences, see, e.g., Apple, *Ideology and Curriculum,* and Apple, ed., *Cultural and Economic Reproduction in Education.*

36. Hall, 'The Schooling — Society Relationship,' p. 7.

37. The argument here is similar to that of Finn, Grant, and Johnson when they state that one's analysis must 'grasp the relations between schools and other sites of social relations . . . within a particular social formation.' Dan Finn, Neil Grant, Richard Johnson, and the C.C.C.S. Education Group, 'Social Democracy, Education and the Crisis,' (Birmingham: University of Birmingham Centre for Contemporary Cultural Studies, mimeo, 1978), p. 4.

38. It is important to keep in mind, though, that capital is *not* a thing, but a set of relationships.

39. Apple, *Ideology and Curriculum.*

40. *Ibid.*, p. 14.

41. Collins, *The Credential Society.*

42. David Noble, *America By Design* (New York: Alfred A. Knopf, 1977) and Castells, *The Economic Crisis and American Society.*

43. Here I was arguing in part with Bourdieu since he did not go far enough into the way cultural capital was produced.

44. Erik Olin Wright, *Class, Crisis and the State* (London: New Left Books, 1978).

45. Paul Willis, *Learning to Labour* (Westmead: Saxon House, 1977) and Robert Everhart, *The In-Between Years: Student Life in a Junior High School* (Santa Barbara, California: Graduate School of Education,

University of California, 1979).

46. There is a danger in employing concepts like penetration, however, especially given the manner in which sexist words and images dominate our linguistic usage. See Noelle Bisseret, *Education, Class Language and Ideology* (London: Routledge & Kegan Paul, 1979).

47. Everhart, *The In-Between Years.*

48. Apple, 'Analyzing Determinations: Understanding and Evaluating the Production of Social Outcomes in Schools,' *Curriculum Inquiry* X (Spring 1980), 55-76. There are other important ways of conceiving of cultural production as a process of production, *per se.* See, for instance, the essays in Barrett *et al.,* eds, *Ideology and Cultural Production,* Rosalind Coward and John Ellis, *Language and Materialism* (London: Routledge & Kegan Paul, 1977), and Philip Wexler, 'Structure, Text, and Subject: A Critical Sociology of School Knowledge,' in Apple, ed., *Cultural and Economic Reproduction In Education.*

49. Bob Jessop, 'Recent Theories of the Capitalist State,' *Cambridge Journal of Economics* 1 (December 1977), 353-73, and Herbert Gintis, 'Communication and Politics: Marxism and the "Problem" of Liberal Democracy,' *Socialist Review* X (March — June 1980), 189-232.

50. See Roger Dale, 'Education and the Capitalist State: Contributions and Contradictions,' in Apple, ed., *Cultural and Economic Reproduction in Education.*

51. I do not wish to denigrate such work totally. Some of it is quite helpful and interesting. See, e.g., Michael Kirst and Decker Walker, 'An Analysis of Curriculum Policy-Making,' *Review of Educational Research* XLI (December 1971), 479-509, William Lowe Boyd, 'The Changing Politics of Curriculum Policy-Making for American Schools,' *Review of Educational Research* XLVIII (Fall 1978), 577-92, and, especially, Arthur E. Wise, *Legislated Learning: The Bureaucratization of the American Classroom* (Berkeley: University of California Press, 1979). For criticisms of liberal theories of the state, see Ralph Miliband, *Marxism and Politics* (New York: Oxford University Press, 1977).

52. Castells, *The Economic Crisis and American Society,* p. 125. Castells notes that if we take into account the amount of employment that is dependent on the production of military goods and services, we would find nearly one-third of our labor force is dependent to a large degree on the economic activity of the state. See pp. 125-30.

53. Mouffe, ed., *Gramsci and Marxist Theory,* p. 10. See, as well, Gitlin's argument that there is of course a serious danger — one that we should clearly recognize — in overusing concepts such as hegemony in explaining cultural and economic reproduction.
Gitlin expresses this concern rather well when he says:

> [We need to] bring the discussion of cultural negemony down to earth. For much of the discussion so far remains abstract, almost as if cultural hegemony were a substance with a life of its own,

a sort of immutable fog that has settled over the whole public life of capitalist societies to confound the truth of the proletarian telos. Thus to the questions, 'Why are radical ideas suppressed in the schools?', 'Why do workers oppose socialism?', and so on comes a single Delphic answer: hegemony. 'Hegemony' becomes the magical explanation of last resort. And as such it is useful neither as an explanation nor as a guide to action. If 'hegemony' explains everything in the sphere of culture, it explains nothing.

His own analysis draws heavily upon the concept, however, and does document the continued power of its use. See Todd Gitlin, 'Prime Time Ideology: The Hegemonic Process in Television Entertainment,' *Social Problems* XXVI (February 1979), 252.

54. Mouffe, ed., *Gramsci and Marxist Theory*, p. 10. See also, Dale, 'Education and the Capitalist State', and Martin Carnoy, 'Education, Economy and the State,' in Apple, ed., *Cultural and Economic Reproduction in Education*.

55. Mouffe, ed., *Gramsci and Marxist Theory*, p. 182.

56. *Ibid.*, p. 193 and James Donald, 'Green Paper: Noise of a Crisis,' *Screen Education* XXX (Spring 1979).

57. John Holloway and Sol Picciotto, 'Introduction: Towards a Materialist Theory of the State,' in *State and Capital*, John Holloway and Sol Picciotto, eds (London: Edward Arnold, 1978), p. 24. Whether the state can be conceived as a set of institutions is part of a larger controversy. See, for example, Jessop, 'Recent Theories of the Capitalist State,' the articles collected in the afore-mentioned volumes edited by Holloway and Picciotto, Mouffe, and Apple, and Alan Wolfe, 'New Directions in the Marxist Theory of Politics,' *Politics and Society* IV (Winter 1974), 131-59.

58. Bob Jessop, 'Capitalism and Democracy,' in *Power and the State*, Gary Littlejohn *et al.*, eds (New York: St Martin's Press, 1978), p. 45.

59. Pierre Macherey, *A Theory of Literary Production* (London: Routledge & Kegan Paul, 1978).

60. See Williams, *Marxism and Literature*, and Apple, *Ideology and Curriculum*.

61. Gitlin, 'Prime Time Ideology,' 254.

62. *Ibid.*, 255.

63. See, e.g., Raymond Williams, *Television: Technology and Cultural Form* (New York: Schocken Books, 1974).

64. Gitlin, 'Prime Time Ideology,' 255.

CHAPTER 2
TECHNICAL KNOWLEDGE, DEVIANCE, AND THE STATE:
THE COMMODIFICATION OF CULTURE

1. See the review of research on the relationship between schooling and inequality in Caroline H. Persell, *Education and Inequality* (New York:

Free Press, 1977).

2. See, for example, Peter Woods and Martin Hammersly, eds, *School Experience* (New York: St Martin's Press, 1977).

3. For instance, David Hargreaves *et al.*, *Deviance in Classrooms* (London: Routledge & Kegan Paul, 1975) and Rachel Sharp and Anthony Green, *Education and Social Control* (London: Routledge & Kegan Paul, 1975).

4. I have argued elsewhere that the very distinction we make between macro and micro explanations is not helpful. See Michael W. Apple, 'The New Sociology of Education: Analyzing Cultural and Economic Reproduction,' *Harvard Educational Review* XLVIII (November 1978), 495-503.

5. Raymond Williams, *Marxism and Literature* (New York: Oxford University Press, 1977).

6. Michael W. Apple, *Ideology and Curriculum* (London: Routledge & Kegan Paul, 1979).

7. *Ibid*. See also Basil Bernstein, *Class, Codes and Control Volume 3: Towards a Theory of Educational Transmissions* (London: Routledge & Kegan Paul, 1977).

8. Michael Olneck and James Crouse, *Myths of the Meritocracy: Cognitive Skill and Adult Success in the United States* (Madison, Wisconsin: University of Wisconsin Institute for Research on Poverty, Discussion Paper 485-78, March 1978), pp. 13-14.

9. *Ibid.*, p. 15. See also Martin Carnoy and Derek Shearer, *Economic Democracy* (White Plains, New York: M.E. Sharpe, 1980).

10. I am not totally subscribing to the Althusserian view here, however. For criticisms of such a view see Michael Erben and Denis Gleesen, 'Education as Reproduction', in Michael Young and Geoff Whitty, eds, *Society, State, and Schooling* (Guildford, England: Falmer Press, 1977), pp. 73-92, Paul Willis, *Learning to Labour* (Lexington, Mass.: D.C. Heath, 1977), and R.W. Connell, 'A Critique of The Althusserian Approach to Class,' *Theory and Society* VIII (November 1979), 303-45.

11. Williams, *Marxism and Literature*.

12. John Meyer, 'The Effects of Education as an Institution,' *American Journal of Sociology* LXXIII (July 1977). See also Randall Collins, 'Some Comparative Principles of Educational Stratification,' *Harvard Educational Review* XLVII (November 1977), 601-2.

13. Jerome Karabel and A.H. Halsey, 'Educational Research: A Review and Interpretation', in Jerome Karabel and A.H. Halsey, eds, *Power and Ideology in Education* (New York: Oxford University Press, 1977), pp. 12-16.

14. See, e.g., Samuel Bowles and Herbert Gintis, *Schooling in Capitalist America* (New York: Basic Books, 1976).

15. Michael W. Apple, 'The Politics of School Knowledge,' *Review of Education* V (Winter 1979).

16. Michael W. Apple and Nancy King, 'What Do Schools Teach?' *Curriculum Inquiry* VI (Number 4, 1977).

17. Bowles and Gintis, *Schooling in Capitalist America*. See also Christian Baudelot and Roger Establet, *La Escuela Capitalista* (Mexico City: Siglo

Vientiuno Editores, 1975) and Jean Anyon, 'Social Class and the Hidden Curriculum of Work,' *Journal of Education* CLXII (Winter 1980), 67-92.

18. Karabel and Halsey, 'Educational Research: A Review and Interpretation,' James O'Connor, *The Fiscal Crisis of the State* (New York: St Martin's Press, 1973), and Manuel Castells, *The Economic Crisis and American Society* (Princeton: Princeton University Press, 1980).

19. Erik Olin Wright, *Class, Crisis and the State* (London: New Left Books, 1978), p. 111.

20. *Ibid.*, p. 112. Wright does argue, though, that the need for a constantly rising process of capital accumulation is not always functional for reproduction. It may in fact generate structural crises within itself. See pp. 111-80.

21. Pierre Bourdieu and Jean-Claude Passeron, *Reproduction in Education, Society and Culture* (London: Sage Publications, 1977).

22. Apple, *Ideology and Curriculum*, pp. 36-7. I am indebted to Walter Feinberg for the idea that schools serve to maximize the production of technical knowledge. See his 'A Critical Analysis of the Social and Economic Limits to the Humanizing of Education,' in *Humanistic Education*, Richard Weller, ed. (Berkeley: McCutchan, 1977), pp. 249-69.

23. David Noble, *America by Design: Science, Technology, and the Rise of Corporate Capitalism* (New York: Alfred A. Knopf, 1977), p. xxvi.

24. Andre Gorz, ed., *The Division of Labour* (Atlantic Highlands, New Jersey: Humanities Press, 1976), p. ix.

25. Il Manifesto, 'Challenging the Role of Technical Experts,' in Gorz, ed., *The Division of Labour*, p. 124.

26. Stephen Marglin, 'What Do Bosses Do?', in Gorz, ed., *The Division of Labour*, pp. 13-54.

27. Braverman, *Labor and Monopoly Capital* (New York: Monthly Review Press, 1974).

28. Noble, *America By Design*, p. 6.

29. *Ibid.*, p. 95.

30. *Ibid.*, pp. 128, 147.

31. Jerome Karabel, 'Community Colleges and Social Stratification,' *Harvard Educational Review* XLII (November 1972), 521-62.

32. See Nicos Poulantzas, *Classes in Contemporary Capitalism* (London: New Left Books, 1975), p. 238.

33. For an investigation of how these internal programs work, see James Rosenbaum, *Making Inequality* (New York: John Wiley, 1976).

34. Wright, *Class, Crisis and the State*, p. 38.

35. Erik Olin Wright delimits six modes of determination, including the ones — structural determination and selection — that I am implying here. These include structural limitation, selection, reproduction/ nonreproduction, limits of functional compatibility, transformation, and mediation. See Wright, *Class, Crisis and the State*, pp. 15-23. I shall return to this point in Chapter 3. Other *status group* interests also enter into this, of course. For an interesting discussion of this, see Randall Collins, *The Credential Society* (New York: Academic Press, 1979).

36. Goran Therborn, *What Does The Ruling Class Do When It Rules?*

(London: New Left Books, 1978), p. 11.

37. Wright, *Class, Crisis and the State*, p. 162. This is not to say that the state and industry will necessarily be successful in regulating these various aspects of production and the economy. As I noted, it is becoming more clear, as well, that the state has a variety of functions to perform, not just its aforementioned increasingly active role in stimulating accumulation, some of which may be in contradiction with each other. For interesting discussions on the varying functions the state performs, see Claus Offe and Volker Ronge, 'Theses on the Theory of the State,' *New German Critique* VI (Fall 1975), 137-47, James O'Connor, *The Fiscal Crisis of the State* (New York: St Martin's Press, 1973), and Roger Dale, 'The Politicization of School Deviance,' in *Schools, Pupils and Deviance*, Len Barton and Roland Meighan, eds (Driffield, England: Nafferton Books, 1979).

38. Castells, *The Economic Crisis and American Society*, p. 69.

39. *Ibid.*, p. 70.

40. *Ibid.*, pp. 70-1.

41. *Ibid.*, p. 71.

42. *Ibid.*, p. 104.

43. *Ibid.*, p. 130.

44. *Ibid.*, p. 125. On the other hand, we can recognize the existence of 'lemon socialism,' where the state takes over industries that are failing and absorbs the costs. The very fact the nationalized industries are nearly always in poor shape when they are taken over means a high rate of failure and poor quality service and product. This is then used to argue against socialism in general. Obviously, this is a rather circular process of reasoning.

45. See Basil Bernstein, *Class, Codes and Control Volume 3* (London: Routledge & Kegan Paul, 1977).

46. Randall Collins's discussion of a credential marketplace is interesting here. See Collins, *The Credential Society*. For some of the discussion of where this group actually is placed within the class structure, see Pat Walker, ed., *Between Labor and Capital* (Boston: South End Press, 1979).

47. See the useful discussion about education in Arthur E. Wise, *Legislated Learning* (Berkeley: University of California Press, 1979).

48. Vicente Navarro, *Medicine Under Capitalism* (New York: Neale Watson Academic Publications, 1976), p. 91.

49. Noble, *American By Design*, p. xxv.

50. *Ibid.*, p. 258.

51. Apple, 'The New Sociology of Education: Analyzing Cultural and Economic Reproduction,' and Michael W. Apple, 'Analyzing Determinations: Understanding and Evaluating the Production of Social Outcomes in Schools,' *Curriculum Inquiry* X (Spring 1980), 55-76.

52. Karabel and Halsey, 'Educational Research: A Review and Interpretation,' p. 25.

53. Erving Goffman, *Asylums* (New York: Doubleday, 1961). See also Rosenbaum, *Making Inequality*.

54. The point is similar to Whitty's argument that the focus in the early

1970s on teacher autonomy and teacher professionalism acted to defuse any conflict between school research and the economic and political demands placed upon the schools. See Geoff Whitty, 'School Examinations and the Politics of School Knowledge,' in Len Barton and Roland Meighan, eds, *Sociological Interpretations of Schooling and Classrooms: A Reappraisal* (Driffield: Nafferton Books, 1978), p. 131.

55. Bertell Ollman, *Alienation* (New York: Cambridge University Press, 1971) and Erik Olin Wright, *Class Structure and Income Determination* (New York: Academic Press, 1979).

56. Paul Willis, *Learning To Labour* (Lexington: D.C. Heath, 1977).

57. See, for example, Apple, *Ideology and Curriculum*.

58. Wright, *Class, Crisis and the State*, p. 237.

59. Castells, *The Economic Crisis and American Society*, p. 57.

60. *Ibid.*, p. 58. My stress. Castells is being a bit too economistic here himself, but his arguments are still persuasive.

61. Martin Carnoy and Derek Shearer, *Economic Democracy* (White Plains, New York: M.E. Sharpe, 1980), p. 232.

62. *Ibid.*

63. Quoted in Lilian B. Rubin, *Worlds of Pain* (New York: Basic Books, 1976), p. ix.

CHAPTER 3
THE OTHER SIDE OF THE HIDDEN CURRICULUM:
CULTURE AS LIVED – 1

1. See Basil Bernstein, *Class, Codes and Control Volume 3* (London: Routledge & Kegan Paul, 1977). Jerome Karabel and A.H. Halsey, eds, *Power and Ideology in Education* (New York: Oxford University Press, 1977), Pierre Bourdieu and Jean Claude Passeron, *Reproduction in Education, Society and Culture* (Beverly Hills, California: Sage, 1977), Ted Tapper and Brian Salter, *Education and the Political Order* (New York: Macmillan, 1978), and Michael W. Apple, *Ideology and Curriculum* (London: Routledge & Kegan Paul, 1979).

2. I am indebted to Erik Olin Wright's discussion of these six modes of determination in his *Class, Crisis and the State* (London: New Left Books, 1978), pp. 15-29. Wright's analysis is more complex theoretically than I have presented here, especially his treatment of the roles that the state and economic and ideological crises play in these processes of determination.

3. See Nicos Poulantzas, *Classes in Contemporary Capitalism* (London: New Left Books, 1975) and Amy B. Bridges, 'Nicos Poulantzas and the Marxist Theory of the State,' *Politics and Society* IV (Winter 1974), 161-90.

4. Harry Braverman, *Labor and Monopoly Capital* (New York: Monthly Review Press, 1974).

5. David Montgomery, 'Workers' Control of Machine Production in the Nineteenth Century,' *Labor History* XVII (Fall 1976), 485-509.

6. Michael Burawoy, 'Toward a Marxist Theory of the Labor Process: Braverman and Beyond,' *Politics and Society* VIII (Number 3-4, 1979), p. 5 in mimeo copy. The basic elements of scientific management were actually rather simple and can be laid out in four basic principles. (1) There should be centralized planning and centralized routing of each of the successive phases of production. (2) Each distinct operation should be systematically analyzed and broken down into its simplest components or tasks. (3) In the performance of his or her task, each worker should be subject to detailed instruction and supervision. (4) Wage payments should be carefully designed to induce workers to do what the centralized planners and supervisors instructed them to do. See David Montgomery, *Workers' Control in America* (New York: Cambridge University Press, 1979), p. 114. For a more detailed look at Taylor's personal relationship to scientific management see Daniel Nelson, *Frederick W. Taylor and Scientific Management* (Madison: University of Wisconsin Press, 1980).

7. Burawoy, 'Toward a Marxist Theory of the Labor Process,' 89.

8. *Ibid.*, 33-4.

9. *Ibid.*, 34.

10. *Ibid.*, 40. See also the analysis of the 'failure' of Taylorism in David Noble, *America By Design* (New York: Alfred A. Knopf, 1977).

11. David Montgomery, *Workers' Control in America* (New York: Cambridge University Press, 1979), p. 24.

12. *Ibid.*, p. 103. See also Noble, *America By Design*.

13. *Ibid.*, p. 104.

14. *Ibid.*, pp. 143-51.

15. *Ibid.*, p. 10.

16. Daniel Clawson, 'Class Struggle and the Rise of Bureaucracy,' unpublished doctoral dissertation, State University of New York, Stony Brook, 1978. The relationship between the growth of bureaucratic management and the control of labor is also well documented in Clawson's study. See also, Richard Edwards, *Contested Terrain* (New York: Basic Books, 1979).

17. Edwards, *Contested Terrain*, p. 123.

18. *Ibid.*, p. 124. Edwards distinguishes between three types of control – simple, technical, and bureaucratic. Each of these lends itself to and in part is a result of specific kinds of resistance. His analysis of these varying kinds of control will provide a good deal of the foundation for my own investigation in Chapter 5.

19. Montgomery, *Workers' Control in America*, p. 4.

20. *Ibid.*

21. Susan Porter Benson, 'The Clerking Sisterhood: Rationalization and the Work Culture of Saleswomen in American Department Stores,' *Radical America* XII (March-April 1978), 41. My stress.

22. Stanley Aronowitz, 'Marx, Braverman and the Logic of Capital,' *The Insurgent Sociologist* VIII (Fall 1978), 142.

23. Quoted in Aronowitz, 'Marx, Braverman and the Logic of Capital,' 142. See also Steve Packard, *Steelmill Blues* (San Pedro, California: Singlejack

Books, 1978) and Reg Theriault, *Longshoring on the San Francisco Waterfront* (San Pedro, California: Singlejack Books, 1978).

24. Aronowitz, 'Marx, Braverman and the Logic of Capital,' 143.
25. See Stanley Aronowitz, *False Promises* (New York: McGraw-Hill, 1973).
26. However, we should not forget that even such resistances can be 'incorporated' by management (and our more conservative unions) so that resistance turns toward paths that do not threaten production. See, e.g., Michael Burawoy, 'The Politics of Production and the Production of Politics: A Comparative Analysis of Piecework Machine Shops in the United States and Hungary,' in *Political Power and Social Theory*, in press.
27. David Noble, 'Social Choice in Machine Design,' unpublished paper, 1979, p. 11.
28. *Ibid.*, p. 48.
29. *Ibid.*, pp. 45-6.
30. Montgomery, 'Workers' Control of Machine Production in the Nineteenth Century,' 500-1.
31. See Sheila Rothman, *Woman's Proper Place* (New York: Basic Books, 1978) and Edith Altbach, *Women in America* (Lexington: D.C. Heath, 1974).
32. Benson, 'The Clerking Sisterhood,' 49.
33. *Ibid.*
34. *Ibid.*, 50.
35. *Ibid.*, 51.
36. I have further discussed the problems of seeing institutions as if they were black boxes in Michael W. Apple, ed., *Cultural and Economic Reproduction in Education* (London: Routledge & Kegan Paul, 1982.
37. Jeremy Brecher, 'Uncovering the Hidden History of the American Workplace,' *Review of Radical Political Economics* X (Winter 1978), 3.
38. Manuel Castells, *The Economic Crisis and American Society* (Princeton: Princeton University Press, 1980), p. 48. It is important to remember that the forms of such resistance will change over time, however, depending on altered material and ideological conditions.
39. John Ehrenreich and Barbara Ehrenreich, 'Work and Consciousness,' in R. Baxendall *et al.*, eds, *Technology, the Labor Process, and the Working Class* (New York: Monthly Review Press, 1976), p. 13.
40. *Ibid.*, p. 14.
41. On the creation of an abstract individual as an ideological form, see Michael W. Apple, 'Ideology and Form in Curriculum Evaluation,' in George Willis, ed., *Qualitative Evaluation* (Berkeley: McCutchan, 1978), Apple, *Ideology and Curriculum*, Raymond Williams, *The Long Revolution* (London: Chatto & Windus, 1961), and Steven Lukes, *Individualism* (Oxford: Basil Blackwell, 1973).
42. Montgomery, *Workers' Control in America*, p. 27.
43. See Martin Carnoy and Derek Shearer, *Economic Democracy* (White Plains, New York: M.E. Sharpe, 1980) and David Moberg, 'Work in American Culture: The Ideal of Self-Determination and the Prospects for Socialism,' *Socialist Review* X (March-June 1980), 19-56.

44. See the interesting discussion in Nelson Lichtenstein, 'Auto Worker Militancy and the Structure of Factory Life, 1937-1955,' *The Journal of American History* LXVII (September 1980), 335-53.

45. Brecher, 'Uncovering the Hidden History of the American Workplace,' 7-14.

46. The literature on the creation and recreation of ideological hegemony is becoming quite extensive and is obviously helpful in unpacking this issue. Among the most recent analyses that might be useful in pursuing this issue are Raymond Williams, *Marxism and Literature* (New York: Oxford University Press, 1977), Raymond Williams, *Television: Technology and Cultural Form* (New York: Schocken, 1975), Will Wright, *Sixguns and Society* (Berkeley: University of California Press, 1975), R.W. Connell, *Ruling Class, Ruling Culture* (New York: Cambridge University Press, 1977), Center for Contemporary Cultural Studies, *On Ideology: Working Papers in Cultural Studies X* (Birmingham, England: University of Birmingham Centre for Contemporary Cultural Studies, 1977), John Brenkman, 'Mass Media: From Collective Experience to the Culture of Privatization,' *Social Text* I (Winter 1979), 94-109, Stanley Aronowitz, 'Film — The Art Form of Late Capitalism,' *Social Text* I (Winter 1979), 110-29, Fredric Jameson, 'Reification and Utopia in Mass Culture,' *Social Text* I (Winter 1979), 130-48, and Todd Gitlin, 'Television's Screens: Hegemony in Transition,' in Apple, ed., *Cultural and Economic Reproduction in Education*.

47. Burawoy, 'The Politics of Production and the Production of Politics.'

48. I am indebted to a discussion with Paul Willis for my basic point here.

49. Paul Willis, 'Shop Floor Culture, Masculinity and the Wage Form,' in John Clarke, Chas Critcher, and Richard Johnson, eds, *Working Class Culture: Studies in History and Theory* (London: Hutchinson, 1979), p. 187.

50. See James O'Connor, *The Fiscal Crisis of the State* (New York: St Martin's Press, 1973), Erik Olin Wright, *Class, Crisis and the State* (London: New Left Books, 1978), and Castells, *The Economic Crisis and American Society*.

51. Hinton's discussion of 'fanshen' is interesting here. See William Hinton, *Fanshen* (New York: Vintage, 1966).

52. Within mainstream curriculum work Fred Newmann's continuing emphasis on public issues and community action programs deserves mention here. See also the discussion between Newmann and myself in Richard Weller, ed., *Humanistic Education* (Berkeley: McCutchan, 1977).

53. Williams, *Marxism and Literature*.

54. Montgomery, *Workers' Control in America*, p. 155.

55. See, for example, Pal Rydlberg, *The History Book* (Culver City, California: Peace Press, 1974) and Quebec Education Federation, *Pour Une Journee Au Service De La Class Ouvriere* (Toronto: New Hogtown Press, no date).

56. Jean Anyon, 'Ideology and U.S. History Textbooks,' *Harvard Educational Review* XLIX (August 1979), 361-86, and Rich Fantasia,

'The Treatment of Labor in Social Studies Textbooks,' unpublished paper, Department of Sociology, University of Massachusetts, Amherst, 1979.

57. I have purposely undertheorized my arguments in this chapter for ease of readability. On a theoretical level, my points here constitute part of a larger debate within the analysis of the relationship between economic and cultural reproduction. In essence, I want to claim that it is not only an epistemological possibility, but an actual accomplishment that large numbers of working people can create alternative and 'relatively autonomous' forms of knowledge that are not merely representations of 'bourgeois social categories.' This is done even in the face of both the power of the economic and cultural capital of dominant classes and the state apparatus in its various forms. My position here is similar to Willis and Aronowitz, who also argue strongly against both traditional base/ superstructure formulas, and the overly deterministic theories of Althusser, the capitalistic logic school, and others. See, for example, Paul Willis, *Learning to Labor* (Lexington: D.C. Heath, 1977), Paul Willis, 'Class Struggle, Symbol and Discourse,' unpublished paper, University of Birmingham, 1979, and Aronowitz, 'Marx, Braverman and the Logic of Capital.'

58. See Apple, *Ideology and Curriculum.*

CHAPTER 4
RESISTANCE AND CONTRADICTIONS IN CLASS, CULTURE, AND THE STATE: CULTURE AS LIVED – II

1. I wish to thank Geoff Whitty of the University of London for his help in shaping the arguments that appear in this chapter.

2. The difficulties with the more economistic models now in use to describe this process of reproduction are described in considerably more detail in Michael W. Apple, ed., *Cultural and Economic Reproduction in Education* (London: Routledge & Kegan Paul, 1982). It is important to note an obvious but too often forgotten point here. Economic and cultural reproduction go on in other than corporate economies. The more significant questions to ask about this are: What specific cultural patterns and social and economic structure are reproduced? For whose benefit? And, to what extent is there a critical awareness on the part of the affected groups of what is being reproduced?

3. This is not the place to enter into a prolonged discussion of whether class has lost its potency as a central category of one's approach to studying the United States. Needless to say, I am satisfied that it has not. For a thorough, though sometimes technical discussion of many of the empirical and conceptual issues involved here, see Erik Olin Wright, *Class, Crisis and the State* (London: New Left Books, 1978) and Erik Olin Wright, *Class, Structure and Income Determination* (New York: Academic Press, 1979). See also Jerome Karabel, 'The Failure of American Socialism Reconsidered,' in *The Socialist Register 1979*,

Ralph Miliband and John Saville, eds (London: Merlin Press, 1979), pp. 204-27.

4. Stanley Aronowitz, 'Marx, Braverman and the Logic of Capital,' *The Insurgent Sociologist* VIII (Fall 1978), pp. 126-46, and Wright, *Class, Crisis and the State*, Chapter 1. See also Raymond Williams, *Marxism and Literature* (New York: Oxford University Press, 1977), Michael W. Apple, *Ideology and Curriculum* (London: Routledge & Kegan Paul, 1979) and the excellent overview of some of the disparate traditions in Centre for Contemporary Cultural Studies, *On Ideology: Working Papers in Cultural Studies 10* (Birmingham, England: University of Birmingham Centre for Contemporary Cultural Studies, 1977).

5. Richard Johnson, 'Histories of Culture/Theories of Ideology,' in *Ideology and Cultural Production*, Michele Barrett *et al.*, eds (New York: St Martin's Press, 1979), p. 43.

6. *Ibid.*, p. 75.

7. I have discussed the culturalist/structuralist controversy and its unfortunate impact on educational research in Apple, ed., *Cultural and Economic Reproduction in Education*. Richard Johnson's discussion of this 'split' is exemplary. See Johnson, 'Histories of Culture, Theories of Ideology.'

8. Paul Willis, *Learning to Labour: How Working Class Kids Get Working Class Jobs* (Lexington: D.C. Heath, 1977).

9. Robert Everhart, *The In-Between Years: Student Life in a Junior High School* (Santa Barbara: Graduate School of Education, University of California, 1979).

10. Angela McRobbie, 'Working Class Girls and the Culture of Femininity,' in *Women Take Issue*, Women's Studies Group, ed. (London: Hutchinson, 1978), pp. 96-108.

11. See, for example, Apple, ed., *Cultural and Economic Reproduction in Education*, Apple, *Ideology and Curriculum*, Samuel Bowles and Herbert Gintis, *Schooling in Capitalist America* (New York: Basic Books, 1976), Jerome Karabel and A.H. Halsey, eds, *Power and Ideology in Education* (New York: Oxford University Press, 1977) and Caroline Hodges Persell, *Inequality and Education* (New York: Free Press, 1977).

12. See, among others, Michael W. Apple and Nancy King, 'What Do Schools Teach?', *Curriculum Inquiry* VI (Number 4, 1977), 341-58, Philip Jackson, *Life in Classrooms* (New York: Holt, Rinehart & Winston, 1968), Michael Young and Geoff Whitty, eds, *Society, State and Schooling* (Guildford, England: Falmer Press, 1977), and Jean Anyon, 'Social Class and the Hidden Curriculum of Work,' *The Journal of Education* CLXII (Winter 1980), 67-92.

13. For further discussion of how even some of the analyses that focus on contradiction do not go far enough, see Philip Wexler, 'Structure, Text and Subject: A Critical Sociology of School Knowledge,' in *Cultural and Economic Reproduction in Education*, Apple, ed.

14. Often this takes the form of an almost unconscious cynical bargain between teachers and students. See Linda McNeil, 'Economic Dimensions of Social Studies Curriculum: Curriculum as Institutionalized

Knowledge,' unpublished Ph.D. thesis, University of Wisconsin, Madison, 1977.

15. Willis, *Learning to Labour*, p. 175. Thus, a good deal of his argument can be read as an express debate with Marxist structuralists such as Althusser and the late Nicos Poulantzas. See, e.g., Louis Althusser's essay 'Ideology and Ideological State Apparatuses' in his *Lenin and Philosophy and Other Essays* (London: New Left Books, 1971), pp. 127-86, and Nicos Poulantzas, *Classes in Contemporary Capitalism* (London: New Left Books, 1975).

16. Willis, *Learning to Labour*, p. 19.

17. Elsewhere I have criticized Willis for assuming that the ear'oles and the girls the lads interact with are, in fact, totally compliant. See Michael W. Apple, 'What Correspondence Theories of the Hidden Curriculum Miss,' *The Review of Education* V (Spring 1979), 101-12, an essay on which the current section of this chapter is based. I shall make this point even more clearly in my discussion of Everhart's and McRobbie's research shortly.

18. Willis, *Learning to Labour*, p. 100.

19. Harry Braverman, *Labor and Monopoly Capital* (New York: Monthly Review Press, 1974).

20. Again, I am wary of employing a concept like penetration given the role of sexist metaphors in organizing our linguistic usage. However, I shall continue to employ Willis's own terms here. As Bisseret has recently demonstrated, though, we should be aware that gender relations may be reproduced in the referential system encoded in our very language. See Noelle Bisseret, *Education, Class Language and Ideology* (London: Routledge & Kegan Paul, 1979).

21. See Pierre Bourdieu and Jean Claude Passeron, *Reproduction in Education, Society and Culture* (Beverly Hills, California: Sage Publications, 1977), Basil Bernstein, *Class, Codes and Control Volume 3* (London: Routledge & Kegan Paul, 1977), Apple, *Ideology and Curriculum*, and Basil Bernstein, 'Codes, Modal Ties and Cultural Reproduction: A Model,' in *Cultural and Economic Reproduction in Education*, Apple, ed.

22. Willis, *Learning to Labour*, p. 146.

23. Braverman, *Labor and Monopoly Capital*.

24. This may increasingly hold true for more scientific and technical occupations, as science and engineering are further organized under a corporate context as part of the process I analyzed in Chapter 2. See also David Noble, *America by Design: Science, Technology, and the Rise of Corporate Capitalism* (New York: Alfred A. Knopf, 1977).

25. Willis, *Learning to Labour*, p. 180.

26. Everhart, *The In-Between Years*.

27. *Ibid.*, p. 116.

28. *Ibid.*, p. 213.

29. *Ibid.*, p. 218.

30. *Ibid.*, p. 220.

31. *Ibid.*, p. 260.

32. *Ibid.*, p. 337.
33. *Ibid.*, p. 446.
34. *Ibid.*, pp. 451-2.
35. *Ibid.*, p. 451. Thus, if there is any serious structural correspondence between the workplace and schools it is on this level.
36. Mike Brake, *The Sociology of Youth Culture and Youth Subcultures* (London: Routledge & Kegan Paul, 1980), p. 142.
37. See Gail Kelly and Ann Nihlen, 'Schooling and the Reproduction of Patriarchy,' in *Cultural and Economic Reproduction in Education*, Apple, ed.
38. McRobbie, 'Working Class Girls and the Culture of Femininity,' p. 97. See also Madeleine MacDonald, 'Schooling and the Reproduction of Class and Gender Relations,' in *Education and the State Volume 1*, Roger Dale, Geoff Esland, Ross Furgusson, and Madeleine MacDonald, eds (Sussex: Falmer Press, 1981) and Madeleine MacDonald, 'Socio-Cultural Reproduction and Women's Education,' in *Schooling for Women's Work*, Rosemary Deem, ed. (London: Routledge & Kegan Paul, 1980).
39. McRobbie, 'Working Class Girls and the Culture of Femininity,' p. 98.
40. *Ibid.*, p. 101. See also Raymond Williams's discussion of residual and emergent cultures in *Marxism and Literature*.
41. *Ibid.*, p. 102. See also the interesting analysis in Wally Seccombe, *Domestic Labour and the Working Class Household* (Toronto: Canadian Women's Press, in press) and Wally Seccombe, *The Expanded Reproduction Cycle of Labour Power in Twentieth Century Capitalism* (Toronto: Canadian Women's Press, in press).
42. *Ibid.*, p. 103.
43. *Ibid.*
44. *Ibid.*, p. 104.
45. *Ibid.*, p. 106.
46. Brake, *The Sociology of Youth Culture and Youth Subcultures*, p. 166.
47. *Ibid.*, p. vii. In his review of the major literature on working-class subcultures and youth, Brake goes further, noting that one of the reasons such groups are formed is because 'subcultures try to retrieve lost socially cohesive elements destroyed in the parent culture, and to combine these with elements from other class fractions symbolizing one or other of the options confronting it,' p. 67.
48. Women's Studies Group, ed., *Women Take Issue* (London: Hutchinson, 1978), p. 10.
49. Lucy Bland, Charlotte Brunsdon, Dorothy Hobson, and Janice Winship, 'Women "Inside" and "Outside" the Relations of Production,' in *Women Take Issue*, Women's Studies Group, ed., p. 61. See also, Apple, ed., *Cultural and Economic Reproduction in Education*.
50. See Brake's discussion of these cultural patterns in *The Sociology of Youth Culture and Youth Subcultures*.
51. *Ibid.*, pp. 118-19.
52. *Ibid.*, pp. 135-6.
53. Goran Therborn, 'The Ideology of Power and the Power of Ideology,'

speech given at the University of Wisconsin, Madison, October 17, 1980.

54. Brake, *The Sociology of Youth Culture and Youth Subcultures*, pp. 137-8.

55. Lesley Johnson, *The Cultural Critics* (London: Routledge & Kegan Paul, 1979), p. 206.

56. Richard Johnson, 'Histories of Culture/Theories of Ideology,' p. 74.

57. *Ibid.*, p. 70.

58. *Ibid.*, p. 75.

59. Todd Gitlin, 'Prime Time Ideology: The Hegemonic Process in Television Entertainment,' *Social Problems* XXVI (February 1979), 264.

60. James O'Connor, *The Fiscal Crisis of the State* (New York: St Martin's Press, 1973).

61. The most clearly articulated arguments for proposals such as the voucher plan can be found in John E. Coons and Stephen D. Sugarman, *Education By Choice: The Case for Family Control* (Berkeley: University of California Press, 1978).

62. Randall Collins, *The Credential Society* (New York: Academic Press, 1979).

63. Wright, *Class, Crisis and the State*, and Manuel Castells, *The Economic Crisis and American Society* (Princeton: Princeton University Press, 1980).

64. Herbert Gintis, 'Communication and Politics: Marxism and the "Problem" of Liberal Democracy,' *Socialist Review* X (March-June 1980), 191. Gintis's stress.

65. *Ibid.*, pp. 194-5.

66. *Ibid.*, p. 195. Gintis's stress.

67. *Ibid.*, pp. 196-7. Gintis's stress.

68. *Ibid.*, pp. 198-9.

69. Murray Edelman, *Political Language* (New York: Academic Press, 1977), p. xxi.

70. Vicente Navarro, *Medicine Under Capitalism* (New York: Neale Watson Academic Publications, 1976), p. 91.

71. Andrew Gamble, 'The Free Economy and the Strong State: The Rise of the Social Market Economy,' in *The Socialist Register*, Ralph Miliband and John Saville, eds (London: Merlin Press, 1979), p. 22.

72. *Ibid.*

73. On the nature and impact of contestation within the state, see Ann Showstack Sassoon, 'Hegemony and Political Intervention,' in *Politics, Ideology and the State*, Sally Hibbin, ed. (London: Lawrence & Wishart, 1978), pp. 9-39.

74. *Ibid.*, p. 39.

75. On suggestions for using the current struggles of workers and others for pedagogical and curricular purposes, see Peter Dreier, 'Socialism and Cynicism: An Essay on Politics, Scholarship, and Teaching,' *Socialist Review* X (September-October 1980), 105-31.

76. See John Clark, Chas Critcher, and Richard Johnson, eds, *Working Class Culture: Studies in History and Theory* (London: Hutchinson, 1979).

77. Brake, *The Sociology of Youth Culture and Youth Subcultures*, p. 171.

See also Brake's discussion of using, say, rock music and other elements of popular culture to 'win spaces from the dominant culture' on pp. 155-61. These possibilities are also pointed to in Paul Willis, *Profane Culture* (London: Routledge & Kegan Paul, 1978).

78. McRobbie, 'Working Class Girls and the Culture of Femininity,' pp. 102-3.

79. See Willis, *Learning to Labour*, pp. 185-93.

80. Chantal Mouffe, ed., *Gramsci and Marxist Theory* (London: Routledge & Kegan Paul, 1979).

CHAPTER 5
CURRICULAR FORM AND THE LOGIC OF TECHNICAL CONTROL: COMMODIFICATION RETURNS

1. James Donald, 'Green Paper: Noise of a Crisis,' *Screen Education* XXX (Spring 1979), 44.

2. *Ibid.*, 36-7.

3. J. Ryerson and Son, Inc., 'The Ryerson Plan: A Teacher Work-Learn Program' (Chicago: Ryerson and Son Inc., unpublished advertisement, no date). I wish to thank Linda McNeil for bringing this material to my attention.

4. *Ibid.*

5. Diane Downing, 'Soft Choices: Teaching Materials for Teaching Free Enterprise,' (Austin, Texas: University of Texas, Institute for Constructive Capitalism, 1979, mimeo).

6. This is not to deny the importance of analyzing official documents emanating from the state. James Donald's essay on the Green Paper noted above provides an excellent example of the power of discourse analysis, for example, in unpacking what these documents mean and do.

7. Raymond Williams, *Marxism and Literature* (New York: Oxford University Press, 1977).

8. Dan Finn, Neil Grant, Richard Johnson, and the C.C.C.S. Education Group, 'Social Democracy, Education and the Crisis,' Birmingham, England: University of Birmingham Centre for Contemporary Cultural Studies, 1978, mimeo, pp. 3-4.

9. James O'Connor, *The Fiscal Crisis of the State* (New York: St Martin's Press, 1973).

10. See, for example, Fredric Jameson, *Marxism and Form* (Princeton: Princeton University Press, 1971), Williams, *Marxism and Literature*, and Michael W. Apple, 'Ideology and Form in Curriculum Evaluation,' in *Qualitative Evaluation*, George Willis, ed. (Berkeley: McCutchan, 1978), pp. 495-521.

11. John Clarke, 'Capital and Culture: The Post War Working Class Revisited,' in *Working Class Culture*, John Clarke, Chas Critcher, and Richard Johnson, eds (London: Hutchinson, 1979). See also the impressive discussions in Harry Braverman, *Labor and Monopoly Capital* (New York: Monthly Review Press, 1974) and Michael Burawoy,

'Toward a Marxist Theory of the Labor Process: Braverman and Beyond,' *Politics and Society* VIII (Number 3/4, 1979).

12. Richard Edwards, *Contested Terrain: The Transformation of the Workplace in the Twentieth Century* (New York: Basic Books, 1979), p. 17.

13. *Ibid.*, pp. 19-21.

14. *Ibid.*, p. 110.

15. See David Noble, *America By Design: Science, Technology and the Rise of Corporate Capitalism* (New York: Alfred A. Knopf, 1977) and Burawoy, 'Toward a Marxist Theory of the Labor Process.'

16. Stanley Aronowitz, 'Marx, Braverman and the Logic of Capital,' *The Insurgent Sociologist* VIII (Fall, 1978), 126-46, and David Montgomery, *Workers' Control in America* (New York: Cambridge University Press, 1979).

17. Edwards, *Contested Terrain*.

18. Jane Barker and Hazel Downing, 'Word Processing and the Transformation of Patriarchal Relations,' Birmingham, England: University of Birmingham Centre for Contemporary Cultural Studies, 1979, unpublished paper.

19. Roger Dale, 'The Politicization of School Deviance,' in *Schools, Pupils and Deviance*, Len Barton and Roland Meighan, eds (Driffield, England: Nafferton Books, 1979), pp. 95-112.

20. Todd Gitlin, 'Prime Time Ideology: The Hegemonic Process in Television Entertainment,' *Social Problems* XXVII (February 1979), 251-66. Philip Wexler's forthcoming volume, *Critical Social Psychology* (London: Routledge & Kegan Paul, in press) on the commodification of intimate relations is important here as well.

21. This is not only an American phenomenon. The foreign subsidiaries of the companies who produce these materials are translating and marketing their products in the Third World and elsewhere as well. In many ways it is similar to the cultural imperialism of Walt Disney Productions. See, e.g., Ariel Dorfman and Armand Mattelart, *How To Read Donald Duck* (New York: International General Editions, 1975).

22. *Science . . . A Process Approach: Module One* (Lexington: Ginn and Co., 1974), pp. 3-4.

23. *Ibid.*, p. 7.

24. *Ibid.*

25. See, for example, my analysis of science curricula in Michael W. Apple, *Ideology and Curriculum* (London: Routledge & Kegan Paul, 1979).

26. I do not mean to romanticize that past, however. Many teachers probably simply followed the textbook before. However, the level of specificity and the integration of curricular, pedagogical, and evaluative aspects of classroom life into *one* system is markedly different. The use of the system brings with it much more technical control of every aspect of teaching than previous text-based curricula. Obviously, some teachers will not follow the system's rules. Given the level of integration, though, it will undoubtedly be much more difficult to ignore it since many systems constitute the core or only program in that curricular area in the

entire school or district. Thus, accountability to the next grade level or to administrators makes it harder to ignore. I shall return to this point later on.

For an interesting theoretic discussion of the historical development of and reasons for what others have called the 'alienation of the teacher from his or her products' in this deskilling process, see Henry Levin, 'Education Production Theory and Teacher Inputs,' in *The Analysis of Educational Productivity Volume II*, Charles Bidwell and Douglas Windham, eds (Cambridge, Mass.: Ballinger Press, 1980), pp. 203-31.

27. This may be similar to what happened in the early mills in New England, when standardized production processes drastically reduced the contact among workers. See Edwards, *Contested Terrain*, p. 114. A recent study by Andrew Gitlin, however, points out that in some settings interaction increases but it is always over the technical questions raised by the material. Teachers deal primarily with issues of organizational efficiency in the study due to the constraints of the curricular form itself. See Andrew Gitlin, 'Understanding the Work of Teachers,' unpublished Ph.D. thesis, University of Wisconsin, Madison, 1980.

28. *Ibid.*, p. 181.

29. Apple, *Ideology and Curriculum*, and Noble, *America By Design*. One could also claim that schools operate to create use value not exchange value. Erik Olin Wright, personal communication.

30. Erik Olin Wright, *Class, Crisis and the State* (London: New Left Books, 1978).

31. Therefore, any outcomes of schooling must be analyzed as the 'products' of cultural, political, and economic resistances as well as sets of structural determinations, as I argued in Chapter 4. See Michael W. Apple, 'Analyzing Determinations: Understanding and Evaluating the Production of Social Outcomes in Schools,' *Curriculum Inquiry* X (Spring 1980), 55-76.

32. I do not want to ignore the question of the relationship between capitalism and bureaucracy. Weber and others were not wrong when they noted that there are needs for rationalization specific to bureaucratic forms themselves. However, neither the *way* bureaucracy has grown in corporate economies nor its effects have been neutral. This is treated in considerably more detail in Daniel C. Clawson, 'Class Struggle and the Rise of Bureaucracy,' unpublished Ph.D. dissertation, State University of New York, Stony Brook, 1978. See also, Wright, *Class, Crisis and the State*.

33. Barker and Downing, 'Word Processing and the Transformation of Patriarchal Relations.' See also Noble, *America By Design*, for his account of standardization and its relationship to capital accumulation.

34. Joel Spring, *The Sorting Machine* (New York: David McKay, 1976).

35. Apple, *Ideology and Curriculum*.

36. See, e.g., O'Connor, *The Fiscal Crisis of the State*.

37. Among the reasons for the fact that the state has slowly but surely backed away from such production and distribution is the controversy surrounding 'Man: A Course of Study' and, no doubt, the intense

lobbying efforts on the part of publishing firms. Corporations will let the government socialize the costs of development, but obviously would prefer to package and distribute the curricula for themselves. See Michael W. Apple, 'Politics and National Curriculum Policy,' *Curriculum Inquiry* VII (Number 7, 1977), 351-61.

38. Donald, 'Green Paper: Noise of a Crisis,' 44.
39. This is not meant to imply that the state always directly serves the needs of industrial capital. As I argued in Chapter 4, it, in fact, does have a significant degree of relative autonomy and is the site of class conflict as well. See Donald, 'Green Paper: Noise of a Crisis,' Wright, *Class, Crisis and the State*, and Roger Dale, 'Education and the Capitalist State: Contributions and Contradictions,' in *Cultural and Economic Reproduction in Education: Essays on Class, Ideology and the State*, Michael W. Apple, ed. (London: Routledge & Kegan Paul, 1982).
40. As I noted earlier, however, we should remember that accumulation and legitimation may be in conflict with each other at times. See Wright, *Class, Crisis and the State*, for a discussion of these possible contradictions and for an argument about the importance of understanding the way the state and bureaucracies mediate and act back on 'economic determinations.' Though I have not specifically noted it here, the transformation of discourse in schools is similar to, and needs to be analyzed in the light of, the process described by Habermas in his discussion of the constitutive interests of purposive/rational action. I have dealt with this at length elsewhere in Apple, *Ideology and Curriculum*.
41. Clarke, 'Capital and Culture: The Post War Working Class Revisited,' p. 241.
42. Raymond Williams, *The Long Revolution* (London: Chatto & Windus, 1961) and C.B. MacPherson, *The Political Theory of Possessive Individualism* (New York: Oxford University Press, 1972).
43. Richard Johnson, 'Three Problematics: Elements of a Theory of Working Class Culture,' in *Working Class Culture*, John Clarke, Chas Critcher, and Richard Johnson, eds (London: Hutchinson, 1978), p. 232.
44. Will Wright, *Sixguns and Society* (Berkeley: University of California Press, 1975), p. 187.
45. Bernstein's work on class and educational codes is interesting here. As he notes, 'The pacing of educational knowledge is class based.' Basil Bernstein, *Class, Codes and Control Volume 3* (London: Routledge & Kegan Paul, 1977), p. 113.
46. Stanley Aronowitz, *False Promises* (New York: McGraw-Hill, 1973), p. 95.
47. Wright, *Class, Crisis and the State*, p. 79.
48. *Ibid.*, p. 59.
49. *Ibid.*, p. 81. See also Braverman, *Labor and Monopoly Capital*.
50. Edward, *Contested Terrain*, p. 151. Of course, this does not mean that important resistances and countervailing practices do or will not occur. As I demonstrated in Chapter 3, exactly the opposite is often the case. However, they usually occur on the terrain established in large part by

capital.

51. Richard Johnson, 'Histories of Culture/Theories of Ideology: Notes on an Impasse,' in *Ideology and Cultural Production*, Michele Barrett *et al.*, eds (New York: St Martin's Press, 1979), p. 70.
52. Paul Willis, *Profane Culture* (London: Routledge & Kegan Paul, 1978).
53. Geoff Whitty has been particularly helpful in enabling me to see this point.
54. Colin Sumner, *Reading Ideologies* (New York: Academic Press, 1979), p. 134.
55. *Ibid.*, p. 149.
56. John Hill, 'Ideology, Economy and the British Cinema,' in *Ideology and Cultural Production*, Michele Barrett *et al.*, eds (New York: St Martin's Press, 1979), p. 114.
57. *Ibid.*, p. 115.
58. *Ibid.*, p. 122.
59. Terry Eagleton, *Criticism and Ideology* (London: New Left Books, 1976), p. 89.
60. These 'internalistic' readings can be taken too far, of course. For to focus our attention only on the contradictions and ideologies within and produced by such material, or on the contradictions produced by the relationship between form and content, has a serious danger. We may forget how very important are the forces that 'determine' the actual production of curricular material in this way, a point I made earlier in my discussion of the way the school has become a rather lucrative market. See, for example, the essays on the political economy of cultural production by Golding and Murdock and others in Barrett *et al.*, eds, *Ideology and Cultural Production*.
61. Johnson, 'Three Problematics: Elements of a Theory of Working Class Culture.'
62. Edwards, *Contested Terrain*, p. 154.
63. Donald, 'Green Paper: Noise of a Crisis.'
64. Herbert Gintis, 'Communication and Politics: Marxism and the "Problem" of Liberal Democracy,' *Socialist Review* X (March-June 1980), 189-232.
65. Johnson, 'Histories of Culture/Theories of Ideology.'
66. See, for example, some of the suggested material in Miriam Wolf-Wasserman and Kate Hutchinson, *Teaching Human Dignity* (Minneapolis: Education Exploration Center, 1978). Also helpful here is Ira Shor, *Critical Teaching and Everyday Life* (Boston: South End Press, 1980).

CHAPTER 6
EDUCATIONAL AND POLITICAL WORK: IS SUCCESS POSSIBLE?

1. I have discussed these debates in considerably more detail in Michael W. Apple, ed., *Cultural and Economic Reproduction in Education* (London: Routledge & Kegan Paul, 1982).

2. Dan Finn, Neil Grant, Richard Johnson, and the C.C.C.S. Education Group, 'Social Democracy, Education and the Crisis,' Birmingham, England: University of Birmingham Centre for Contemporary Cultural Studies, mimeo, 1978, p. 4.
3. *Ibid.*, p. 34.
4. Philip Wexler, 'Structure, Text and Subject: A Critical Sociology of School Knowledge,' in *Cultural and Economic Reproduction in Education*, Apple, ed. See also Henry Giroux, 'Beyond the Correspondence Theory: Notes on the Dynamics of Educational Reproduction and Transformation,' *Curriculum Inquiry* X (Fall 1980), 225-47.
5. One could in fact claim that such correspondences are actually clearer now given the emerging power of the new right and capital during the current structural crisis. See, for example, Roger Dale, 'The Politicization of School Deviance,' in *Schools, Pupils and Deviance*, Len Barton and Roland Meighan, eds (Driffield: Nafferton Books, 1979), pp. 95-112.
6. The role of the media in constructing the issues on which people act is very important in this regard. See the interesting discussion in C.C.C.S. Education Group, *Unpopular Education: Schooling and Social Democracy in England Since 1944* (London: Hutchinson, 1981).
7. The necessity of looking at the *totality* of cultural, political, and economic conditions is pointed out in David Hogan, 'Education and Class Formation: The Peculiarities of the Americans,' in *Cultural and Economic Reproduction in Education*, Apple, ed. See also Martin Carnoy, 'Education, Economy and the State,' in *Cultural and Economic Reproduction in Education*, Apple, ed., for a further discussion of the impact of action in the 'superstructure' on the 'base.'
8. I am indebted to my colleague Jeffrey Lukowsky for reminding me of what Habermas can contribute in our attempt to theorize these issues.
9. For an insightful study of how technical expertise is used in the family, especially on women, see Rima D. Apple, 'To Be Used Only Under the Direction of a Physician: Commercial Infant Feeding and Medical Practice 1870-1940,' *Bulletin of the History of Medicine* LIV (Fall 1980), 402-17.
10. Basil Bernstein makes a similar point in *Class, Codes and Control Volume 3* (London: Routledge & Kegan Paul, 1977). The literature on the 'new middle class' is also helpful here. See the debate in Pat Walker, ed., *Between Labor and Capital* (Boston: South End Press, 1979).
11. One result of the crisis in accumulation, however, is that the employment possibilities for these people will also be significantly more limited. As I mentioned in Chapter 2, as long as the technical/administrative knowledge is made available for use by capital, it is not really imperative that large numbers of people be employed who have it, *unless* they are needed to control labor. The fact is, however, that the most rapid growth in employment in the United States is in the service sector where a considerably smaller number of, say, supervisory staff is needed. Why this is often the case can be seen in the growth of fast food restaurants. A very large percentage of the work is mechanized, using techniques of

technical control for cooking and so on. Thus, while it is essential for these industries to have a continual flow of new knowledge and techniques, the successful incorporation of it may actually threaten the growth of positions for the new petty bourgeoisie. This will create its own problems of legitimation. On the growth of the service sector and the decline in the need for supervisory personnel, see Emma Rothschild, 'Reagan and the Real America,' *New York Review of Books* XXVIII (February 5, 1980), 12-18.

12. Manuel Castells, *The Economic Crisis and American Society* (Princeton: Princeton University Press, 1980), p. 51.

13. *Ibid.*, p. 47.

14. *Ibid.*, pp. 235-6. See also Rothschild, 'Reagan and the Real America.' On the state, the labor market, and economic conditions and their impact on hispanic workers, see Mario Barrera, *Race and Class in the Southwest: A Theory of Racial Inequality* (Notre Dame, Indiana: University of Notre Dame Press, 1979).

15. Richard Edwards, *Contested Terrain* (New York: Basic Books, 1979), pp. 211-12.

16. *Ibid.*, p. 215.

17. *Ibid.*

18. *Ibid.*, pp. 215-16.

19. Martin Carnoy and Derek Shearer, *Economic Democracy* (White Plains, New York: M.E. Sharpe, 1980), p. 360.

20. Rachel Sharp, *Knowledge, Ideology and the Politics of Schooling* (London: Routledge & Kegan Paul, 1980), p. 164. This is not just for teachers. Indeed, that might subvert some of the conditions of a transitional program. I would include working-class youth and their parents here.

21. C.C.C.S. Education Group, *Unpopular Education*, p. 67.

22. Castells, *The Economic Crisis and American Society*, p. 259.

23. Carnoy and Shearer, *Economic Democracy*, describes many of these alternatives, some of which are clearly 'reformist' while others are just as clearly what I have called non-reformist reforms.

24. Peter Dreier, 'Socialism and Cynicism: An Essay on Politics, Scholarship, and Teaching,' *Socialist Review* LIII (September-October 1980), 128-9.

25. The exceptional film, *Harlan County, U.S.A.*, shows how vital and alive these traditions are today.

26. See, e.g., Carnoy and Shearer, *Economic Democracy*, p. 384.

27. For a discussion of socialist feminist principles of organizing, see Diana Adlam, 'Socialist Feminism and Contemporary Politics,' in *Politics and Power I* (London: Routledge & Kegan Paul, 1980), pp. 81-102.

28. See William Reese and Kenneth Teitelbaum, 'American Socialist Pedagogy and Experimentation in the Progressive Era: The Socialist Sunday School,' unpublished paper presented at Teachers College, Columbia University, January, 1981.

29. One interesting description can be found in Ira Shor, *Critical Teaching and Everyday Life* (Boston: South End Press, 1980). Some have claimed that Dewey provides much of what is necessary here. Certainly, a good

deal can be learned from him, no matter what his ultimate political weaknesses. See Richard Smith and John Knight, eds, 'The Right Side: A Reader in the Theory and Practice of Knowledge and Control,' unpublished manuscript, University of Queensland, Australia, 1980.

30. This will always involve walking a tightrope between teaching and learning, providing intellectual and political leadership and following. The role of organic intellectuals here, then, is never settled, never a simple path. See the discussions of Gramsci's position on this in Chantal Mouffe, ed., *Gramsci and Marxist Theory* (London: Routledge & Kegan Paul, 1979).

31. C.C.C.S. Education Group, *Unpopular Education*, Conclusion, p. 11, in manuscript copy.

32. *Ibid.*, p. 12.

33. One example of needed research that might go on in this regard is on women's resistance in the home, perhaps something similar to the points I brought out in Chapter 3.

34. Carnoy and Shearer, *Economic Democracy*, p. 385.

35. *Ibid.*, p. 386.

36. *Ibid.*, pp. 394-5.

BIBLIOGRAPHY

Adlam, Diana, 'Socialist Feminism and Contemporary Politics,' in *Politics and Power* I, London: Routledge & Kegan Paul, 1980, pp. 81-102.

Altbach, Edith, *Women in America*, Lexington: D.C. Heath, 1974.

Althusser, Louis, 'Ideology and Ideological State Apparatuses,' in *Lenin and Philosophy and Other Essays*, London: New Left Books, 1971, pp. 127-86.

Anyon, Jean, 'Ideology and U.S. History Textbooks,' *Harvard Educational Review* XLIX (August 1979), 361-86.

Anyon, Jean, 'Social Class and the Hidden Curriculum of Work,' *Journal of Education* CLXII (Winter 1980), 67-92.

Apple, Michael W., 'Politics and National Curriculum Policy,' *Curriculum Inquiry* VII (Number 7, 1977), 351-61.

Apple, Michael, W., 'Ideology and Form in Curriculum Evaluation,' in *Qualitative Evaluation*, George Willis (ed.), Berkeley: McCutchan, 1978, pp. 492-521.

Apple, Michael W., 'The New Sociology of Education: Analyzing Cultural and Economic Reproduction,' *Harvard Educational Review* XLVIII (November 1978), 495-503.

Apple, Michael W., 'What Correspondence Theories of the Hidden Curriculum Miss,' *Review of Education* V (Spring 1979), 101-12.

Apple, Michael W., 'The Politics of School Knowledge,' *Review of Education* V (Winter 1979), 1-14.

Apple, Michael W., *Ideology and Curriculum*, London: Routledge & Kegan Paul, 1979.

Apple, Michael W., 'Analyzing Determinations: Understanding and Evaluating the Production of Social Outcomes in Schools,' *Curriculum Inquiry* X (Spring 1980), 55-76.

Apple, Michael W. (ed.), *Cultural and Economic Reproduction in Education: Essays on Class, Ideology and the State*, London: Routledge & Kegan Paul, 1982.

Apple, Michael W., and Nancy King, 'What Do Schools Teach?' *Curriculum Inquiry* VI (Number 4, 1977), 341-69.

Apple, Michael W., and Joel Taxel, 'Ideology and the Curriculum,' in *Educational Studies and Social Science*, Anthony Hartnett (ed.), London: Heinemann, 1982.

Apple, Rima D., 'To Be Used Only Under the Direction of a Physician: Commercial Infant Feeding and Medical Practice 1870-1940,' *Bulletin of the History of Medicine* LIV (Fall 1980), 402-17.

Aronowitz, Stanley, *False Promises*, New York: McGraw-Hill, 1973.

Aronowitz, Stanley, 'Marx, Braverman and the Logic of Capital,' *Insurgent Sociologist* VIII (Fall 1978), 126-46.

Aronowitz, Stanley, 'Film — The Art Form of Late Capitalism,' *Social Text* I (Winter 1979), 110-29.

Barrera, Mario, *Race and Class in the Southwest: A Theory of Racial Inequality*, Notre Dame, Indiana: University of Notre Dame Press, 1979.

Barrett, Michele *et al.* (eds), *Ideology and Cultural Production*, New York: St Martin's Press, 1979.

Barton, Len, and Roland Meighan (eds), *Sociological Interpretations of Schooling and Classrooms: A Reappraisal*, Driffield, England: Nafferton Books, 1978.

Barton, Len, and Roland Meighan (eds), *Schools, Pupils and Deviance*, Driffield, England: Nafferton Books, 1979.

Baudelot, Christian, and Roger Establet, *La Escuela Capitalista*, Mexico City: Siglo Vientiuno Editores, 1975.

Baxendall, R. *et al.* (eds), *Technology, the Labor Process, and the Working Class*, New York: Monthly Review Press, 1976.

Benson, Susan Porter, 'The Clerking Sisterhood: Rationalization and the Work Culture of Saleswomen in American Department Stores,' *Radical America* XII (March-April 1978), 41-55.

Bernstein, Basil, *Class, Codes and Control Volume 3: Towards a Theory of Educational Transmissions*, London: Routledge & Kegan Paul, 1977.

Bernstein, Basil, 'Codes, Modal Ties and Cultural Reproduction: A Model,' in *Cultural and Economic Reproduction in Education*, Michael W. Apple (ed.), London: Routledge & Kegan Paul, 1982.

Bisseret, Noelle, *Education, Class Language and Ideology*, London: Routledge & Kegan Paul, 1979.

Bland, Lucy, Charlotte Brunsdon, Dorothy Hobson, and Janice Winship, 'Women "Inside" and "Outside" the Relations of Production,' *Women Take Issue*, Women's Studies Group (ed.), London: Hutchinson, 1978, pp. 35-78.

Bourdieu, Pierre, and Jean-Claude Passeron, *Reproduction in Education, Society and Culture*, London: Sage Publications, 1977.

Bourdieu, Pierre, and Jean-Claude Passeron, *The Inheritors*, Chicago: University of Chicago Press, 1979.

Bowles, Samuel, and Herbert Gintis, *Schooling in Capitalist America*, New York: Basic Books, 1976.

Boyd, William Lowe, 'The Changing Politics of Curriculum Policy-Making for American Schools,' *Review of Educational Research* XLVIII (Fall 1978), 577-628.

Brake, Mike, *The Sociology of Youth Culture and Youth Sub-Cultures*, London: Routledge & Kegan Paul, 1980.

Braverman, Harry, *Labor and Monopoly Capital*, New York: Monthly Review

Press, 1974.

Brecher, Jeremy, 'Uncovering the Hidden History of the American Workplace,' *Review of Radical Political Economics* X (Winter 1978), 1-23.

Brenkman, John, 'Mass Media: From Collective Experience to the Culture of Privatization,' *Social Text* I (Winter 1979), 94-109.

Bridges, Amy B., 'Nicos Poulantzas and the Marxist Theory of the State,' *Politics and Society* IV (Winter 1974), 161-90.

Burawoy, Michael, 'Toward a Marxist Theory of the Labor Process: Braverman and Beyond,' *Politics and Society* VIII (Number 3-4, 1979), 247-312.

Burawoy, Michael, 'The Politics of Production and the Production of Politics: A Comparative Analysis of Piecework Machine Shops in the United States and Hungary,' in *Political Power and Social Theory*, in press.

Carnoy, Martin, 'Education, Economy and the State,' *Cultural and Economic Reproduction in Education*, Michael W. Apple (ed.), London: Routledge & Kegan Paul, 1982.

Carnoy, Martin, and Derek Shearer, *Economic Democracy*, White Plains, New York: M.E. Sharpe, 1980.

Castells, Manuel, *The Economic Crisis and American Society*, Princeton: Princeton University Press, 1980.

C.C.C.S. Education Group, *Unpopular Education: Schooling and Social Democracy in England Since 1944*, London: Hutchinson, 1981.

Centre for Contemporary Cultural Studies, *On Ideology: Working Papers in Cultural Studies* X, Birmingham, England: University of Birmingham Centre for Contemporary Cultural Studies, 1977.

Clarke, John, 'Capital and Culture: The Post War Working Class Revisited,' in *Working Class Culture*, John Clarke, Chas Critcher, and Richard Johnson (eds), London: Hutchinson, 1979, pp. 238-53.

Clarke, John, Chas Critcher, and Richard Johnson (eds), *Working Class Culture*, London: Hutchinson, 1979.

Clawson, Daniel, 'Class Struggle and the Rise of Bureaucracy,' unpublished doctoral dissertation, State University of New York, Stony Brook, 1978.

Collins, Randall, 'Some Comparative Principles of Educational Stratification,' *Harvard Educational Review* XLVII (February 1977), 1-27.

Collins, Randall, *The Credential Society*, New York: Academic Press, 1979.

Connell, R.W., *Ruling Class, Ruling Culture*, New York: Cambridge University Press, 1977.

Connell, R.W., 'A Critique of the Althusserian Approach to Class,' *Theory and Society* VIII (November 1979), 303-45.

Coons, John E., and Stephen D. Sugarman, *Education by Choice: The Case for Family Control*, Berkeley: University of California Press, 1978.

Coward, Rosalind, and John Ellis, *Language and Materialism*, London: Routledge & Kegan Paul, 1977.

Dale, Roger, 'The Politicization of School Deviance,' in *Schools, Pupils and Deviance*, Len Barton and Roland Meighan (eds), Driffield, England: Nafferton Books, 1979, pp. 95-112.

Dale, Roger, 'Education and the Capitalist State: Contributions and
    Contradictions,' in *Cultural and Economic Reproduction in Education*,
    Michael W. Apple (ed.), London: Routledge & Kegan Paul, 1982.
DiMaggio, Paul, 'Review Essay: On Pierre Bourdieu,' *American Journal of
    Sociology* LXXXIV (May 1979), 1460-74.
Donald, James, 'Green Paper: Noise of a Crisis,' *Screen Education* XXX
    (Spring 1979), 13-49.
Dorfman, Ariel, and Armand Mattelart, *How To Read Donald Duck*, New
    York: International General Editions, 1975.
Downing, Diane, 'Soft Choices: Teaching Materials for Teaching Free
    Enterprise,' Austin, Texas: University of Texas, Institute for
    Constructive Capitalism, 1979, mimeo.
Dreier, Peter, 'Socialism and Cynicism: An Essay on Politics, Scholarship, and
    Teaching,' *Socialist Review* X (September-October 1980), 105-31.
Eagleton, Terry, *Criticism and Ideology*, London: New Left Books, 1976.
Edelman, Murray, *Political Language*, New York: Academic Press, 1977.
Edwards, Richard, *Contested Terrain*, New York: Basic Books, 1979.
Ehrenreich, John, and Barbara Ehrenreich, 'Work and Consciousness,' in
    Technology, the Labor Process, and the Working Class, R. Baxendall
    et al. (eds), New York: Monthly Review Press, 1976, pp. 10-18.
Erben, Michael, and Denis Gleesen, 'Education as Reproduction,' in *Society,
    State, and Schooling*, Michael Young and Geoff Whitty (eds),
    Sussex: Falmer Press, 1977, pp. 73-92.
Everhart, Robert, *The In-Between Years: Student Life in a Junior High
    School*, Santa Barbara, California: Graduate School of Education,
    University of California, 1979.
Fantasia, Rich, 'The Treatment of Labor in Social Studies Textbooks,'
    unpublished paper, Department of Sociology, University of
    Massachusetts, Amherst, 1979.
Featherman, David, and Robert Hauser, 'Sexual Inequalities and Socio-
    Economic Achievement in the U.S., 1962-1973,' *American
    Sociological Review* XLI (June 1976), 462-83.
Feinberg, Walter, 'A Critical Analysis of the Social and Economic Limits to
    the Humanizing of Education,' in *Humanistic Education*, Richard
    Weller (ed.), Berkeley: McCutchan, 1977, pp. 247-69.
Feldberg, Roslyn, L., 'Union Fever: Organizing Among Clerical Workers,
    1900-1930,' *Radical America* XIV (May-June 1980), 53-67.
Finn, Dan, Neil Grant, Richard Johnson, and the C.C.C.S. Education Group,
    'Social Democracy, Education and the Crisis,' Birmingham, England:
    University of Birmingham Centre for Contemporary Cultural Studies,
    1978, mimeo.
Gamble, Andrew, 'The Free Economy and the Strong State: The Rise of the
    Social Market Economy,' in *The Socialist Register*, Ralph Miliband and
    John Saville (eds), London: Merlin Press, 1979, pp. 1-25.
Gintis, Herbert, 'Communication and Politics: Marxism and the "Problem" of
    Liberal Democracy,' *Socialist Review* X (March-June 1980), 189-232.
Giroux, Henry, 'Beyond the Correspondence Theory: Notes on the Dynamics
    of Educational Reproduction and Transformation,' *Curriculum Inquiry*

X (Fall 1980), 225-47.

Gitlin, Andrew, 'Understanding the Work of Teachers,' unpublished Ph.D. thesis, University of Wisconsin, Madison, 1980.

Gitlin, Todd, 'Prime Time Ideology: The Hegemonic Process in Television Entertainment,' *Social Problems* XXVI (February 1979), 251-66.

Gitlin, Todd, 'Television's Screens: Hegemony in Transition,' in *Cultural and Economic Reproduction in Education*, Michael W. Apple (ed.), London: Routledge & Kegan Paul, 1982.

Goffman, Erving, *Asylums*, New York: Doubleday, 1961.

Gorz, Andre (ed.), *The Division of Labour*, Atlantic Highlands: New Jersey: Humanities Press, 1976.

Hall, Stuart, 'The Schooling-Society Relationship: Parallels, Fits, Correspondences, Homologies,' mimeo, no date.

Hargreaves, David, *et al.*, *Deviance in Classrooms*, London: Routledge & Kegan Paul, 1975.

Hartnett, Anthony (ed.), *Educational Studies and Social Science*, London: Heinemann, 1982.

Haubrich, Vernon (ed.), *Freedom, Bureaucracy and Schooling*, Washington, D.C.: Association for Supervision and Curriculum Development, 1971.

Hill, John, 'Ideology, Economy and the British Cinema,' in *Ideology and Cultural Production*, Michele Barrett *et al.* (eds), New York: St Martin's Press, 1979, pp. 112-34.

Hinton, William, *Fanshen*, New York: Vintage, 1966.

Hirst, Paul, *On Law and Ideology*, London: Macmillan, 1979.

Hogan, David, 'Education and Class Formation: The Peculiarity of the Americans,' in *Cultural and Economic Reproduction in Education*, Michael W. Apple (ed.), London: Routledge & Kegan Paul, 1982.

Holloway, John, and Sol Picciotto (eds), *State and Capital*, London: Edward Arnold, 1978.

Holloway, John, and Sol Picciotto, 'Introduction: Towards a Materialist Theory of the State,' in *State and Capital*, John Holloway and Sol Picciotto (eds), London: Edward Arnold, 1978, pp. 1-31.

Jackson, Philip, *Life in Classrooms*, New York: Holt, Rinehart & Winston, 1968.

Jameson, Fredric, *Marxism and Form*, Princeton: Princeton University Press, 1971.

Jameson, Fredric, 'Reification and Utopia in Mass Culture,' *Social Text* I (Winter 1979), 130-48.

Jencks, Christopher *et al.*, *Who Gets Ahead?*, New York: Basic Books, 1979.

Jessop, Bob, 'Recent Theories of the Capitalist State,' *Cambridge Journal of Economics* I (December 1977), 353-73.

Jessop, Bob, 'Capitalism and Democracy,' in *Power and the State*, Gary Littlejohn *et al.* (eds), New York: St Martin's Press, 1978.

Johnson, Lesley, *The Cultural Critics*, London: Routledge & Kegan Paul, 1979.

Johnson, Richard, 'Histories of Culture/Theories of Ideology: Notes on an Impasse,' in *Ideology and Cultural Production*, Michele Barrett *et al.* (eds), New York: St Martin's Press, 1979, pp. 49-77.

207

Johnson, Richard, 'Three Problematics: Elements of a Theory of Working Class Culture,' in *Working Class Culture*, John Clarke, Chas Critcher, and Richard Johnson (eds), London: Hutchinson, 1979, pp. 201-37.

Karabel, Jerome, 'Community Colleges and Social Stratification,' *Harvard Educational Review* XLII (November 1972), 521-62.

Karabel, Jerome, 'The Failure of American Socialism Reconsidered,' in *The Socialist Register 1979*, Ralph Miliband and John Saville (eds), London: Merlin Press, 1979, pp. 204-27.

Karabel, Jerome, and A.H. Halsey, 'Educational Research: A Review and Interpretation,' in *Power and Ideology in Education*, Jerome Karabel and A.H. Halsey (eds), New York: Oxford University Press, 1977, pp. 1-85.

Karabel, Jerome, and A.H. Halsey (eds), *Power and Ideology in Education*, New York: Oxford University Press, 1977.

Kelly, Gail, and Ann Nihlen, 'Schooling and the Reproduction of Patriarchy,' in *Cultural and Economic Reproduction in Education*, Michael W. Apple (ed.), London: Routledge & Kegan Paul, 1982.

Kirst, Michael, and Decker Walker, 'An Analysis of Curriculum Policy-Making,' *Review of Educational Research* XLI (December 1971), 479-509.

Kliebard, Herbert, 'Bureaucracy and Curriculum Theory,' in *Freedom, Bureaucracy and Schooling*, Vernon Haubrich (ed.), Washington, D.C.: Association for Supervision and Curriculum Development, 1971, pp. 74-93.

Levin, Henry, 'Education Production Theory and Teacher Input,' in *The Analysis of Educational Productivity Volume II*, Charles Bidwell and Douglas Windham (eds), Cambridge, Mass.: Ballinger Press, 1980, pp. 203-31.

Lichtenstein, Nelson, 'Auto Worker Militancy and the Structure of Factory Life, 1937-1955,' *The Journal of American History* LXVII (September 1980), 335-53.

Lukes, Steven, *Individualism*, Oxford: Basil Blackwell, 1973.

MacDonald, Madeleine, 'Socio-Cultural Reproduction and Women's Education,' in *Schooling for Women's Work*, Rosemary Deem (ed.), London: Routledge & Kegan Paul, 1980.

MacDonald, Madeleine, 'Schooling and the Reproduction of Class and Gender Relations,' in *Education and the State*, Roger Dale, Geoff Esland, Ross Furgusson and Madeleine MacDonald (eds), Sussex: Falmer Press, 1981.

Macherey, Pierre, *A Theory of Literary Production*, London: Routledge & Kegan Paul, 1978.

McNeil, Linda, 'Economic Dimensions of Social Studies Curriculum: Curriculum as Institutionalized Knowledge,' unpublished Ph.D. thesis, University of Wisconsin, Madison, 1977.

MacPherson, C.B., *The Political Theory of Possessive Individualism*, New York: Oxford University Press, 1962.

McRobbie, Angela, 'Working Class Girls and the Culture of Femininity,' in *Women Take Issue*, Women's Studies Group (ed.), London: Hutchinson, 1978, pp. 96-108.

Il Manifesto, 'Challenging the Role of Technical Experts,' in *The Division of Labour*, Andre Gorz (ed.), New York: Humanities Press, 1976, pp. 123-43.

Marglin, Stephen, 'What Do Bosses Do?' in *The Division of Labour*, Andre Gorz (ed.), New York: Humanities Press, 1976, pp. 13-54.

Meyer, John, 'The Effects of Education as an Institution,' *American Journal of Sociology* LXXXIII (July 1977), 55-77.

Miliband, Ralph, *Marxism and Politics*, New York: Oxford University Press, 1977.

Moberg, David, 'Work in American Culture: The Ideal of Self-Determination and the Prospects for Socialism,' *Socialist Review* X (March-June 1980), 19-56.

Montgomery, David, 'Workers' Control of Machine Production in the Nineteenth Century,' *Labor History* XVII (Fall 1976), 485-509.

Montgomery, David, *Workers' Control in America*, New York: Cambridge University Press, 1979.

Mouffe, Chantal, 'Hegemony and Ideology in Gramsci,' in *Gramsci and Marxist Theory*, Chantal Mouffe (ed.), London: Routledge & Kegan Paul, 1979, pp. 168-204.

Mouffe, Chantal (ed.), *Gramsci and Marxist Theory*, London: Routledge & Kegan Paul, 1979.

Navarro, Vicente, *Medicine Under Capitalism*, New York: Neale Watson Academic Publications, 1976.

Nelson, Daniel, *Frederick W. Taylor and Scientific Management*, Madison: University of Wisconsin Press, 1980.

Noble, David, *America By Design*, New York: Alfred A. Knopf, 1977.

Noble, David, 'Social Choice in Machine Design,' unpublished paper, Massachusetts Institute of Technology, Cambridge, 1979.

O'Connor, James, *The Fiscal Crisis of the State*, New York: St Martin's Press, 1973.

Offe, Claus, and Volker Ronge, 'Theses on the Theory of the State,' *New German Critique* VI (Fall 1975), 137-47.

Ollman, Bertell, *Alienation*, New York: Cambridge University Press, 1971.

Olneck, Michael, and James Crouse, *Myths of the Meritocracy: Cognitive Skill and Adult Success in the United States*, Madison, Wisconsin: University of Wisconsin Institute for Research on Poverty, Discussion Paper 485-78, March 1978.

Packard, Steve, *Steelmill Blues*, San Pedro, California: Singlejack Books, 1978.

Persell, Caroline H., *Education and Inequality*, New York: Free Press, 1977.

Piven, Francis Fox, and Richard Cloward, *Poor People's Movements*, New York: Vintage, 1977.

Poulantzas, Nicos, *Classes in Contemporary Capitalism*, London: New Left Books, 1975.

Quebec Education Federation, *Pour Une Journee Au Service De La Class Ouvriere*, Toronto: New Hogtown Press, no date.

Reese, William, and Kenneth Teitelbaum, 'American Socialist Pedagogy and Experimentation in the Progressive Era: The Socialist Sunday School,' unpublished paper presented at Teachers College, Columbia University, January 1981.

Rosenbaum, James, *Making Inequality*, New York: John Wiley, 1976.

Rothman, Sheila, *Woman's Proper Place*, New York: Basic Books, 1978.

Rothschild, Emma, 'Reagan and the Real America,' *New York Review of Books* XXVIII (February 5, 1980), 12-18.

Rubin, Lilian, *Worlds of Pain*, New York: Basic Books, 1976.

Rydlberg, Pal, *The History Book*, Culver City, California: Peace Press, 1974.

Sassoon, Anne Showstack, 'Hegemony and Political Intervention,' in *Politics, Ideology and the State*, Sally Hibbin (ed.), London: Lawrence & Wishart, 1978, pp. 9-39.

Seccombe, Wally, *Domestic Labor and the Working Class Household*, Toronto: Canadian Women's Press, in press.

Seccombe, Wally, *The Expanded Reproduction Cycle of Labour Power in Twentieth Century Capitalism*, Toronto: Canadian Women's Press, in press.

Selden, Steven, 'Conservative Ideologies and Curriculum,' *Educational Theory* XXVII (Summer 1977), 205-22.

Sharp, Rachel, *Knowledge, Ideology and the Politics of Schooling*, London: Routledge & Kegan Paul, 1980.

Sharp, Rachel, and Anthony Green, *Education and Social Control*, London: Routledge & Kegan Paul, 1975.

Shor, Ira, *Critical Teaching and Everyday Life*, Boston: South End Press, 1980.

Smith, Richard, and John Knight (eds), 'The Right Side: A Reader in the Theory and Practice of Knowledge and Control,' unpublished manuscript, University of Queensland, Australia, 1980.

Spring, Joel, *The Sorting Machine*, New York: David McKay, 1976.

Sumner, Colin, *Reading Ideologies*, New York: Academic Press, 1979.

Tapper, Ted, and Brian Salter, *Education and the Political Order*, New York: Macmillan, 1978.

Tepperman, Jean, 'Organizing Office Workers,' *Radical America* X (January-February 1976), 3-20.

Therborn, Goran, *What Does the Ruling Class Do When It Rules?*, London: New Left Books, 1978.

Theriault, Reg, *Longshoring on the San Francisco Waterfront*, San Pedro, California: Singlejack Books, 1978.

Useem, Michael, 'Corporations and the Corporate Elite,' *Annual Review of Sociology* VI (1980), 41-77.

Walker, Pat (ed.), *Between Labor and Capital*, Boston: South End Press, 1979.

Weller, Richard (ed.), *Humanistic Education*, Berkeley: McCutchan Publishing, 1977.

Wexler, Philip, *Critical Social Psychology*, London: Routledge & Kegan Paul, in press.

Wexler, Philip, 'Structure, Text, and Subject: A Critical Sociology of School Knowledge,' in *Cultural and Economic Reproduction in Education*, Michael W. Apple (ed.), London: Routledge & Kegan Paul, 1982.

210

Whitty, Geoff, 'School Examinations and the Politics of School Knowledge,' in *Sociological Interpretations of Schooling and Classrooms: A Reappraisal*, Len Barton and Roland Meighan (eds), Driffield, England: Nafferton Books, 1978, pp. 129-44.

Williams, Raymond, *The Long Revolution*, London: Chatto & Windus, 1961.

Williams, Raymond, *Television: Technology and Cultural Form*, New York: Schocken Books, 1974.

Williams, Raymond, *Marxism and Literature*, New York: Oxford University Press, 1977.

Willis, Paul, *Learning to Labour*, Westmead: Saxon House, 1977.

Willis, Paul, *Profane Culture*, London: Routledge & Kegan Paul, 1978.

Willis, Paul, 'Shop Floor Culture, Masculinity and the Wage Form,' in *Working Class Culture: Studies in History and Theory*, John Clarke, Chas Critcher, and Richard Johnson (eds), London: Hutchinson, 1979, pp. 185-98.

Willis, Paul, 'Class Struggle, Symbol and Discourse,' unpublished paper, University of Birmingham, 1979.

Wise, Arthur, *Legislated Learning: The Bureaucratization of the American Classroom*, Berkeley: University of California Press, 1979.

Wolfe, Alan, 'New Directions in the Marxist Theory of Politics,' *Politics and Society* IV (Winter 1974), 131-59.

Wolf-Wasserman, Miriam, and Kate Hutchinson, *Teaching Human Dignity*, Minneapolis: Education Exploration Center, 1978.

Woods, Peter, and Martin Hammersly (eds), *School Experience*, New York: St Martin's Press, 1977.

Wright, Erik Olin, *Class, Crisis and the State*, London: New Left Books, 1978.

Wright, Erik Olin, *Class Structure and Income Determination*, New York: Academic Press, 1979.

Wright, Will, *Sixguns and Society*, Berkeley: University of California Press, 1975.

Young, Michael, and Geoff Whitty (eds), *Society, State and Schooling*, Sussex: Falmer Press, 1977.

INDEX